MUSEUMS IN CHINA

THE POLITICS OF REPRESENTATION AFTER MAO

HERITAGE MATTERS

ISSN 1756–4832

Series Editors
Peter G. Stone
Peter Davis
Chris Whitehead

Heritage Matters is a series of edited and single-authored volumes which addresses the whole range of issues that confront the cultural heritage sector as we face the global challenges of the twenty-first century. The series follows the ethos of the International Centre for Cultural and Heritage Studies (ICCHS) at Newcastle University, where these issues are seen as part of an integrated whole, including both cultural and natural agendas, and thus encompasses challenges faced by all types of museums, art galleries, heritage sites and the organisations and individuals that work with, and are affected by them.

Previously published titles are listed at the back of this book

Museums in China

The Politics of Representation after Mao

MARZIA VARUTTI

THE BOYDELL PRESS

The right of Marzia Varutti to be identified
as the author of this work has been asserted in accordance with
sections 77 and 78 of the Copyright, Designs and Patents Act 1988

First published 2014
The Boydell Press, Woodbridge

ISBN 978–1–84383–888–3

The Boydell Press is an imprint of Boydell & Brewer Ltd
PO Box 9, Woodbridge, Suffolk IP12 3DF, UK
and of Boydell & Brewer Inc.
668 Mt Hope Avenue, Rochester, NY 14620–2731, USA
website: www.boydellandbrewer.com

The publisher has no responsibility for the continued existence or accuracy
of URLs for external or third-party internet websites referred to in this book,
and does not guarantee that any content on such websites is,
or will remain, accurate or appropriate.

A CIP record for this book is available
from the British Library

Papers used by Boydell & Brewer Ltd are natural, recyclable products
made from wood grown in sustainable forests

Printed and bound in Great Britain by
CPI Group (UK) Ltd, Croydon, CR0 4YY

Contents

	List of Illustrations	vi
	Acknowledgments	ix
	Chronology	x
	List of Abbreviations	xi
	Introduction	1
1	Cultural Heritage in China	9
2	Museums in China: Origins and Development	25
3	New Actors in the Chinese Museum World	43
4	Museum Objects and the Chinese Nation	59
5	The Nation in the Museum	77
6	The Politics of the Past	89
7	The Representation of the Past in China's Museums	103
8	The Politics of Identity	121
9	The Museum Representation of Ethnic Minorities	129
10	Techniques and Sites of Display of Ethnic Minorities	145
	Conclusions: The New Museums of China	159
	Appendix: List of Museums in China Visited by the Author	165
	Bibliography and References	167
	Index	183

Illustrations

COVER IMAGES

(Top) Cultural relic of the ancient Shu culture, Sanxingdui Museum, Sichuan Province.
Photo: Marzia Varutti

(Middle) Detail of painting representing Chinese ethnic groups.
Photo: Marzia Varutti, taken at the Minzu Museum, Minzu University of China, June 2012. Reproduced with kind permission of Minzu University

(Bottom) Sculpture at the entrance of a Buddhist temple in Jinghong, Yunnan Province.
Photo: Marzia Varutti

FIGURES

1.1.   Visitors examining ancient calligraphic texts, National Museum of China, Beijing.   14
Photo: Marzia Varutti. Reproduced with kind permission of the National Museum of China

1.2.   *Zun* bronze wine vessel from the Shang Dynasty (c. 1600–1046 BC), National Museum of China, Beijing.   18
Photo: Marzia Varutti. Reproduced with kind permission of the National Museum of China

3.1.   The Tobacco Museum, Shanghai.   46
Photo: Marzia Varutti

3.2.   Entrance of the Shanghai History Museum in the basement of the Oriental Pearl Tower, Shanghai.   46
Photo: Marzia Varutti

3.3.   Donors are acknowledged in the lobby of the Shanghai Museum.   53
Photo: Marzia Varutti

4.1.   Soil with fragments of projectile become 'witnesses of history' at the National Museum of China, Beijing.   61
Photo: Marzia Varutti. Reproduced with kind permission of the National Museum of China

4.2.   Example of 'wonder' approach to displays at the Shanghai Museum.   65
Photo: Marzia Varutti

4.3.   Example of 'resonance' approach at the National Museum of China, Beijing.   65
Photo: Marzia Varutti. Reproduced with kind permission of the National Museum of China

4.4.   The unique architectural style of the Shanghai Museum.   72
Photo: Marzia Varutti

6.1. Cultural relic of the ancient Shu culture, Sanxingdui Museum, Sichuan Province.   93
       Photo: Marzia Varutti

7.1. Encountering Mao at the National Museum of China, Beijing.   110
       Photo: Marzia Varutti. Reproduced with kind permission of the National Museum of China

7.2. The National Museum of China, Beijing.   114
       Photo: Marzia Varutti. Reproduced with kind permission of the National Museum of China

7.3. Young members of the Chinese military admire the National Museum of China's   116
       reconstructed section of the Imperial Palace from which Mao declared the birth
       of the People's Republic of China in 1949.
       Photo: Marzia Varutti. Reproduced with kind permission of the National Museum of China

8.1. The majestic entrance to the Shanghai Science and Technology Museum.   126
       Photo: Marzia Varutti

9.1. Mural depicting Chinese nationalities at the Minzu Museum, Minzu University   136
       of China, Beijing.
       Photo: Marzia Varutti. Reproduced with kind permission of the Minzu Museum, Minzu University of China

9.2. Mannequins representing ethnic minority groups at the Shanghai Museum.   142
       Photo: Marzia Varutti

10.1. Miniature figurines of ethnic groups at the Museum of the Southwest University   146
       for Nationalities in Chengdu, Sichuan Province.
       Photo: Marzia Varutti

The author and publisher are grateful to all the institutions listed for permission to reproduce the materials in which they hold copyright. Every effort has been made to trace the copyright holders; apologies are offered for any omission, and the publisher will be pleased to add any necessary acknowledgment in subsequent editions.

Acknowledgments

Many people contributed, in various ways, to the completion of this book. Although it is not possible to name them all here, I wish to thank all the museum curators and academics who opened the doors of their museums and offices to an inquisitive stranger, and showed curiosity and interest in museums and museology in Europe. Fieldwork research in China was made possible through the support of the Swiss Commission for Research Partnership with Developing Countries (KFPE), and the Swiss Agency for Development and Cooperation (SDC). I also wish to acknowledge the support of the Swiss National Science Foundation, which enabled me to conduct research at the Museum of Archaeology and Anthropology of the University of Cambridge, UK.

I gratefully acknowledge the following publishers and journals for allowing me to reprint articles and book chapters: Routledge, MuseumsEtc, Linköping University Electronic Press, *Museum and Society, Culture Unbound: Journal of Current Cultural Research, Outlines: Critical Practice Studies* and *The International Journal of the Inclusive Museum*.

In China, many people generously set aside time to answer my questions. Among others, I wish to acknowledge the availability and kindness of Professor Song Xiangguang at Peking University; Professor Qian Zonghao at the Shanghai Museum of History/Tongji University; Professor Hua Jian at the Shanghai Academy of Social Sciences; Professor Guo Qingshen at the Shanghai Museum; and Professor Lu Jiansong at Fudan University. I gratefully acknowledge the help of students at the Shanghai Academy of Social Sciences, Fudan University and Yunnan University, who not only helped me with the translation of academic texts but, most importantly, through their friendship offered me some of the most invaluable insights into Chinese culture. I particularly wish to thank Mr Li Yihai and Ms Li Li from the International Programs Office at the Shanghai Academy of Social Sciences (SASS) for facilitating my stay there. My heartfelt thanks go to Professor Yu Jinyiao at the Chinese Academy of Social Sciences, Beijing, for his generosity and friendship, and for providing a home away from home.

I wish to express my gratitude to Dr Helen Loveday at the Collection Baur, Geneva, for her advice, insights and encouragement, especially during the first phases of research. I also wish to thank the curatorial and academic staff at the Museum of Archaeology and Anthropology (MAA) of the University of Cambridge. During my extended research visit there, the MAA provided an ideal framework for my research, offering me invaluable opportunities to gain insights into, and first-hand experience of, museum practice and pioneering collaborative curatorship.

In Cambridge, my reflections were greatly enriched by conversations with friends and colleagues; I especially wish to thank Professor Alan Macfarlane of the Department of Social Anthropology, University of Cambridge, his wife Sarah, and Yan Xiaoxiao for sharing their knowledge of Chinese history and culture with me.

I am sincerely grateful to Professor Peter Davis and Catherine Dauncey of the International Centre for Cultural and Heritage Studies at Newcastle University for their insightful comments on the manuscript draft and for patiently guiding me through the publication process.

Finally, my deepest thanks go to my parents for their unremitting support and to my husband, Geoffrey, who shared every moment, every doubt and every laugh of this journey.

Chronology

c. 2100–1600 BC	Xia Dynasty
c. 1600–1046 BC	Shang Dynasty
1046–256 BC	Zhou Dynasty
1046–771 BC	*Western Zhou*
770–475 BC	*Spring and Autumn Annals*
475–221 BC	*Warring States*
221–206 BC	Qin Dynasty
206 BC–AD 220	Han Dynasty
AD 220–589	Period of disunity
AD 220–265	*Three Kingdoms*
AD 581–618	Sui Dynasty
AD 618–906	Tang Dynasty
AD 907–960	Five Dynasties
AD 960–1279	Song Dynasty
960–1127	*Northern Song*
1127–1279	*Southern Song*
1279–1368	Yuan Dynasty
1368–1644	Ming Dynasty
1644–1911	Qing Dynasty
1912–1949	Republic of China
1949–	People's Republic of China

Abbreviations

CCP	Chinese Communist Party
ICOM	International Committee of Museums
NAMOC	National Art Museum of China, Beijing
SACH	State Administration of Cultural Heritage
UNESCO	United Nations Educational, Scientific and Cultural Organization
UNIDROIT	International Institute for the Unification of Private Law
V&A	Victoria and Albert Museum, London

Introduction

Standing in the middle of Tian An Men Square is a moving experience. The concrete landscape and empty sky are overwhelming in their immensity. Space, form, textures, perspectives and colours are defined in an authoritative tone. A millennial history of power struggles, collective tragedies and dreams seems to exude from this vast esplanade. Yet Tian An Men is actually only just over half a century old. In its time, very little seems to have changed: the austerity of the concrete façade has remained unaltered. Like the eye of a tornado, Tian An Men has retained an appearance of immobility in a national context characterised by a thorough, high-paced process of transformation. One only needs to walk a few hundred metres from Tian An Men, along one of the arteries that cross Beijing, to encounter the unmistakable signs of a buoyant country spinning spectacularly ahead.

This book examines the transformations occurring in China through the prism of museums, their objects and narratives. Encompassing the social, political, economic and artistic spheres, museums are at the same time trustees of tradition – embodying historical memory and preserving cultural and artistic heritage – and symbols of modernity: showcases of the achievements of a civilisation. Mirroring the past, the present and the future of societies, museums are ideal tools through which to examine the complexity of social change. By casting light on the political role that museums have historically played within the country, this book aims to contribute to a better understanding of contemporary China.

Since the early 1990s, China has witnessed a considerable increase in the number of its museums. At the end of the 1990s, the municipality of Shanghai adopted a plan to supply all 20 city districts with a 'public culture centre' composed of a library, a cinema, a youth centre and a museum. Successively, the planned creation of new museums in Shanghai was further fuelled by the 2010 World Expo (Zheng 2007). In 2010, the National Museum of China in Beijing underwent major renovation work, transforming it into 'the world's largest arts and history museum' (*People's Daily* 2007). The Military Museum of the Chinese People's Revolution underwent comprehensive renovation in 2011–12, and renovation plans for the Imperial Palace were started in 2002 and are due to be completed by 2020.

The precise number of museums in China at the end of the first decade of the new millennium is difficult to assess. According to official statistics, at the end of 2011 the number of museums totalled 2571, with Beijing ranking second globally for the number of its museums, after London.[1] The objective of the State Administration of Cultural Heritage – a governmental body based in Beijing – is to reach 3000 museums by the year 2015, including 'at least one fully-functional museum for every large or medium-sized city' (*People's Daily* 2002; see also *People's*

---

[1] This news was reported on several websites, including *China News Service*, 'Beijing ranks second in number of museums' [online], 10 October 2011, available from: http://www.ecns.cn/2011/10–10/2883.shtml [1 July 2013]. However, according to Professor Lu Jiansong at Fudan University, the number of museums in China at the end of 2010 totalled 3410, of which 475 were private (Lu 2012, *pers comm*).

Daily 2006). In 2012 in China there was one museum for every 650,000 inhabitants, but government authorities are planning to increase this to one museum for every 400,000 inhabitants over the next decade (Song 2012, *pers comm*).[2] The current fever surrounding the construction and renovation of museums in China points to a change in the way museums are perceived, conceived and evaluated in the framework of governmental cultural policies. Although museums had been to some extent left in the shadows during the years of Deng Xiaoping reforms, they have regained the attention of authorities. Why have museums become so important? And for whom? How does this swell of interest for museums reflect the country's ongoing social and political transformations?

The re-evaluation of museums, and of China's cultural heritage and ancient past, has broad political ramifications. The announcement of the creation of new museums is only an index, a symptom of a complex process of change affecting the realms of culture, politics, ideology, economics and Chinese society at large. One needs to first disentangle this knot in order to make sense of the contemporary museum frenzy.

Museums, Ideological Crisis and Cultural Nationalism

Recent decades of Chinese history have been marked by enormous changes in all aspects of social and political life. In the late 1970s and early 1980s, the end of the Maoist economic system brought about the disappearance of communal cooperatives and a gradual opening to the market economy. The events of 1989 in Tian An Men and the fall of Communist regimes in Eastern Europe and the former USSR shook the basis of the Communist political system, engendering an ideological crisis, the effects of which have not completely dissipated. Internationally, the entry of China into the World Trade Organisation in December 2001 and the designation, the following year, of Hu Jintao as Secretary General of the Communist Party marked major steps in the process of transition towards a post-Maoist China and the gradual integration of the country in the world economic system.

Considered as a whole, these events not only reshaped the entire economic structure of the country, but also fostered a mounting disenchantment with Communist ideals, resulting in an increasing distance between the Chinese government and its citizenry. Although Chinese political rhetoric remains imbued with references to Communist principles and values, these no longer carry real emotional resonance (Friedman 1994; Hwang and Schneider 2011; Schwarcz 1991; Suresh 2002; Tu 1993). Communist ideology is no longer the main cohesive force in Chinese society, nor the primary vehicle of public authority. The government is turning to other tools to justify its authority and secure its power, both factual and symbolic. In spite of astonishing rates of production growth, general increases in quality of life and easier access to goods for mass-consumption, social disparities are widening against the background of an increasing developmental gap between the industrialised coastal areas and the rural interior, further eroding the pillars of the Communist social project. Old slogans and Marxist theories are no longer enough to ensure the level of popular consent needed by the government to legitimise its authority. A

---

[2]　According to the owner of the Guanfu Classical Art Museum in Beijing, 'the per capita ratio of museums is an important indicator of the level of civilisation of a modern society' (Ma 2003, 100).

new discourse,[3] a new vocabulary, a new rationale and, ultimately, new sources of political legitimation are required.

Although resistant to change, the Chinese political intelligentsia has been compelled to reformulate its ideological bases. Since the rhetorical tones of Communist utopia have been abandoned, an ideological foundation is now provided by the nationalist discourse, of which cultural nationalism is a major tenet. The re-evaluation of the past and the connected reformulation of the discourse on China's national identity are part and parcel of such legitimating strategies. Thus, the immensely rich Chinese cultural heritage becomes a source of political legitimation insofar as the associations established with ancient cultural and artistic traditions contribute to inscribing the authority of the current government in a line of continuity harking back to imperial rule. Such claims are central to cultural nationalist discourses aimed at instilling a sense of belonging to the Chinese nation, and fostering social cohesion. In both discursive and representational practices, museum narratives consistently promote a sense of Chinese national identity through references to the longevity and continuity of Chinese civilisation, and the unity and diversity of the Chinese nation. In this context, museums and their content are recast as cultural treasure houses, symbols of national prestige, tokens of modernity, and even measures of civic development, as well as being tools to attract foreign capital and tourists. This book endeavours to unravel the modalities through which museums take part in such processes.

Through a focus on how museum objects are selected, exhibited and interpreted, this study shows how the search for new sources of political legitimation has ultimately led to a reinterpretation of the past, notably of ancient history, and a consequent reformulation of Chinese national identity. While museum narratives on the revolutionary past and the ethnic components of the Chinese nation have remained consistent with the post-1949 directive, renewed emphasis is placed on the progressive and modern facets of the Chinese nation (associated with industrial and service sectors, science and technology) and the celebration of China's ancient past. Through the inscription of manufactured versions of the past into the 'official' national history (as well as the imposition of collective amnesia concerning specific historical periods), and by enforcing a definition of Chinese national identity that emphasises ethnic diversity and unity, the state is actively constructing an image of the Chinese nation that is substantiated, sustained and disseminated through museums.

In light of this, the inconsistencies, discontinuities and hiatuses among museum representations and narratives over time and space open up valuable analytical dimensions where the politics of identity and the role that museums play in its implementation become visible and intelligible. Crucially, the changes in museum narratives are the manifestation of broader changes affecting the whole museum system in China. More museums are constructed, and with increasingly 'modern' features; to some extent China resembles, at present, an extraordinary 'museum laboratory'. New actors are entering the museum scene and new museum objects, narratives, display techniques and architectural styles are appearing. By considering the overall process of changes within museums from the perspective of the changes in their components, this book aims to capture the multidimensional complexity of the transformation of museums in contemporary China.

---

3   Reference is made here to the anthropologist Yang Mei-hui's (1994, 50) definition of 'official discourse' as 'the style of language which projects the authority and political correctness which plays a hegemonic role in unifying public discourse'.

WRITING ABOUT CHINESE MUSEUMS

In recent decades, the focus of theoretical reflection in museum studies[4] has revolved around issues of representation and the changing social roles of museums (see, for example, Bennett 1995; Hooper-Greenhill 1992; Kaplan 1994; Karp *et al* 1992; Sandell 2002; Sandell and Nightingale 2012). In most instances, these themes have been framed through colonial and postcolonial perspectives (see, for example, Barringer and Flynn 1998; Henare 2005), as museums constituted not only an import of the coloniser, but also an emblem of colonial power, a tool by means of which cultural paradigms were imposed (or dismissed) under the elusive claims of a 'civilising mission'. A significant part of the literature has focused on the aptitude of museums to become a tool of social control. Through such lenses, museums are seen as technologies of governance. The power of control, coercion and even repression attributed to museums by Tony Bennett (1995, mainly drawing from Antonio Gramsci and Michel Foucault) needs, however, to be critically addressed in light of the increasing participation of communities in museum work. Increasingly, museums are becoming arenas where different visions, interests, concerns and objectives co-exist, albeit not without friction.

Locating Chinese museums within this literature is neither obvious nor necessarily appropriate. Indeed, the Chinese case study eludes easy classification. While a thickening strand of museum studies explores the gradual opening up of museums to source communities (see Clifford 1997; Peers and Brown 2003), this finds little application in a country like China, where the movement claiming rights of inclusion in the process of museum representation is still at an embryonic stage. While the 'frontier' of museum studies has long been challenging museums' authority and addressing the chasm between narrator and narrated by means of a self-reflexive (or 'new') museology (Vergo 1989), museums in China largely remain enshrined in an authoritative, monodirectional paradigm.

A significant part of the literature on the political role of museums has developed around the cases of countries that have become independent relatively recently, where the experience of postcolonialism is linked to the urge to sever ties with the colonial past and to construct an independent national identity. In contrast, China has experienced a peculiar form of colonialism, whereby the foreign administration of resources was not widespread through the territory, but, rather, was concentrated geographically (with a focus on important harbour centres such as Tianjin, Shanghai, Hong Kong and Macau) and thematically (the colonial presence mainly focused on the control of trade and related institutions, such as banks, markets and stock exchanges). Without underestimating the dramatic consequences of the colonial presence in China, its containment in time and space meant that it did not lead, as in the case of other colonised countries, to a radical disruption of the country's traditions, nor to the annihilation of its cultural coordinates. The fissures in the Chinese political, economic, social and cultural system during the 19th century and the subsequent 'decline' up to the 1911 Republican Revolution were as much a consequence of internal problems as of colonialism. During the 20th century, China's historical trajectory took such unforeseen and dramatic turns that in approaching its study one is very soon deprived of valuable comparative references. Additionally, over the course of recent decades, the scenario has been further complicated by the Chinese transition. As the quest for

---

[4]   In a narrow interpretation, 'museum studies' focuses on the study of the historical, social and cultural dimensions of museums.

legitimacy and the need for popular consensus (formal, if not substantial) exert pressure on the government, the expectations and the functions with which museums and the cultural heritage are invested are further amplified and exacerbated by the pace of socio-economic transformation.

The corpus of literature specifically addressing museums in China is relatively little developed, especially if one considers publications in languages other than Mandarin. Chinese monographs and volumes on museology remain sparse and tend to privilege historical rather than critical perspectives (cf H Wang 2001; Li 2007; Zheng 1985). Discussions on museums in China are sometimes included in works on Chinese heritage, in essays on Chinese nationalism, or in treaties on the wider topic of art and power in China. Research that focuses on the evolution of museums in China and their relation to the political and social sphere is relatively scant.[5] All in all, the debate on Chinese museums, both in China and beyond, is still in its infancy.

The arguments presented in this book are based on observations from over 50 museums in various regions of China (Beijing, Shanghai, and Zhejiang, Jiangsu, Yunnan and Sichuan provinces).[6] The museums considered in this study are those dealing with aspects of the Chinese nation, specifically the representation of the national past and of national identity. They include art, history, scientific, industrial and ethnographic museums, at the national, provincial, county and local level. Rather than conducting in-depth research on one or more museums, the main concern was to capture the overall dynamic of change within Chinese museums through a comparative perspective applied to a composite museum sample. While the sample of museums studied is in no way representative of all museums in China, it provides valuable insights into the current museum landscape in the country.

The study is based on over ten months of field research in China between September 2003 and May 2008, with a return visit in 2012. The research methodology and the theoretical frameworks of reference are those of museum studies and social anthropology. The data has been collected through direct observation of museum exhibitions, discourse analysis of displays, and interviews with museum academics and professionals. The analysis is based on the assumption that the way in which objects are displayed (or excluded from display) and the narratives that are woven around them constitute a platform from which to tackle underlying questions, such as which objects are considered important and which are not (and why), the meanings that are attributed to them (and by whom), and how they are interpreted. In turn, these questions cast light on how such interpretations are used to manufacture broader narratives centred on the Chinese nation and, in a diachronic perspective, how such narratives have changed over time.

An array of factors combine to determine the direction, twists and shortcuts of a research project lasting several years. Field research is a combination of planned arrangements and haphazard events. Although I have striven for scientific reliability and objectivity, in an enquiry of this breadth, 'findings' remain to a large extent dependent on arbitrary factors – the people one meets along the way, the specific circumstances of the encounters, the kind of information that becomes available in those contexts and moments, and so on. The Chinese language represented a considerable difficulty, especially at the onset of the research. Although I was able to interact in everyday conversations with Chinese people, my language skills were not advanced enough to enable me to conduct structured research interviews in Chinese, nor to read specialised literature

---

[5] Authors addressing similar issues to this work include Vickers (2007); Watson (1992; 1994; 1998); Hamlish (2000); and Tythacott (2011).

[6] The museums included in the sample are listed in the Appendix.

without help. My understanding of facts and opinions has therefore been biased by the inaccuracies that inevitably occur in processes of translation and interpretation.[7] I have tried to contain these biases by double-checking the main points with my interlocutors and by submitting similar questions to different interviewees.

Obviously, the perception and interpretation of the data gathered have been affected by my own subjective vision, as a Western European academic interested in museums. Thus, the ideas put forward in this book should be read less as definitive statements than as informed interpretations contributing to the collective scholarly endeavour of understanding contemporary China and its millennial civilisation.

STRUCTURE OF THE BOOK

The book is structured across ten chapters; these explore the concepts of cultural heritage and museums in China, and examine the link between museums and the nation in historical and contemporary perspectives. The first chapter, 'Cultural Heritage in China', aims to provide readers with references to better understand Chinese approaches to cultural heritage and artistic production. The importance of gesture and the written word, concepts of authenticity and imitation, philosophical notions of flexibility and adaptation are all points of entry into a unique artistic and philosophical system. These considerations are important premises for the discussion of the tradition of collecting in China. The historical depth of the relations linking art production, collecting practice and political authority can be appreciated by considering the political relevance of bronze vessels and, more broadly, of imperial collections, which continue to have a strong resonance in contemporary Chinese museums.

Chapter 2, 'Museums in China: Origins and Development', traces the historical development of museums in China, from their appearance in the late 19th century as an 'import' from abroad, to the gradual transformation of museums into a Chinese institution during the 20th century. The chapter also introduces the most important Chinese laws and regulations relating to museums, and sheds light on the origins, development and main tenets of museology in China.

Chapter 3, 'New Actors in the Chinese Museum World', provides an overview of the main actors on the Chinese museum scene, including the Chinese government, private and state-owned enterprises, museum professionals, museum donors and museum audiences.

Chapter 4, 'Museum Objects and the Chinese Nation', examines the relationships that link museums, their objects and the Chinese nation. The analysis focuses on how museum objects are contextualised, displayed and interpreted in museums in order to create and disseminate specific narratives of the Chinese nation. Specific attention is paid to the role of aesthetics as a mode of display in contemporary representations and narratives of the Chinese nation. The increasing importance of spectacular museum architecture is also discussed as a facet of museums' enhanced visibility in Chinese cities.

Chapter 5, 'The Nation in the Museum', takes analysis of the links between museums and the nation a step further through an anthropologically inspired conceptualisation of museum objects as substitutes for the Chinese nation. This theoretical stance offers a fresh perspective on the topic of repatriation and the role of travelling exhibitions of Chinese art and cultural heritage.

---

[7]   The Pinyin transliteration system has been used for Chinese terms.

In museums, Chinese national identity is represented in both the depth of its history and the breadth of its civic project and ethnic composition. To reflect these two aspects, the core of the analysis of museum representations develops around critical discussion of the politics of the past and the politics of identity.

Chapter 6, 'The Politics of the Past', investigates the role of the past as a source of political legitimation. Reference to the past is particularly important in framing the quest for the origins of Chinese civilisation, the imperial concept of the 'Mandate of Heaven', Communist ideology and the recent ideological crisis and nationalist turn. Crucially, such historical influences find expression in museums.

Chapter 7, 'The Representation of the Past in China's Museums', takes a critical look at museums' historical narratives, paying special attention to the discontinuities and inconsistencies engendered by the juxtaposition of the Marxist–Leninist view of ancient history as a dark era, and the ongoing movement of re-evaluation of antiquity.

In Chapter 8, 'The Politics of Identity', the focus shifts to discourses on national identity. These discourses unfold on several levels: cultural (centred on a Han culture-based definition of national identity); civic (China 'is' the Chinese state, portrayed as an efficient, technologically advanced apparatus of production fulfilling its citizens' needs and dreams); and ethnic (whereby China is presented as a multi-ethnic country).

Museums' treatment of ethnic minorities is discussed in the last two chapters of the book. Chapter 9, 'The Museum Representation of Ethnic Minorities', introduces readers to the official discourse on ethnic minorities in contemporary Chinese political rhetoric and illustrates how this discourse affects museum narratives. Chapter 10, 'Techniques and Sites of Display of Ethnic Minorities', examines the main display techniques used by museums in exhibitions of ethnic minorities and discusses their implications.

The concluding chapter develops a longitudinal and critical perspective on the development of museums in China as part of a broader reflection on the changes that have occurred over the last century within Chinese museums and Chinese society more generally.

1

Cultural Heritage in China

This chapter considers the relevance of cultural heritage in Ancient and Imperial China,[1] and its ties to political authority. An appreciation of the historical relationship between heritage and power in China is a useful preamble to the discussion of the forms that this same relationship takes in today's museums.

HERITAGE, MUSEUMS AND CULTURAL RELICS: SOME DEFINITIONS

The concept of heritage is steeped in the specific cultural and historical trajectory of a country. As such, it cannot be transposed across different cultural contexts. It is therefore useful to recast the notion of heritage in light of its conceptualisation within the Chinese cultural milieu.

The term 'heritage' is translated in Mandarin by the word *wenwu*, encompassing both built heritage and objects, and bearing a historical connotation as 'anything coming from the past' (see also Chang 1999, 85). The Western meaning of heritage, which includes historical monuments, only appears in China after the end of the imperial era, when the process of identifying and cataloguing monuments began. However, a number of authors (Chang 1999; Zhang 2003) argue that the concept of heritage, understood as a corpus of historical monuments, does not have a direct equivalent within Chinese cultural tradition. In China, priority is not given to the physical aspect of historical buildings, but rather to their cultural-symbolic dimension. In other words, the cultural values that are transmitted through heritage are more important than their materiality. This is illustrated by the example of the Temple of Issei in Japan (Chang 1999, 81). The temple is reconstructed every 20 years in accordance with the traditional architectural design and using traditional building techniques. The temple building, then, is not regarded as a feature to maintain or conserve: it is the traditional knowledge and the symbolic values that it encapsulates that are preserved and renewed by means of its cyclical reconstruction. The Chinese term for tradition, *chuantong*, conveys the idea of the transmission of fundamental values for the continuity of a civilisation (Chang 1999, 86). Indeed, the idea of keeping a tradition and a collective memory constitutes a key aspect of the Chinese approach to heritage, characterised by a concern to remember. The emphasis on remembrance is in turn linked to the importance of Confucian principles in the Chinese cosmology. Preaching respect for the elderly and for ancestors, and imposing the observance of morality lessons gained through past mistakes, Confucianism significantly contributed to shaping Chinese attitudes towards the past and its material manifestations.

---

[1] Joseph Alsop (1982) distinguishes between a first period in Chinese history corresponding to 'Ancient China' (roughly from 2000 BC to the establishment of the Empire in 221 BC) and a second period corresponding to 'Imperial China' (from 220 BC to AD 1911).

In Mandarin, 'museum' is translated by the term *bowuguan*, which is composed of three characters, referring respectively to a large number (*bo*), of things or objects (*wu*) placed in a large room or house (*guan*).[2] The semantic roots of the term suggest the notion of 'a house of many objects'. The term was imported from Japan around the second half of the 19th century; the original Japanese term *hakubutsukan* – bearing the same characters as *bowuguan* – appeared towards 1860 and was officially adopted in 1867 to designate the objects that had been exhibited at the Universal Exhibition held in Paris that same year.

The notion of a museum object, as a component of a museum collection, appears relatively late in China. Valuable objects were essentially meant to be part of private collections – that is, to be a source of personal delight for the owner and an audience of a select few. The emergence of museums (notably of public museums) introduced a notion of the museum object associated with ideas of education and edification. The object was no longer intended simply to generate pleasure in the viewer, but to perform an educational and didactic function. This approach to the museum object is linked to Marxist–Leninist theory and notably to historical materialism, whereby the object is considered to be evidence of social change. This becomes clearer when we look at the definition of cultural relics.

The term 'cultural relic' is used extensively in China to indicate cultural heritage items. The law on the protection of cultural relics passed in October 2002 broadly defines cultural relics as 'anything produced before 1949'. Usually, a distinction is made between historical cultural relics – those pre-dating 1750 – and modern cultural relics. Other sources offer further insights on the idea. The *Chinese Encyclopedia of Cultural Relics and Museums* states that 'the cultural relics refer to those historical objects as well as sites [that have] survived during the process of historical development of mankind' (quoted by Shen 1994, 1). The Chinese scholar Ruan Jiaxing (1994, 1), curator of China's Military Museum, adds that a cultural relic can be 'any object created by human beings in the social development [...] anything which is constituted by man or has connection with human beings and the social development. A natural thing, once discovered, collected and studied by human beings, can also become a cultural relic.'

These definitions emphasise two elements: the human being and the ideas of development and progress. The centrality assigned to human beings has interesting theoretical implications. According to the definition, it is owing to the intervention of human beings, through knowledge and appropriate interpretation, that natural specimens (which have no innate value) acquire value. Similarly, handicrafts are seen as 'embodiments of man's labor' and, as such, they are called to testify to the progress of human development. Indeed, the final aim of collecting cultural relics is 'reflecting the continuity, variety and regularity in the development of man-centered society' (Ruan 1994, 2).

This approach reveals the underlying Marxist–Leninist vision of human development as a linear path, marked by a succession of developmental phases. This perspective is characterised by a scientific concern to document human evolution through objects. In this framework, objects become witnesses of a specific moment in human history. The very fact of collecting is seen in itself as a statement of progress: 'the more civilized and developed a society is, the more atten-

---

2   Although the term *guan* has the meaning today of a large room or house, it originally meant 'the place for the hosts'. The fact that this specific term has been chosen to define the museum seems meaningful if one remembers that China's first museums were considered a foreign import, created by and for foreigners, rather than for the Chinese.

tion will it pay to cultural relics' (ibid, 2). Such a perspective contributes to the understanding of museums in China as evidence of social development.

A UNIQUE APPROACH TO ART AND HERITAGE

According to the scholar Edmund Capon (1977, 15), Chinese thought is framed by adjustment and intuition. Adjustment is defined as 'the maintenance of ideas and concepts, and amending them to suit the conditions, fashions and attitudes of the day'. Such a quality is represented by the image of bamboo: thanks to its flexibility, it 'bends but never breaks'. Capon extends these characteristics to Chinese artists and art production and links them to China's relative artistic continuity. Such continuity, Capon argues, is based on 'firstly, a basically hieratic and formal structure; secondly, independence; and thirdly, a tendency to conservatism' (ibid, 16).

On a more general note, Chang Wan-Chen (1999) maintains that, in Chinese art, priority is given to the meaning held by objects rather than to their material value. The Chinese scholar Feng Chengbo (1993, 13) corroborates Chang's point of view when he cites the Song Dynasty (AD 960–1279) philosopher Zhu Xi – 'rationality comes before the things' – suggesting that the notion and significance of objects take priority over their physical dimension. This principle is exemplified by bronze vessels, the historical, cultural and ritual importance of which is ascribed to the inscriptions they bear. This also explains why, for centuries, bronzes have been among the most sought-after objects, and, still today, no museum of Chinese antiquities would be complete without a few exemplars of ancient bronzes. The same principle of 'rationality over materiality' could be extended to other art domains, such as calligraphy and painting. Interestingly, this approach to art objects contrasts with the materialism of Marxism–Leninism, which became dominant during the Maoist era.

A brief digression on the status of calligraphy and painting in Chinese art is useful in understanding their prominence in contemporary exhibitions. The ascent of calligraphy (the 'art of arts') to the status of 'art' is linked to the power of the scholar-officials. Firstly, calligraphy was a key element of official examinations for admission to public office and, secondly, both scholar-officials' duties and artistic activities (be they calligraphy or painting) required the same tool: the writing brush (Alsop 1982, 220). The development of calligraphy as an art form was facilitated by the harmonisation and simplification of Chinese characters at the dawn of the imperial era. However, it was only between the 2nd and 3rd centuries AD that calligraphy achieved the status of a commonly recognised art form, gaining the affirmation of painters and calligraphers still known and admired today. One of the major themes in calligraphy appreciation is the idea of 'bone energy'. Such energy is embodied by strong ink traits, which are supposed to reflect the strength and the skill of the calligrapher (Alsop 1982, 234). Although requiring a huge amount of repetition, calligraphy also leads to the elaboration of a personal style; artistic calligraphy surpasses technical perfection and displays variation and spontaneity in the brush stroke, in an attempt to transcend pure form.

The principles of Chinese painting support even more explicitly the principle of the primacy of substance over form:

the Chinese philosophy of painting […] rather than being concerned with representation of the subject based on form, volume light and colour […] is an art founded on fidelity to the spirit or essence of the subject in which intangible space is as 'true to life' as solid form. A painting is

great only if it succeeds in nourishing the spirit, setting the imagination wandering – in a way
a European judges a poem or piece of music. The Chinese artist is interested in depicting the
accumulation of experience: 'mountain-ness' rather than faithfully rendering the actual shape
of the mountains. [...] Chinese landscape is intended to be contemplated over time. (Dunedin
Public Art Gallery 1999, 18)

During the Song Dynasty (AD 960–1279) the art of painting reached its apex; later in the
Ming (AD 1368–1644) and Qing (AD 1644–1911) dynasties, painting was marked by the creative manipulation of old forms and conventions. For centuries, calligraphy and painting were
the only two recognised forms of art in China, while craft activities in materials such as jade,
porcelain, lacquer, textiles and wood only started to be considered as legitimate arts during the
Song Dynasty. Almost ironically, it is precisely these art forms, considered in Western artistic
tradition as 'minor arts' (as opposed to 'fine arts'),[3] that have become the symbol of Chinese
artistic production outside China.

THE QUESTION OF AUTHENTICITY

Just as the Chinese approach to heritage differs from Western approaches, so notions of authenticity and copy also hold unique significance in the Chinese cultural realm. In China, an
authentic item and a forgery are not antithetical; indeed, it is often almost impossible to separate the two. Thus, it follows that authenticity is a conceptual category that calls for a culturally
specific approach.

Artistic continuity over centuries has been assured by the practice of creating reproductions
of artworks. For instance, since the Song Dynasty (AD 960–1279), Chinese collectors have
welcomed the reproduction of masterpieces. The reproduction of originals was considered neither
a diminishing nor a dubious practice, but a way to prolong the object's life and to improve its
qualities: for example, in the case of literary texts to which grammatical or stylistic corrections
were made during the reproduction process. Replicas and transcriptions also, crucially, allowed
important texts to survive; this is the case, for instance, for many inscribed stelae, from which
rubbings were made. Tellingly, the reproduction of classic artworks is a task usually undertaken
by the most skilled artists.

Bronzes, ceramics, paintings and literary texts are not only 'copied' but also reinterpreted,
improved and even corrected. Imitation therefore implies full understanding and appreciation of
the original work. Moreover, reproductions also contributed significantly to the coalescence of a
corpus of artworks regarded as 'classics'.

Ultimately, the reproduction of artworks constitutes a means of transmission of cultural
heritage. The principle underlying reproduction practices is that the original artwork is not so
much a unique masterpiece as a *support*: more attention is devoted to its meanings and spiritual
values than to its materiality. But what happens when this approach is extended to cultural relics
and museum objects, where there is usually an expectation of authenticity?

Authenticity is seemingly a requirement for cultural relics: 'a cultural relic must strictly remain
in its initial shape and cannot be reproduced. No matter how similar is a replica to the original

---

[3]   In China, the 'fine arts' include calligraphy, painting, music and poetry, but not sculpture.

one, it cannot be a cultural relic' (Ruan 1994, 2). Yet replicas are often included in exhibitions in China, sometimes without indication on their labels. For instance, according to Professor Qian Zonghao at the Shanghai History Museum, some clothing items exhibited at the Site of the First Congress of the Communist Party of China, in Shanghai, are reproductions made according to photographs from the time and witnesses' descriptions and memories; yet this is not always acknowledged in the display (Qian 2004b, *pers comm*). Museum authorities justify the use of reproductions by advocating their educational role: 'museums in China play an essentially teaching role and because of this, the authentic object, whether unique or simply rare, is less significant than its didactic meaning. Collections therefore contain many replicas and copies of objects belonging to other museums' (Museums Department of the State Administrative Bureau of Museums and Archaeological Data 1980, 171).

Professor Song Xiangguang at Peking University explains that Chinese curators and conservators of the 1950s and 1960s fostered the restoration of artefacts with a view to re-establishing their original form and function (Song 2004b, *pers comm*). Here, restoration has an educational goal: to supply the visitor with more information about the object in its integrity and original function. The reproduction of the object's original appearance is perceived as an improvement of its aesthetics.

From another point of view, the preference for complete, polished, 'perfect' exhibits may also imply a willingness to 'make the old new'; that is, to show the past as new, to present antiquity with the tones of modernity (Claypool 2005, 589). However, visible, high-impact restoration is practised less and less, and the tendency today is not to intervene too invasively (Song 2004b, *pers comm*).

THE IMPORTANCE OF INSCRIPTIONS

A Western visitor in Chinese gardens or temples may be surprised to see locals reaching for characters engraved on rocks or stone walls, and repeatedly following the inscriptions with their hands, as if to retrace the lines of the characters. This attention is reserved for specific characters bearing auspicious connotations, such as 'joy', 'luck', 'happy marriage', 'longevity' or 'fertility'. For instance, in the Forbidden City, Chinese visitors can be seen queuing to touch the character meaning 'happiness' (*xǐ*) that appears on a door in the emperor's nuptial room. Such rocks with characters carved into them have become smooth and shiny, polished by the passage of thousands upon thousands of hands. These practices are based on the belief that the concepts conveyed by the character are somehow 'incorporated' in the carving, and by touching the character one may 'absorb' part of its meaning.

The importance attributed to inscriptions is indeed one of the most striking features of Chinese art and civilisation (see Yen 2005). One of the main reasons for their prominence is the remarkable stability of Chinese characters, making it possible to decipher, to some extent, an inscription dating back several hundreds, if not thousands, of years. Within Chinese cosmology, almost any object bearing an inscription is considered more valuable than its non-inscribed counterpart. As Chang Kwang-Chih (1983, 81) explains of Ancient China:

The written record held the secret of the governance of the world; the inscriptions were identified with the information they contained because when writing began, they themselves were part of the instruments of the all-important heaven-earth communication. In other words, the medium was at least part of the message.

FIG 1.1. VISITORS EXAMINING ANCIENT CALLIGRAPHIC TEXTS, NATIONAL MUSEUM OF CHINA, BEIJING.

As a result, those individuals who mastered the skill of writing were considered highly: 'the power of the written word came from its association with knowledge – knowledge from the ancestors, with whom the living communicated through writing; which is to say, knowledge from the past, whose wisdom was revealed through its medium' (Chang 1983, 88).

The profound esteem in which inscriptions and writing are held is reflected in museums. At the entrance of museums in China it is usual to find auspicious calligraphic inscriptions, often created by an important personality. For instance, at the entrance of the Site of the First Congress of the Communist Party of China, in Shanghai, visitors can admire the calligraphic quality of inscriptions by Deng Xiaoping and Jiang Zemin (produced in 1984 and 1999 respectively). Inscriptions by such prominent political figures also contribute to setting the tone of the museum, providing evidence of the site's political importance. Such inscriptions are valuable museum objects due to their associations.

When an item in an exhibition bears inscriptions, it is common practice in China to transcribe these; the characters are represented graphically next to the object, often as a rubbing or in an enlarged photograph to make them legible. It is not surprising then that visitors pay at least as much attention to labels and inscriptions as to the objects themselves. This is also due to the fact that inscriptions very often bear historical, literary or metaphorical references that enhance appreciation of the object.

THE TRADITION OF COLLECTING IN CHINA

Some objects, such as bronzes or calligraphy scrolls, have had particular significance and value attributed to them by their makers, users, collectors and art-lovers throughout Chinese history. This section considers the reasons behind such sustained interest by exploring the corpus of cultural references that some artworks in today's museum collections continue to encapsulate.

Collecting in China is considered a cultural tradition (He 2000); indeed, the historian Joseph Alsop (1982) calls it a 'rare art tradition'. Government officials and elites since the earliest dynastic periods are known to have collected antiquities (Tong 1995, 183). However, it was not until the Song Dynasty (AD 960–1279) that a widespread interest in the past and antiquities developed (Capon 1977, 16). At that time, collecting was inspired by an attempt to retrieve the 'image of the great traditions of the Han and Tang dynasties' (Capon 1977, 31). It was notably the Song emperor Huizong (1101–25) who, being an art-lover and supposedly a painter himself, is thought to have started collecting paintings as well as commissioning works by important artists, thereby initiating the tradition of imperial collections.

The Chinese museologist Guo Changhong (2008, 80) distinguishes between imperial, elite and scholarly collections. The three types of collections are characterised by different modes of acquisition (inheritance, gifts and confiscation in the case of imperial collections, and marketplace purchase and exchange in the case of elite and scholarly collections), and different collection criteria (imperial collections emphasised the historical value of artefacts, elite collections were mostly driven by the economic value of collectibles, while scholarly collections were structured around concerns for the pedagogic and aesthetic dimensions of objects). Interestingly, as Guo (2008, 80) notes, 'growth or decline in these three collections often reflected political changes'.

From a Marxist–Leninist perspective, the dawn of collecting practices is linked to the crystallisation of the idea of the art object, which in turn developed with the appearance of private property (Su 1995, 61). From this viewpoint, the introduction of private property is seen as a disruptive moment leading to the dismantlement of communal society, the appearance of elitist classes and, with them, categories such as art objects. The accumulation of art objects (such as those found in funerary sites, for example) is considered indicative of social status.

From another point of view, Feng Chengbo (1993, 15) points out that the main motivation for collecting in China is to remember ancestors and ancient rituals. The habit of retaining and passing down ancient objects from one generation to the next (especially in the highest strata of society, such as elite governing families) is most probably linked to the cult of ancestors. Preserving the objects and symbols of ancestors was perceived as an act of deference, a way of 'paying respect' to one's ancestors. Professor Wang Hongjun[4] maintains that a concern for remembering the past (more so than preserving it) has always been central to Chinese culture. He describes remembering as 'one of the Chinese traditions', intimately linked to the ideas of knowledge, cultivation and respect for ancestors (Wang 2004, *pers comm*).

Not all antique objects however were (or are) attributed the same importance. Objects were especially highly valued when presenting a patina of age: 'although artificial patinating was prac- tised during the Song Dynasty (960–1279), connoisseurs agreed that only great age gave bronzes the desired mellowness' (Lowenthal 1985, 156). Some objects, such as ancient funerary relics, including glazed earthenware tomb figures or ceramic pillows, were not considered of much value during the Ming Dynasty (AD 1368–1644) because their close connection to funerary rites made them unsuitable for collection purposes. Not all collected ancient objects were destined to be exhibited. Some were used – for instance, during the Ming Dynasty, ancient bronzes were actually used as incense burners – while others were kept private, if not secret, and reserved for the gaze of the collector himself and for that of an invited few.

Perhaps a remnant of such secrecy can be found in the ongoing practice of keeping valuable objects wrapped in silk and cased in beautiful and precious boxes, rather than exhibited on full view in glass cases. This is particularly true of tea and tea sets (especially when offered as gifts) or ink sets (usually composed of ink, an ink slab and a writing brush). Tellingly, collections of calligraphy and paintings were called *biji*, meaning 'secret book-box'. From imperial times to the creation of the People's Republic, it was common for the richest and most powerful families to own private collections of art objects, passed on from generation to generation. Although access to the family collection was usually restricted, the simple fact of owning a collection was considered a symbol of power and social prestige. After 1949, most of these wealthy families fled – with their art collections – to Taiwan, Hong Kong, Australia or the United States, which explains why today's major Chinese collectors of Chinese art are based in these countries. Most 21st-century Chinese collectors are successful businessmen who consider collections a tasteful, philanthropic way to invest their fortunes, while improving their social profile. Mr Yi Jiang, for instance, is a private collector and famous ceramics artist based in Dingshan, Jiangsu Province.[5] Mr Yi's collection occupies two large rooms on the first floor of his house; the walls are lined with glass cases within which the objects are carefully illuminated by spotlights. Mr Yi has been collecting cultural relics for more than 30 years. The objects – including teapots, decorative oil

---

[4] Professor Wang, now retired, is the former director of the Chinese Cultural Relics Bureau; a former member of the Committee of Chinese History Museums; former Professor at the Department of History at Peking University; and honorary member of the Chinese Society of Museums.

[5] I visited Mr Yi's collection in October 2004. The market value of Mr Yi's creations can easily reach US $2000. Some of his teapots are exhibited at the New York State Museum.

lamps, sculptures, ornamental pots and other vessels – date from the Qing, Ming and, in some cases, even earlier dynasties. Some of the pieces in his collection are reproduced and described in art books which are also on display in the rooms. In these art objects, Mr Yi finds a source of inspiration for his own artistic creation. To some extent, Mr Yi's private collection epitomises his success, wealth and taste in a way that is perhaps not too dissimilar from the aristocratic European cabinets of curiosities of the Middle Ages.

Collection practices appear to be sustained by a plurality of factors: a deep interest in the past, reflected in the cult of ancestors, but also, according to the Marxist–Leninist theory, the existence of a bourgeois class that has the financial wealth necessary to set up private art collections. There is, however, a question that remains unanswered: in spite of such an important collecting tradition, why did China not develop a similar tradition of museums? According to the museologist An Laishun (1999), this is due to the elitist character of art: art and art appreciation were the prerogative of the imperial family and aristocrats. Moreover, early Chinese collections were not centred on natural or scientific specimens (as was the case in the European cabinets of curiosities) but on items linked to 'humanist' features such as literature, history, ethics and philosophy. This focus, in An's (1999) view, implied an orientation towards a cultivated, personal reflection on objects, rather than an aesthetic or scientific appreciation that could be shared with others. The museologist Su Donghai (1995, 65) has a slightly different view, and attributes the absence of a tradition of museums in China to social and economic factors: 'In China feudalism lasted until the end of the 19th century, so the conditions for a modern museum did not exist. [...] China lagged behind in the establishment of modern museums as a result of its later industrialisation.' Art objects in private collections were strictly connected to political authority; indeed, they became the tokens of such authority. The most powerful illustration of this is ritual bronzes.

RITUAL BRONZES AS SYMBOLS OF POLITICAL AUTHORITY

In the Chinese universe of references, ritual bronzes are among the objects most strongly associated with political power. Unsurprisingly, they feature in most exhibitions of ancient Chinese art, both within China and abroad. Consistently, bronzes are one of the most in-demand antiquities with collectors, as testified by the stellar prices achieved by some bronzes in art auctions.

The dawn of the Bronze Age is usually dated back to the 21st century BC, and associated with the establishment of the Xia Dynasty (although the existence of this dynasty remains a subject of debate among historians) (Dunedin Public Art Gallery 1999, 14). Bronze production reached its peak during the Shang (c. 1600–1046 BC) and Zhou (1046–256 BC) dynasties. The importance of bronzes has been clearly expressed in the preface to the catalogue of the touring exhibition *Treasures from the Bronze Age of China: An exhibition from the People's Republic of China*, held at the Metropolitan Museum of Art, New York, from 12 April to 9 July 1980, and subsequently touring major museums in the United States. The Committee for the Preparation of Exhibitions of Archaeological Relics states: 'The bronze objects of the Shang and Zhou periods represent the level of cultural development achieved during the early times of Chinese slave society. They possess a unique national style' (Metropolitan Museum of Art 1980, 6). It is worth noting that in this definition the quality of the bronzes does not refer to the technological or artistic skills displayed. Rather, in a much broader sense, the bronzes testify to the *cultural level* attained by the Chinese *nation*. In other words, in the Committee's interpretation, the bronzes are the tokens of a cultural system and they are attributed political meaning by virtue of their link to the nation.

FIG 1.2. *ZUN* BRONZE WINE VESSEL FROM THE SHANG DYNASTY (C. 1600–1146 BC), NATIONAL MUSEUM OF CHINA, BEIJING.

But why are bronzes ascribed such political relevance? According to legend, King Yu of the Xia Dynasty ordered that nine different bronzes be created, one for each of the nine provinces of his kingdom. Each province was requested to supply the bronze necessary for the creation of the objects. According to Williams (1976, 50), each bronze was engraved with the map of a province. These nine tripod bronze vessels (*jiu ding*) became the symbol of legitimate dynastic rule and as such were passed on from dynasty to dynasty (first to the Shang and later to the Zhou). The number nine was used to express the idea of a multitude of objects, so that those who possessed a multitude of *ding* were thought to hold the necessary wealth to access power. The association with wealth is also probably due to the fact that this kind of bronze vessel was used to cook and serve meat courses: the more bronzes one could boast, the greater the wealth displayed and the higher the rank (Thorp 1988, 25). Moreover, in the mythical narrative, the weight of the tripods was a metaphoric measure of the virtue of the government, and the transfer of these nine bronzes implied the transfer of power. On another level, bronzes symbolised the control of metal 'which meant control of exclusive access to the ancestors and to political authority' (Metropolitan Museum of Art 1980, 97). The Chinese scholar Chang Kwang-Chih (1983, 95) explains that in Ancient China (Xia, Shang and Zhou dynasties), access to power was granted to those 'controlling a few key resources – above all, bronzes – and [...] amassing the means to control them'.

As bronzes became a symbol of individual wealth and prestige, they were included in the funerary regalia of members of the elite. In the burial context, bronzes were a tool to immortalise the memory of a person and his or her virtues and merits, often detailed in the inscriptions featured on the vessels. Classic texts confirm this point: 'when the powerful have conquered the weak, they use their bounty to make ritual vessels and to cast inscriptions to record the deed, to show to their descendants, to publicise the bright and the virtuous, and to penalise those without rituals' (Chang 1983, 100). The Sinologist Chang Wan-Chen (1999, 92, my translation) further details the symbolism of bronzes:

> the bronzes symbolised the reality and the orthodoxy of power. Since the Western Zhou, the use of a *ding*, a kind of bronze tripod, was regulated to qualify the hierarchical status between the king and his subjects. Therefore, since, the bronzes, notably the *ding*, were considered symbols of power, the owners of a *ding* are the holders of the power.

The practice of inscribing bronzes dates back to the Shang Dynasty and was fully developed under the Western Zhou. Many centuries later, Song antiquarians would be particularly 'interested in the inscriptions on these vessels since they were considered to be messages, possibly even instructions, concerning the maintenance and performance of the ritual which was so vital a part of the system of government in China' (Capon 1977, 31). Thanks to their inscriptions, bronzes are extraordinary historical documents, allowing a better understanding of the historical, political and social structures of Ancient China. Although bronzes have always been considered as objects of special value, it was only in the 18th century that the importance of their inscriptions began to be recognised and to be used as a means of identification.

During the 'brilliance period' (late Shang Dynasty), particular emphasis was placed on the decoration of bronzes. The development of decoration and bronze-making skills is associated with the political stability of the Shang period. Designs emphasise symmetry and revolve around the figure of the *taotieh* – a mythical animal that appears in stylised form on many bronzes. The mystery that characterises this motif contributes to the object's charm, even in today's museums.

Charged with such a corpus of mythical, historical, political, social and artistic references, bronzes hold great evocative and communicative power. In the words of Rubie Watson (1998, 167), 'Shang bronzes and oracle bones, serve as a link to the very core of Chinese civilisation itself; they have a significance that goes beyond the representational force of even the most precious Song paintings'. Ritual bronzes were key items in imperial collections which, by extension, became the ultimate symbols of authority not only in Ancient and Imperial China, but also in the China of today.

THE POLITICAL RELEVANCE OF IMPERIAL COLLECTIONS

Craig Clunas (1997a, 45) clearly explains the relationship between art and power in Ancient China: '[rulers] needed ideological justification and support for their rule, needs which the symbolic resources of works of art could often satisfy'. Moreover, he continues, 'possession of ancient things stood for an equivalence with the wise rulers of ancient times' (1997a, 58). According to Rubie Watson (1998, 168), artefacts that made '"heaven and earth communication" possible (i.e. bronze offering vessels and the implements of writing and music) conferred special powers on those who possessed them […] the emperors' art collection both reflected and constituted imperial power and authority'.

The association of collections with imperial and political power is so strong that a link can be made between the size of imperial collections and the legitimacy of the ruler. Periods of collection and/or addition to the existing collections corresponded with periods of political strength, while periods of dispersion of the collection corresponded with a certain weakness and crisis within the central power. As the scholar Tamara Hamlish (2000, 150, 158) explains:

> [The imperial collections] would serve to represent the legitimacy of a modern Chinese nation possessed of a distinctive culture and a lengthy history […] What the state 'preserves' is not the collections themselves but their symbolic significance as a sign of political authority and legitimacy. In resisting the hegemony of a universalizing heritage, the state asserts its own hegemony over the construction of the Chinese past, instilling in museum visitors a memory of imperial rule that ultimately leads directly to the legitimization of the current state.

Interestingly, the long series of mysterious 'accidents' that led to the destruction and loss of parts of imperial collections were paralleled by corresponding attempts to de-legitimise the emperor's power. And, conversely, 'it was a form of lèse-majesté to possess a really important work of art and *not* to contribute it to the collection of the ruling dynasty' (Alsop 1982, 245).

Imperial collections continue to act as a barometer of political authority and legitimacy. Controversy over the detention of the imperial collections between the Palace Museum in Beijing and the National Palace Museum in Taipei exemplifies the political and symbolic importance that collections, to this day, still hold. The controversy was generated by the appropriation of the best items by the Nationalist government (Kuomintang, or KMT) and their move to Taiwan on the occasion of the Nationalist government's retreat to the island in 1949.[6] The dispute between

---

[6]   The best items in the imperial collections had left the Palace Museum in Beijing in 1933 when, on sensing the approaching danger of a Japanese invasion, the Chinese government moved a selection of the most valuable pieces to the southern city of Nanjing. Over 600,000 objects (including imperial thrones)

Communist and Nationalist China, and after 1949 between China and Taiwan, led to the creation of two separate 'Palace Museums' – one in Beijing and the other in Taipei – each claiming to represent the 'true' Chinese national identity, the 'true' authority, the 'true' China. The collections are not only artistic and historical treasures, but also hold tremendous value as symbols of Chinese civilisation and of moral and political authority. In recent years, however, cross-strait relations have improved and a 'museum diplomacy' has been put in place between the Palace Museum in Beijing and its counterpart in Taipei. The first collaborative projects were initiated in 2010, paving the way for further future joint ventures (see Barboza 2010).

Art, Cultural Heritage and Political Authority in the 20th Century

The complex relationship between cultural heritage and political authority in China throughout the 20th century sets the framework for discussion of the appearance and development of museums in China. Having examined the political role of art and heritage in Imperial China, this chapter now considers the changes brought about by the dissolution of the imperial system and efforts to create a modern China.

The four decades from 1911 to the establishment of Communist rule in 1949 were deeply influenced by the events of the May Fourth Movement in 1919. Until then, art had had a mostly entertaining, pleasurable dimension; the modernist movement of May Fourth attributed a reforming role to art. While references to Confucianism were targeted as obsolete – symbols of the empire's decadence and thus to be rejected – Western technological, military, political and cultural features were considered models for the creation of a new society. Art was meant to embody and interpret the idea of modernity which, in turn, was to be infused into the different social strata to perfect the process of reform. The ideals raised by the revolutionary movement proposed a vision of modernity imbued with Western literature and art. The movement rejected all references to Chinese traditions and philosophy (especially Confucianism) associated with intellectual elitism, as opposed to the proletarian class. As a result, not only all forms of art but also many aspects of social life – religion, leisure, food, New Year's customary celebrations and so on – were purged of any reference to traditional culture. Tradition was associated with the 'feudal' system and considered the ultimate cause of China's 'backwardness'. Attitudes towards the West were ambivalent: while some turned to the West for inspiration in the artistic, political and philosophical domains, others abhorred it as a cause of moral corruption.

Towards the end of the 1930s, with the coalescence of Communist ideals, art and cultural heritage became increasingly enmeshed with politics. In the framework of Marxist–Leninist thought, art had no function but as political and ideological propaganda. Both the Nationalist government and the Communist Party invested artistic expression with a 'social mission': art had to serve the nation, praising its greatness, unity and long history, and becoming a channel for expression of loyalty and patriotism. The Nationalist government encouraged the development of a new form of national painting, a mix of Chinese classical painting and Western styles, of which the major interpreter was Xu Beihong. In 1929, the first National Fine Art Exhibition was organised under the auspices of the Nationalist government in Shanghai.

were moved, first to Nanjing, then to Chongqing in Sichuan when the Japanese approached Nanjing in 1937, and then back to Nanjing following the Japanese retreat. It was from there that the Kuomintang selected the finest items to be moved to Taiwan (see Watson 1995, 11).

With the rise of Communism and Marxist ideology in the late 1930s, and more forcefully after 1949, artistic expression became almost totally subordinated to politics. As the museologist Hung Chang-Tai (2012, 586) puts it, 'in the Maoist aesthetic no distinction was made between art, life, and politics'. Indeed, Maria Galikowski (1998, 9) notes, 'After 1949, the Chinese Communist Party became the exclusive arbiter of cultural policy throughout the country.'

The outlines of Communist cultural policy were drawn in 1942 at the *Yan'an Forum on Literature and Art*. The event represents a milestone in the relationship between art and politics in China. The Communist Party's desire to incorporate art into Communist ideology was dictated by two sets of considerations. Firstly, as the Yan'an talks put forward very clearly, art was to become a tool of ideological legitimation. Secondly, it was imperative to incorporate artists in the revolutionary enterprise in order to secure their support for the system, keep them away from the perils of bourgeois artistic *dérives* and put their activity at the service of the community, integrating them in the proletariat system as 'cultural workers' (Galikowski 1998, 10). The translation of these concerns into propaganda slogans gave way to the well-known principle 'art must serve the people'. In Communist propaganda terms, this meant that 'first, culture and art should reflect people's life [...] and second, culture and art should stress national characteristics and styles so that people will accept and favour them, thus educating, encouraging and entertaining people' (Gao 1999, 3).

The National Art Museum of China (NAMOC) in Beijing – a creation of the newly established Communist government – exemplifies this approach. The Museum focuses on the artistic forms privileged in Communist ideology, such as painting and wood-carving, as well as artistic traditions, such as paper-cutting and theatrical puppetry. The rationale underpinning displays at the NAMOC does not follow conventional historical, chronological or stylistic criteria. Works are selected by virtue of their capacity to evoke Communist values: the spirit of sacrifice and martyrdom, loyalty to the motherland, the ideals of the progress of the nation and of the triumph of Communist ideals.

Although in the first decades of the 20th century arts were purified from the 'burden of tradition', under Communist rule some traditional art forms were kept alive to the extent that they could be reinterpreted to suit the needs of propaganda. Theatre, opera and folk music were used by the Red Army to channel propaganda ideals and to pursue, in the words of Chen Boda, Mao's secretary, 'the combination of new cultural content with old national form' (quoted in Holm 1991, 53). This idea was popularised by the slogan 'putting new wine in old bottles'. In a speech dated 1940, Mao specified that such 'national form' corresponded to a 'national, scientific and mass culture' (Mao 1940). In this definition appear the main themes of Communist political philosophy. Firstly, there is the idea of 'nation' and 'nationality'. As David Holm (1991, 74) explains, 'by calling this new culture "national" Mao meant two things: first, that it was adapted for China's needs; and secondly that it should belong to the peasants'. Secondly, there is the focus on science and scientific attitude. Here again Holm (ibid, 74) clarifies the point: 'by describing New Democratic culture as scientific, Mao meant primarily that it was "opposed to all feudal and superstitious ideas, and stands for seeking the truth from facts"'. Thirdly, the use of the term 'mass' to designate the culture of the nation meant that culture had to be an emanation of the people, reflecting people's needs and expectations, while at the same time addressing the people. In Mao's mind, 'the people' were mainly represented by the peasants, thus the idea of a 'culture for the masses' can be taken to approximate that of a 'culture for the peasants'. The results of decades of Maoism in terms of culture production were scant. As Edward Friedman (1994, 76) notes, because of the censorship on books and culture in general, 'throughout the Mao era, no powerful national literature or culture was produced'.

However, some exceptions apply. In the decade that followed the creation of the People's Republic, southern Chinese provinces started to exert a growing influence at the national level. Notably, a proliferation of propaganda literature brought southern China to the fore in the construction of Chinese national identity by demonstrating its contribution to the formation of Chinese civilisation.

The Second Sino-Japanese War (1937–45) represented an important test for the Communist national spirit that was gradually coalescing: the common enemy contributed to the formation of a Chinese-Communist national identity via a process of cultural differentiation and opposition to the Japanese 'other'. Anti-Japanese propaganda, through songs, leaflets, posters, dances, etc, ultimately gave significant impetus to the creation of what Mao called a 'new democratic culture'. From another point of view, the war against Japan and all the propaganda it entailed helped to crystallise further the status of art as subordinated to politics. In 1942, Mao (1967, 86) adamantly decreed art a tool at the service of politics: 'there is in fact no such thing as art for art's sake, art that stands above classes, art that is detached from or independent of politics'. The absolute nature of this decree suggests an inability (and an unwillingness) to conceive of art as a purely creative form of expression.

Mao's position on foreign literature and art was no less trenchant: 'the completely uncritical rigid transfer, imitation, and substitution of the works of dead men and foreigners is the most useless and harmful literary dogmatism' (quoted in Holm 1991, 96). Although this position was later to be slightly softened, during Maoism, foreign art was regarded with suspicion by public authorities. In a most pragmatic approach, a governmental publication on Chinese cultural policies in the 1950s reported that 'cultural construction needs to absorb active elements from traditional and foreign cultures, mix them with the modern spirit and Chinese characteristics and further develop them' (Gao 1999, 11). This idea was later conveyed in the slogan 'make foreign things serve China' (ibid, 10).

In continuity with these guidelines, the 1950s were marked by the crystallisation and institutionalisation of the links between the government and artists; artists were organised into associations according to activity (associations of writers, painters, calligraphers, potters and so on). At the same time, new journals and specialised periodicals on art were created (among others, *People's Art*, *Popular Arts* and *People's Literature*). These publications were run under strict governmental control. Stern guidelines were imposed upon figurative art, most notably the pictorial dogma of Socialist Realism, according to which art had to reflect the 'material' and 'objective' reality of life (the paintings exhibited at the NAMOC provide good examples of Socialist Realism). In 1958, also as a consequence of the international isolation of China, the Great Leap Forward movement called for even more 'national' and 'popular' forms of art. Feeling threatened by the American alliance with Taiwan and weakened by the rupture of political relations with the Soviet Union, China turned to (artistic) nationalism as an antidote to the crisis. Chinese traditional art, albeit previously condemned as 'bourgeois', was now declared acceptable to the extent that it supported government-approved ideas of Chinese national identity.

The period that followed the Great Leap Forward is probably one of the darkest in Chinese history. During the Cultural Revolution (1966–76), cultural heritage was associated with the 'four old': old ideas, old culture, old customs and old habits. All had to be destroyed. Artists, collectors and art-lovers were persecuted as 'social parasites'. This decade of terror not only annihilated art production, but also inflicted deep wounds on all aspects of social relations and social life in China.

Towards the end of the 1970s and in the early 1980s, under the influence of some ground-breaking international exchanges in the art domain (including exhibitions of foreign art held in Beijing and the translation of foreign art journals),[7] Chinese artists started to advocate the right to free art expression, devoid of political and ideological connotations. This position was shared by museum professionals, who 'said they look forward to a time when artifacts are allowed to speak for themselves without the heavy veneer of political interpretation' (Ferguson 1981, 52).

Partly in response to such claims to artistic freedom, in 1982 the government launched the 'Anti-Spiritual Pollution Campaign', in the name of which a climate of intellectual and artistic repression was once more established. The censorship campaign continued until at least 1985. In the second half of the 1980s, the ideological climate changed again as a result of Deng Xiaoping's campaign of 'spiritual civilisation' (later revived by Jiang Zemin, at the time mayor of Shanghai), which shifted the focus back onto the foundational role of cultural institutions.

The events of June 1989 in Tian An Men Square marked the beginning of another period of repression for art in China. Despite the success of a first national avant-garde art exhibition at the National Gallery in Beijing in February 1989,[8] creative expression was dramatically reduced through the widespread dismissal of art journal employees, censorship of art editions and the closure of art venues.

In 21st-century China, can art be said to be completely disengaged and liberated from political agendas? The curatorial decisions taken in the newly refurbished National Museum of China – currently the country's most prominent site for the display of Chinese art to domestic and international audiences – is telling. In the Museum, artistic production since 1949 is represented by works linked to Communist ideals and history. In particular, the Museum has set up a gallery devoted to the Masterpieces of Modern Chinese Fine Arts from the National Museum Collection. The works on display include paintings and sculptures of revolutionary propaganda, bearing titles such as *Founding Ceremony of People's Republic of China* by Dong Xiwen, *Mao Zedong at the December Meeting* by Jin Shangyi, *Mao Zedong in Jinggang Mountain* by Luo Gongliu, and *Five Heroes in Langya Mountain* by Zhan Jianjun (National Museum of China n.d.b). This selection of works, made to represent 'modern Chinese fine arts', highlights the ongoing politicisation of the arts in China.

This chapter has aimed to introduce key conceptual elements (such as basic definitions of cultural heritage), cultural considerations (such as the importance of inscriptions) and historical background (such as the historic links between imperial collections and political authority) in order to familiarise the reader with the cultural heritage realm in China. These elements provide cultural and historical contextualisation for analysis of the development of the museum institution in China, which is the topic of the next chapter.

---

[7]   A couple of journals in particular became sources of inspiration for Chinese artists. They are the *Review of Foreign Art* (*Guowai meishu ziliao*), which would be renamed the *Journal of Art Translation* (*Meishu yicong*), and *World Art* (*Shijie meishu*).

[8]   The artists' success in gaining permission from the authorities to set up this first exhibition of avant-garde art was, however, only partial, since the authorities closed the exhibition down twice during the few weeks in which it was due to take place.

2

Museums in China: Origins and Development

The Historical Development of Museums in China

The notion of the museum as a public institution has a relatively short history in China, having been imported by the colonial powers Great Britain, France and Japan. Indeed, 'Asian nations are still struggling, with mixed results, to domesticate this somewhat exotic transplant' (Kahn 1998, 226). Referring to museums in early 20th-century China, the Chinese museologist Guo Changhong (2008, 80) notes that, in China, the museums of the time were frequently viewed as 'imported wonders'. The effort to educate the Chinese people, safeguard cultural artefacts and promote research through museums can be directly attributed to an increasing acceptance of Western ideas in early modern China, as well as to the institutional transformations Chinese society underwent in the wake of the Revolution.

In the evolution of museums in China, three phases can be identified.[1] The first phase is associated with forms of proto-museums, such as the Temple of Confucius. Although Chinese museology considers these to be the origins of the institution, strictly speaking, museums did not appear in China until the second half of the 19th century. The establishment of the first museum open to the public, in 1868, marked the dawn of a second phase in the history of Chinese museums. The spread of museums accompanied the transition from the imperial to the republican system, as marked by the emblematic transformation, in 1925, of the Imperial Palace (Forbidden City) into a public museum. The creation of numerous new museums also punctuated the fusion of the republican and nationalist political projects, until the ravages of war against Japan and the civil war dramatically interrupted the rise of museums. The third phase, from 1949 to the present, includes the museums of the 'New China' created under Communist rule. The landscape of museums in China has become increasingly complex in recent decades, so much so that it makes sense to consider developments from the early 1990s onwards as a fourth phase in the evolution of Chinese museums. Let us consider each of these phases in more detail.

According to Chinese museum academics (H Wang 2004, *pers comm*; see also Su 1995, 61), the origins of museums in China can be traced back to the Temple of Confucius in Qufu, Shandong Province. Allegedly, a few years after Confucius' death in 479 BC, his home was transformed into a temple and all his belongings were preserved as 'sacred' objects. Officially, the temple was only assigned the status of museum in 1994. By claiming that the first museum dates back to the 5th century BC, the museum institution is implicitly constructed as a Chinese creation, rather than an import from the West. From another point of view, this narrative on the long history of

---

[1]   This tripartite subdivision in the history of museums is suggested by, among others, the museologist Su Donghai (1995, 61–80).

museums dating back to Confucius suits the ongoing trend of re-evaluation and reinterpretation of Chinese traditional culture and ancient history.

Proto-museums, or embryonic forms of museums, are also associated with the temples that in Ancient China were devoted to mythical figures such as Ma Zu, the divinity that protected sailors. She was considered 'the guardian of the sea', and it is still possible to find a number of temples devoted to her in southern China (as well as in other areas of Southeast Asia). Such proto-museums did not include scientific specimens, as was the case in Europe with the cabinets of curiosities, but were inspired by a concern for remembrance. Professor Wang Hongjun has no hesitation in placing the notion of remembrance at the core of the Chinese conceptualisation of museums (Wang 2004, *pers comm*). According to Professor Wang, the concern for remembrance also explains the large number of museums devoted to historical figures, including writers, artists, philosophers, national heroes and politicians.

MUSEUMS AS A SIGN OF 'MODERNITY'

The first museums appeared in China towards the end of the 19th century, introduced by Western missionaries and researchers. The coastal regions, including the Shanghai area, were privileged locations for these first museums. They were created by non-Chinese on the model of Western (or Japanese) museums and were meant to support the activities of Western researchers in the field of natural sciences. Among them were the Shanghai Xujiahui Museum (a natural history museum), founded by a French missionary, Pierre Heude, in 1868;[2] the Shanghai Museum, created in 1871 by the north China section of the Royal Asiatic Society; the Asian Cultural Association Museum, established by the British in 1876; and the Yidu Museum, founded by the missionary I S Wright in 1887 (Flath 2002, 43).

The opening of these museums occurred in a context of ideological crisis for the country, as the decline of the imperial system triggered a process of deep, often dramatic, transformations affecting Chinese society at large. The 19th century can reasonably be called a century of crisis for China: it brought the colonisation of the major ports (from 1842), civil war between the Qing Dynasty and Christian religious groups known as the Taiping Rebellion (1850–64), and persistent generalised opposition to the Manchu rulers (who had always been considered invaders), accompanied by calls for political and social reform.

Towards the end of the 19th century, an increasingly strong reformist movement started to gain momentum beyond the Imperial Palace walls. The reformist attempts of the Qing court – epitomised by the one-hundred-days reforms of Emperor Guangxu – were frustrated by the conservative position of Empress Cixi. Too superficial, too slow, too late, the reforms did not succeed in restructuring the imperial system.

The end of the imperial era and the transition to the republican system were accompanied by an unprecedented interest in the West. Confucianism and, more generally, traditional culture were considered the cause of China's 'backwardness' in a variety of fields, including political philosophy, economy, science, technology and social relations. The more moderate reformists argued for the need to open up to Western influences and consider them as tools to renew the institutional system. They proposed combining Western ideas on government and citizenry with

---

[2] Originally named Musée Heude, the museum was renamed Xujiahui Museum in 1883.

Confucian values, which would help to 'moralise' and legitimate Western imports (Chevrier 1990, 89).

Around 1915, a movement of urban intellectuals (mainly from the coastal areas), called the 'New Cultural Movement', became one of the major partisans of the spread of Western thought and ideas, leading to the appearance of the first Western publications, books and newspapers. In such an intellectual and political framework, Western and Japanese ideas on museums found fertile ground. Museums appeared as tokens and vehicles of modernity (Song 2004a, *pers comm*).

The pioneer of Chinese museums was the intellectual and industrialist Zhang Qian, who opened the first Chinese museum in 1905 in Nantong (Jiangsu Province).[3] Zhang's original plans for a museum were grander. Before setting up the Nantong Museum, Zhang had unsuccessfully sought authorisation from the Qing court to establish a Chinese Imperial Palace Museum in Beijing, based on the model of the Japanese Imperial Palace Museum. Inspired by Japanese museums, and in particular by the Universal Fair in Japan, Nantong Museum held artistic, historical and natural specimens, and included a botanical garden and zoo. The Museum was to serve pedagogic and didactic purposes. Zhang commented that the educational function of museums had to 'restore the trust of Chinese peoples in themselves, and this way save the motherland, at that time attacked and partially occupied by foreign troops' (quoted in Chang 1999, 106, my translation). In this sense, the Nantong Museum was a nationalistic endeavour. As Lisa Claypool (2005, 569) explains:

> the loss of cultural artifacts posed a real threat to Chinese identity – elite and national. The museum was generally perceived as a protection against such loss [...] The museum exhibited the civilising strength and wealth of a state by demonstrating its ability to explore the globe and extract specimen and objects.

The Nantong Museum appropriated the narratives and modes of classification of the above-mentioned Western-style museums established in Shanghai's foreign settlements at the end of the 19th century. Thus, collections were organised into art, archaeology, history and natural science sections; notions of order and hierarchy were incorporated in this new knowledge system. The Nantong Museum did not aim so much at celebrating China's glorious past as at showing the wealth of the Chinese nation, its moral and intellectual stature, its technological potential and scientific achievement. It attempted to educate its public about the Chinese nation through displays on science and civic education that possessed Western scientific authority (Claypool 2005, 569–70). Following this Museum's lead, the first national exhibition, in Nanjing in 1909, combined aesthetic exhibits which should 'please the eye and warm the heart' with accessibility, education and scientific rigour; displayed items would be 'understood at a glance' (Fernsebner 2006, 109–10).

The opening of the Nantong Museum contributed to cultural reforms that would see China enter the world stage. Under the supervision of Cai Yuanpei, minister of education in Sun Yat-Sen's government, the first years of the Republic of China witnessed the creation of the National Museum of Chinese History in 1912 and the Nanjing Museum in 1915. These two museums were followed by several others at the provincial level: the Provincial Museum of Tianjin, Hebei,

---

[3]   The museum was destroyed by the Japanese in 1938.

in 1918; the Fuzhou Museum, Fujian, in 1923; and the Provincial Museum of Zhejiang in 1929. The concept of public museums paved the way to the dismantling of imperial collections and contributed to the establishment of knowledge as a civic right and a public good. As discussed, in the past, private collections were a symbol of power and social prestige. By fostering exclusivity and restricting access to the aesthetics of arts, they represented the very system of imperial privileges that the reformists aimed to destroy. In this sense, the transformation of the 'Forbidden City' into the Palace Museum in 1925 represents one of the most important events in the history of Chinese museums: the former residence of the emperor, his personal belongings and the most intimate aspects of his daily life were now exposed to everyone's gaze and judgement. As the Chinese museologist Guo Changhong (2008, 82) notes, 'The public's newly-won right to glimpse these valuable artefacts *in situ* was seen as concrete proof of the political importance of this new cultural institution.' The transformation of the Imperial Palace into a public museum was one of the most effective steps taken to achieve the desacralisation of the emperor, contextually marking the end of an era.

In 1935, the process of the institutionalisation of museums was significantly fostered by the creation of the Chinese Museum Association. However, the outbreak of war against Japan in 1937 dramatically disrupted the development of museums. In 1937, on the brink of war, there were around 65 to 70 museums in China; in 1949, only 25 were left (H Wang 2004, *pers comm*).[4] The museums created during the first half of the 20th century have been dismissed by Chinese officials as a facet of the 'old, semi-feudal and semi-colonial China [where] such institutions had little scope for development' (Museums Department of the State Administrative Bureau of Museums and Archaeological Data 1980, 171). Things were set to change with the rise of Communist power.

Museums in Communist China

In the context of Communist China, museums have been mainly conceived as propaganda tools. As mentioned previously, Mao held the primacy of revolutionary ideals over artistic expression: art was officially supposed to serve the cause of the Communist Party. During the years preceding and following the creation of the People's Republic, most aspects of social life – education, employment, as well as leisure activities – were managed or supervised by the army, which also set guidelines in the area of cultural policy.

It was at the 1949 turning point that the very idea of museology as an independent science (that is, independent from history and archaeology) came to the fore. In the Marxist–Leninist view, museums can only develop within a society that has reached a given stage of development (H Wang 2004, *pers comm*). The museologist Su Donghai explains that 'the modern sense of the museum is an outcome of industrial civilisation. Museums in the primitive sense cannot turn into modern museums unless they have gone through the test of modern science and democracy' (Su 1995, 64). Although the reference to democracy may raise eyebrows, these statements suggest that the development of museums is understood to be an achievement made possible by Communist rule.

In line with Mao's focus on 'modernity', in the decades following 1949, museum activities

---

[4]   Other sources (An 1991, 3) report the number of museums in 1949 to be 21.

were carried out under the slogans 'stress the present, not the past' and 'make the past serve the present'. Represented in this way, ancient history appeared as the ultimate token of 'backwardness', and its storehouses – museums – as the emblems of a backward society. As An Laishun (1999, 5) reports, 'to serve for politics and socialism were the basic definition on [sic] museum functions at that time'. In museum exhibitions, the Communist tale, with its martyrs and heroes, was to be an inspiration and a model contributing to the popularisation of Communist ideology and the creation of a shared mythology. Feng Chengbo (1991, 18) reports that 'during the first Five Year Plan [...] museums were set up in the provinces to preserve and illustrate the country's regional and local natural resources, history, and political history'. The themes of the exhibitions set up in these years – bearing titles such as 'Land Reform', 'Revolutionary History' and 'Social Development History' – illustrate how museums at this time were a channel through which historical, social and economic information was spread, contextually conveying new notions of national identity and national unity.

During the Great Leap Forward (1958–61), the development of museums accelerated considerably. In 1959, on the occasion of the tenth anniversary of the founding of the People's Republic, the government allocated funds for the creation of a core of national museums (Su 1995, 65). These included the Museum of Chinese History, the Museum of the Chinese Revolution, the Natural History Museum, the Cultural Palace of Nationalities and the Chinese Military Museum, among others. These institutions would be the pillars of the Chinese museums system for decades. The network was also significantly enhanced by the establishment of museums at the county level. The process was summarised by the slogan 'every county must have its museum, every commune its exhibition hall' (*xianxian you bowuguan, sheshe you zhanlanshi*). The paradox of such a decision was that museums had to be created even in the absence of relevant collections and qualified museum staff. This led to a multitude of museums with poor content and low exhibition quality. Feng Chengbo (1991, 18–19) recalls that:

> almost overnight, thousands of museums emerged without collections, professional staff, or buildings. Most of them dissolved during the economic recession and natural disasters of the years between 1959 and 1961 [...] Numerous exhibits were designed and displayed to meet the needs of political programs such as land reform, the teaching of historical materialism, and anti-corruption and anti-waste campaigns. The political function of museums became an essential tenet, and their missions either were to serve politics or serve production.

During the Cultural Revolution (1966–76), artistic production and cultural expressions not of a propagandistic nature were considered obsolete, remnants of a social system based on the exploitation of the working classes, the reserve of a wealthy bourgeoisie who could devote themselves to unproductive luxury activities such as art. Ancient art in particular became the emblem of the social paradigm that the young Red Guards were urged to crush. Those emblems of an ancient world had to be destroyed in order to make room for the 'New China'. It is no secret that 'during the ten-year "cultural revolution" [...] large numbers of cultural relics were destroyed. However, a few rare objects and nationally protected relics were well preserved by the army' (Min 1989, 104). Almost all museums were at some point during this dark decade, and for varying periods of time, closed down. Although rarely remarked upon, the damage extended not only to objects, but also to people: 'museum workers were physically injured and mentally affected' (Lu 1994, 2).

The end of the Cultural Revolution and the 1978–79 turn towards reforms brought museum experts to a reformulation of the old 'three natures and two tasks' theory.[5] Scientific research, while remaining a key function of museums, was no longer considered the main issue. The collection and preservation of cultural relics were given priority, followed by education and, lastly, scientific research. As James Flath (2002, 50) recalls, 'it was not until 1977 that provincial authorities began to account for cultural relics, initiate protection policies, and build and restore museums and archives'.

The late 1970s were marked by the 'open door' policy, the process of reforms of domestic institutions and cautious opening to the outside world. This corresponded with a temporary relief from artistic and cultural repression: 'class struggle was no longer the key link in Chinese life', thus 'museums resumed their cultural essence again' (An 1999, 6). Economic reforms were pursued through the strategy of 'the four modernisations': modernisation of industry, agriculture, science and technology, and defence. In the museum field, this phase was punctuated by an increase in the number and quality of museums. Several academic courses on museology were established in the early 1980s (notably in Beijing, Shanghai, and Nankai University, Tianjin). At the same time, several museum associations were created: the Chinese Society of Natural Museums was established in 1980, the Chinese Society of Museums in 1982, and the Chinese Society of Agricultural Museums in 1984. These domestic reforms of the museum system coincided with China opening up to Western and international museology. In 1982, China became a member of the International Committee of Museums (ICOM). By joining ICOM, China became attuned to international museology standards. ICOM membership offered unprecedented opportunities for exchanges at international level (exchanges of museum practices, concepts and approaches, but also of museum professionals, exhibitions and data). These exchanges allowed the Chinese government to cast a self-critical gaze on the national museum system; one of the features that emerged was that historical and cultural museums were well represented, to the detriment of scientific and technological ones (H Wang 2004, *pers comm*). This, together with the race to modernisation and industrialisation, helps to explain the large-scale creation of technology museums (transport, aeronautical, naval and military museums, among others) that marked the two decades 1980–2000. It is worth noting, however, that the exchanges and initiatives of cooperation with foreign experts triggered by accession to ICOM mainly revolved around technical aspects (basically, how technology could be used to improve exhibitions), while matters of content, such as the topics of exhibitions, were excluded from discussions.

The eighth five-year plan (covering the years from 1991 to 1995) included some guidelines for museums. Ma Zishu (1994, 2), at that time vice director of the State Bureau of Cultural Relics, offers a summary of such guidelines:

> museums of history and revolution shall mainly show off the national attitude, revolutionary spirit and creative power of the Chinese people. Memorial halls shall highlight their memorial characteristics and record actual events. Nationality and folk custom museums shall emphasise fine traditions and solidarity spirit of this united multinational country.

In spite of the conservatism that these dispositions suggest, it would be misleading to overlook the deep process of change that has been reshaping the profile of Chinese museums since the

---

5   For this theory, see page 36.

early 1990s, most notably the sharp increase in the number of museums. High-level museum authorities such as Zhang Wenbin (2008, 9), former director of the State Administration of Cultural Heritage, have described the exponential growth of museums in contemporary China as 'laudable' and an 'encouraging situation [that] can been attributed to governmental policies of ideological emancipation, pragmatism, opening and reform'.

LEGAL PROVISIONS ON MUSEUMS AND CULTURAL HERITAGE

Since the 1990s, authorities and international observers have been increasingly attentive to the question of the protection of cultural heritage in China. Conspicuous media campaigns have led to an increased social and political awareness surrounding the issues of cultural heritage preservation.[6] The protection of cultural heritage is sanctioned at the constitutional level. Article 22 of the Chinese Constitution (National People's Congress of the People's Republic of China 2004) states:

> The state promotes the development of literature and art, the press, broadcasting and television undertakings, publishing and distribution services, libraries, museums, cultural centres and other cultural undertakings, that serve the people and socialism, and sponsors mass cultural activities. The state protects places of scenic and historical interest, valuable cultural monuments and relics and other important items of China's historical and cultural heritage.

The socialist ideology infusing this constitutional formula becomes even more evident in the Law of the People's Republic of China on the Protection of Cultural Relics (Chinese Government Official Web Portal 2013), passed in October 2002. The first article of the law states:

> With a view to strengthening the protection of cultural relics, inheriting the splendid historical and cultural legacy of the Chinese Nation, promoting the scientific research, conducting education in patriotism and revolutionary tradition, and building the socialist spiritual and material civilisation, this Law is formulated in accordance with the Constitution.

The use of the adjective 'splendid' denotes a subjective judgement, and cultural relics are defined in terms of the 'legacy of the Chinese nation'. The use of the term 'nation', rather than 'state', also has precise connotations, referring to the community of people sharing the features of Chinese civilisation. Similarly, the references to patriotism and the 'revolutionary tradition' unmistakably place this law within the framework of Communist ideology. The stated aims of 'conducting education in patriotism and revolutionary tradition, and building the socialist spiritual and material civilisation' reinstate the pillars of Chinese political ideology: the subordination of education to patriotism and to the Marxist ideals of Communist and socialist society.

In an article that appeared in the journal *Art, Antiquity and Law* in March 2000, the Chinese lawyer He Shuzong (2000, 35) cautions against the dangers of a continuous politicisation of preservation policies:

---

6 This is confirmed by the amount of public funds that are channelled into preservation: 'The special subsidies on the cultural relics protection from the central finance has raised to RMB276 million in 2002 from RMB129 million in 1995' (Academic Exchanges on Conservation of China 2003).

The socialist revolutionary tradition is still the most significant aspect of China's cultural inheritance, and the monuments of the socialist leaders remain the most important cultural properties. Preserving political ideals is important for China. The revolutionary monuments are easier to get support from the government than ordinary cultural sites, and some of the revolutionary monuments are indeed cultural sites of modern history. But if the political ideal is higher than that of a wider culture or history, the protected cultural heritage will become the revolutionary heritage alone.

The total number of cultural relics in Chinese museums and libraries is estimated at approximately 11 million (He 2000). This impressive figure is probably explained by the fact that, as mentioned previously, the 2002 law provides an extremely loose definition of 'cultural relic'. To appreciate the contribution of the 2002 law, it is worth putting it into context and taking a few steps back to briefly consider the evolution of the legislation on the protection of cultural relics since 1949.

The first legal acts of the Communist government in the cultural heritage domain were aimed at limiting the export of Chinese cultural relics, considered crucial in the construction of the 'New China'. As of 1960, a law prohibited the export of all relics pre-dating 1795, as well as a wide range of later relics. In 1967, in the midst of the Cultural Revolution (1966–76), the government issued an order intended to save relics and old books from the ravages of the Revolution; people were asked to donate such items to local authorities, who would forward them to museums (unless they were deemed to be 'superstitious', 'old' or 'traditional', in which case they were destroyed). A Law on the Protection of Cultural Relics (Chinese Government Official Web Portal 2013) was passed in 1982 by the Standing Committee of the National People's Congress. The law was subsequently revised in 1991, and again in 2002. China also ratified the UNESCO (1972) *Convention on the Protection of World Cultural and Natural Heritage* (The World Heritage Convention) (UNESCO 1972) in 1985; the UNESCO (1970) *Convention on the Means of Prohibiting and Preventing the Illicit Import, Export and Transfer of Ownership of Cultural Property* (UNESCO 1970) in 1989; and the UNIDROIT (1995) *Convention on Stolen or Illegally Exported Cultural Objects* (UNIDROIT 1995) in 1997.

As far as museums are concerned, the 2002 Law on the Protection of Cultural Relics defines them as 'cultural relics collection entities'. From a jurisdictional point of view, museums are organised at three levels: national, provincial (in some instances including municipal museums) and local museums (either of prefecture or county level). In most instances, national museums are subordinated to a branch of the central government, usually a ministry. For instance, the Military Museum is controlled by the Central Military Commission, the Museum of Agriculture by the Ministry of Agriculture, the Cultural Palace of Nationalities by the State Commission of Nationalities, the Science and Technology Museum by the State Commission of Science and Technology, and so on (Song 2004b, *pers comm*). The second level – provincial and municipal museums – includes the museums of the autonomous regions (Xinjiang, Tibet, Inner Mongolia, Guangxi and Ningxia).

In the domain of museums, the presiding institution is the State Administration of Cultural Heritage (SACH, formerly State Bureau of Cultural Relics). SACH was established in 2003 under the aegis of the Ministry of Culture. Other museum-related institutions that gravitate around the Ministry of Culture include the Chinese Society of Museums, the Chinese National Committee of ICOM and the National Research Institute of Cultural Heritage.

The main legal tool in the management of museums is the Law on the Protection of Cultural Relics, approved in 2002. The text of Article 40 of the law details the functions of museums: 'Cultural relics collection entities shall make full use of the cultural relics in their collection, and, by holding exhibitions and conducting scientific research, etc., strengthen the propaganda and education of the splendid historical culture and revolutionary traditions of the Chinese Nation' (Chinese Government Official Web Portal 2013). Museum exhibitions and research activities are explicitly framed as tools of political propaganda, a propaganda relying on the celebration of both the recent ('revolutionary') and the ancient past (the 'splendid historical culture').

Article 37 specifies the methods of acquisition of museum objects; these are: '(1) Purchasing; (2) Accepting donations; (3) Exchanging according to law; (4) Other methods provided for by laws and administrative regulations'. In relation to this last point, Article 53 mentions the establishment of cultural relics shops through which the state can sell cultural relics and, significantly, buy precious objects from particular people and organisations: 'the state encourages citizens, legal persons and other organisations other than cultural relics collection entities to donate the cultural relics they collect to collection entities of state-owned cultural relics or lend them to cultural relics collection entities for exhibition and research'. Interestingly, the Shanghai History Museum adopted a similar approach, directly addressing its audiences and inviting them to contribute material for exhibitions. On the Museum's website one could read the following:

> In order to reflect more deeply and accurately the evolution and development of the city of Shanghai and further substantiate, enrich and improve the content and level of exhibition, the Shanghai History Museum sets up a special department to collect materials in kind which mirror the history of Shanghai's local development. We request those at home and abroad who are familiar with or have collected materials concerning Shanghai's historical relics to provide us with relevant clues.[7]   (Shanghai History Museum website 2004)

One can imagine that through this public appeal the Museum was hoping to tap into the collections of wealthy Shanghainese citizens and the diaspora, and divert objects from the antiques market.

Although the 2002 law states that the establishment of private businesses in the field of cultural relics is prohibited (Article 55), many private or semi-private auction houses have appeared in recent years. This is partly as a result of the ambiguity of the law, Article 54 of which authorises 'auction enterprises' to operate next to cultural relic shops on the cultural relics market. In spite of the ambivalent status of domestic auction enterprises, the law clearly forbids the creation of

---

7   The public appeal gave the following further intriguing details: 'Scope of collecting: materials concerning the historical relics reflecting the local development since the founding of the county of Shanghai, and about the foreign settlement and concession, economy, municipal construction, culture, education, hygiene, science and technology, art, journalism, publication, urban residents' customs, and political parties and groups. Varieties for collecting: newspapers, periodicals, books, textbooks, documents, original manuscripts, inscriptions, photographs, certificates, seals, signboards, nameplates, bills, account books, coins, postal stamps, stone tablets, rubbings, works of art, archives, living utensils and articles, and tools of production. Ways of collecting: donation, purchase, borrowing, storing on the owner's behalf, and exchange'. This text featured on the English homepage of the Shanghai History Museum website (http://www.historymuseum.sh.cn/en.php) in 2004. It was later removed following a revamp of the website.

joint ventures with foreign companies.[8] Cultural relics represent a flourishing industry in China today. Until 1992, the 'market of cultural relics' was strictly controlled by the state, which acted through a limited number of authorised antique shops. Through such shops, the state could buy pieces from private collectors and pass them on to museums or individuals. The whole system was controlled and managed by the state. In 1992, in line with a general trend towards liberalisation and the 'open door' policy, the cultural relics market was reformed and private initiative encouraged. As a result, new actors entered the market, including, among others, private auction houses and cultural relic dealers. The 2002 Law on the Protection of Cultural Relics institutionalised these changes. The current situation can be described as follows:

> It is regulated in the new cultural relics law that besides the state-owned cultural relics collection unit, the other citizens, legal representatives and organizations can obtain cultural relics through the following ways, including legal heritage and acceptance from donation, purchase from cultural relics stores, purchase from auction enterprises which engage in such auction business, change or transfer of cultural relics legally possessed by individuals, and other legal ways regulated by the state. (*Beijing Daily* 2003)

The museologist Song Xiangguang explains that 'the current antiques market in China can now be divided into four types of enterprises: 1) government antiques stores and authorised non-governmental antiques stores, 2) auction houses licensed for trading antiques, 3) non-governmental antiques markets under government inspection and 4) the underground antiques trade' (quoted in Nerison-Low 2001). As mentioned previously, the creation of private auction houses is encouraged, but on the condition that they are domestic institutions.

Since the 2002 landmark law, the Chinese government has encouraged a series of initiatives to further regulate museum activities. These include guidelines for museum practice, *Solutions on Museum Management* (*Bowuguan Guanli Banfa*), issued in 2005; a programme run by SACH between 2004 and 2005 to classify cultural relics as first, second or third class according to their cultural, historical and scientific significance; and a system of museum evaluation introduced by SACH in 2008, which also classifies museums as first, second or third level, according to the quality of their infrastructure and activities.

Another noteworthy government decision was the shift to free admission. As of spring 2008, most state-run museums are free to enter. The government's decision – motivated by the wish to increase numbers of museum visitors throughout the country – affects state-owned museums, memorial halls and patriotic educational bases under the jurisdiction of the Ministry of Culture and SACH. However, the provision does not apply to historical architecture and archaeological sites, which amount to roughly half of all the sites categorised as 'museums' in China (Song 2012, *pers comm*). So, for instance, the Forbidden City, one of the most visited sites, will continue to charge admission fees. The central government has also introduced a plan to subsidise museums suffering loss of income from ticket sales (GOV.cn 2008).

---

[8] Article 55 states: 'It is prohibited to establish Chinese–foreign equity joint, Chinese–foreign contractual joint or solely foreign-funded cultural relics shops or auctions enterprises engaging in cultural relics auctions.'

THE ORIGINS OF CHINESE MUSEOLOGY

Chinese museology is a relatively young discipline. Museum experts and academics in China approach the discipline in the following terms: 'a) museology is a frontier science; b) museology is a comprehensive science; c) museology is an administrative science; d) museology is a social applied science' (Yuan 1992, 203). Of particular interest is the association of museology with an 'administrative science', suggesting a vision of museums as administrative units, which is in tune with the importance attributed to museum management, marketing and profitability.

As discussed previously, according to a generally accepted interpretation, several phases may be identified in the development of museums in China.[9] The first refers to the proto-museums; the second covers the period from the inception of Western-style museums (early 20th century) to the establishment of Communist rule in 1949; the third extends to the 1990s; and, finally, a tentative fourth period starting in the late 1990s. The criterion underlying such classification is the predominant source of influence exerted on museology: Japanese and Western in the first phase, Soviet in the second and Chinese in the third, meaning that, by this time, Chinese museology has finally freed itself from foreign influences.

Quite intriguingly, the reading of the evolution of museology as a succession of different phases recalls the Marxist–Leninist evolutionary theory, whereby the development of society is similarly seen as a sequence of different stages. Pushing the parallel a little further, one can identify in the first phase (the proto-museum) the 'primitivism' of the museum, in the second and third phases (Western and Soviet influence) a form of feudalism and subordination, and in the fourth phase the emancipation and accomplishment of the socialist ideal in the form of freedom from any reference model.

The scholar Yuan Kejian (1992, 200) identifies the origins of museology in China with *Yidali Youji* (Travels Around Italy) (Kang 1905), the work of the intellectual Kang Youwei, which appeared at the beginning of the 20th century, and in which Kang reported memories and impressions collected during a series of visits to European museums. Despite this early attempt to address museums from an academic point of view, it was only in the 1930s that museology developed as a discipline in its own right. The text *An Introduction to Museology (Bowuguanxue gailun)* (Fei and Fei 1936), written in 1936 by Fei Yu and Fei Hongnian, an entomologist and an agrobiologist, is considered the first Chinese text of museology. The two scientists were inspired by a text of Japanese museology.[10]

The influences of Soviet museology and Marxist–Leninist ideology became palpable after 1949. In the 1950s, delegations of Chinese Party officials frequently conducted 'study visits' to museums in Moscow, and, conversely, Russian museologists were invited to China to introduce Soviet museums. In addition, Russian museology books such as *Principles of Soviet Museum Management* (1955) were translated into Chinese (Hung 2005, 918). The museologist Su Donghai (1989, 30) synthesises the main features of Soviet museology as follows: 'first, all the historical relics and museums of a country are owned by public society; and second, all the museums should carry out work under the leadership of their governments'. The book *General Discussion*

---

[9] Such an interpretation was elaborated by the museologist Su Donghai, as corroborated by An Laishun (1991, 1).

[10] The Japanese museology text, *Educational institutions having resort to the eyes*, was written by Tanahashigen Taro, as reported by Su Donghai (1989, 30).

on Museology, written in 1957 by the Chinese museologist Fu Zhenlun (Fu 1957), is a cornerstone insofar as it institutionalised the leading role of Soviet museology as an ideological model.

In 1956, a 'National Conference of Museum Work' established the theory of the 'three natures and two tasks' (*sanxing erwu*). The museologist An Laishun (1999, 5) explains the theory as follows: 'a museum is an institution of scientific research, cultural education and an important place to house material and spiritual cultural heritage or natural specimen. The two tasks refer to serving for scientific research and the broad masses of people.' The museologist Su Donghai (1995, 69) adds, 'only with the existence of all the three [natures], a museum can be a museum in its true sense'. The priority accorded to scientific research as a task for museums adheres to a governmental campaign launched shortly before the conference took place, entitled 'March Towards Science' and aimed at strengthening scientific activities. The implementation of the campaign in the museum domain led to the idea that 'scientific research is the foundation of all activities of museums' (Su 1995, 69).

Although the authority of Soviet sources was compromised by the interruption of diplomatic relations between China and the USSR in 1964, Soviet museology and Marxism–Leninism continued to exert a deep influence on Chinese museology. The general principles of Marxism–Leninism combined with Maoism to shape the new profile of Chinese museums. For decades, the reference to Marxist theories (namely, dialectical and historical materialism) and Mao Zedong's ideology has been an implicit dogma for any museum-related activity or publication in China. Maoism and Marxism–Leninism have exerted such a deep, co-extensive and synergic influence on Chinese museology that it is hard to separate the former from the latter. Maoism has led museums to emphasise historical figures whose lives could be considered exemplary. As a result, Chinese museums represent a case in point in the creation of 'ideal types', models of social, political and intellectual engagement.

The museum devoted to the writer Lu Xun in Shanghai (inaugurated in 1999) offers a particularly illuminating instance of intertwining displays and texts unfolding the hagiography of a person. The museum portrays Lu Xun as a model of intellectual engagement supporting Communist ideology. Exhibitions substantiate the myth of the politically engaged intellectual whose writings, rejecting 'feudal traditions', became the literary manifesto of the May Fourth Movement; to use the terms employed in the exhibition, he became 'its intellectual spirit'.[11] Here Lu Xun is celebrated as 'the writer of the New China', and as having fought and died for his motherland (though he actually died of tuberculosis in 1936, well before the Communist era in China, and never joined the Communist Party). Through a form of storytelling that characterises many museums of famous people, Lu Xun's persona is sublimated through the fetishisation of his personal belongings: the visitor can observe closely his books, his writing brush, his clothes, his thermometer, his teacup and even an X-ray of his lungs. Through museum exhibitions the individual trajectories of prominent figures such as Lu Xun are transformed into narratives (sometimes mythologies) that substantiate Marxist ideals and the Marxist vision of history.

In the 1980s, China's accession to ICOM gave a substantial impetus to Chinese museology. Professor Guo Qingshen (2004, *pers comm*) of the Department of Education at the Shanghai Museum explains that, during that decade, Chinese museology focused on the purpose of education, the main issue being how museums could offer wider and more accurate information to

---

[11]   Lu Xun Museum, Shanghai. Last visited in August 2004.

their audiences. However, Professor Guo points out that education was mainly understood as a passive activity, and the possibility of thought-provoking, inquisitive and critical exhibitions was simply not contemplated. In the 1990s, under the pressure of the market economy and the changes affecting Chinese society, museology took a slightly different direction. Professor Guo interprets the change as a turn towards the individual and specific needs, interests and expectations of visitors. This turn towards a 'customer-oriented' museum is a facet of the broader transformation of this institution, with increasing levels of differentiation and specialisation implying unprecedented attention paid to customers' needs. China's museology field is also being increasingly transformed by the new generations of museum scholars and curators receiving their training in Chinese and internationational academic centres, as discussed in the next chapter.

THE FUNCTIONS OF MUSEUMS

'Museums should promote scientific knowledge and the nation's long history while resisting the decadence of feudalism and capitalism.' This statement, issued by Mr Sun Jiazheng, former Minister of Culture (quoted in *China Daily* 2000b), is typical in its use of ideology-laden terms such as 'feudalism' and 'capitalism'. Official statements of museums' functions and roles are often characterised by strong ideological connotations. A more detailed definition of museums' roles can be found in the preface of a publication devoted to museums in China, where the then director of the State Cultural Relics Bureau (now SACH), Zhang Wenbin, explains the functions of museums in the following terms:

> In China, we regard museums as an important part of our cultural and educational undertakings. The primary responsibility of museums is to collect, store and protect cultural relics and specimens, carry out scientific research activities, hold exhibitions, disseminate historical, scientific and cultural knowledge, propagate patriotism, socialism and the revolutionary traditions among the broad masses of the people, enhance the level of understanding of science, culture and moral ethics among the whole nation, increase the nation's self-confidence and cohesive force, and contribute, by way of intellectual support, to the great cause of building socialism with Chinese characteristics.   (quoted in Xiao 2002, 5)

Mr Zhang's definition casts light on the thinking behind museums' activities. In his statement, reference is made to the collection, research and preservation of cultural relics, and the dissemination of historical and cultural knowledge; however, nothing is said about the people legitimated to decide what is worth collecting and researching, what and whose history to tell, whose culture to portray and how. These questions are implicitly addressed in the second part of Mr Zhang's statement: the references to patriotism, socialism, the nation, revolutionary traditions and 'socialism with Chinese characteristics' reveal the political agenda that informs museum activities. Ma Zishu (1994, 2), vice director of the State Bureau of Cultural Relics, corroborates this point: 'a museum shall use the cultural relics to educate the public to patriotism, revolutionary tradition and national conditions'. In a similar vein, the director of SACH asserts that cultural and artistic heritage represent 'a solid base for patriotic education' (*People's Daily* 2002).

Professor Song Xiangguang, a museologist at Peking University, confirms that, in China, museums are eminently meant to perform political functions – 'today museums are a tool to spread socialism' – though they are also increasingly called upon to fulfil other tasks, such as 'introducing new cultural forms and new science' (Song 2004a, *pers comm*). Similarly, Professor Su Donghai, a leading Chinese museologist, argues that 'the basic function of museums is political education. The museum should be able to teach how to appreciate an object or history' (Su 2004, *pers comm*).

Since the discourses surrounding the functions of museums in China are steeped in Marxist–Leninist theories, it is worth pondering what the application of such theories to museums entails. Marxist–Leninist theory considers technology, the economic system and natural resources as the infrastructure of a society. In contrast, museums are seen as belonging to the domain of superstructure – that is, the ideological sphere (H Wang 2001, 3). Infrastructure and superstructure are intimately linked and ultimately interdependent. Through this perspective, the museum is seen as a 'cultural phenomenon' which only occurs once a society has reached a given stage of development. In line with this approach, the museologist Wang Hongjun (2001, 4) defines museology as 'the study of museum exhibits, their layout, the audience, museum cause and relations among museums at different levels' as well as 'the relations between museums and the development of society, and social economy, politics, cultural education, and scientific technology'. Marxist–Leninist theory puts great emphasis on materialism, scientific thought and objectivity; within museum walls these principles lead to objects being viewed as scientific evidence and material proof of social theories, and to a strong concern with classification: 'the issue of museology *is* scientific classification' (H Wang 2001, 3, my emphasis). Concerns for scientific thought, rationale and objectivity also emerge in the way museums are discussed. Numerical figures – of such importance in Chinese cosmology (cf Stafford 2003) – are widely used to describe logistical features: the surface of the museum in square metres, the number of volumes stored in the library, the auditorium capacity and so on.[12]

Marxist–Leninist-inspired museological principles have been articulated by Professor Su Donghai (1994, 1–7) in his paper 'Philosophy of Chinese Museums', where he explains that museums have basically four values or roles. The first is 'the value of verifying history'. Su (ibid, 4) sees cultural relics as 'historical verifiers' and 'those collected and preserved in museums are the most selective ones with higher values of historical memory and verification'. This reading entails a vision of history as a science, whereby objects enable the scientific verification of facts. This position postulates the ability to 'reconstruct' historical events through objects, since objects are thought to carry historical 'truth'.[13] The idea that objects 'possess objectivity and reality' constructs materiality as impervious to time, space and human agency. The second value that Su attributes to museums is the ability to spread knowledge. 'The displays and exhibitions [...] represent a unified body combining thinking both in terms of images and logic and thus form a special knowledge' (ibid, 4). Museums are considered as sources of knowledge, rather than as sites for critical reflection. The third valuable aspect of museums, according to Su, is aesthetic value. The aesthetic dimension of museum objects, in Su's view (and somehow in contradiction with his first point), has long been neglected in favour of their scientific and educational values. The fourth and last value is morality. 'The Chinese museums work rather hard to extol the virtues such as patriotism, collectivism and selfishness devotion by means of their displays and exhibi-

[12] For examples of the emphasis placed on figures when discussing museums, see Ren *et al* (1994, 26–42); Xiao (2000, 23); National Museum of Chinese History (2002).

[13] This approach resists theorisations of objects as carrying multiple layers of meanings. See Tilley *et al* (2006) for a range of alternative theoretical approaches to material culture.

tions' (ibid, 5). Not only are displays a tool 'for the purpose of raising the moral status of the visitors' but also, overall, 'museums are the carriers of the "true", "good" and "beauty"' (ibid, 5). Museums are thus also endowed with the task of establishing canons of authenticity, morality and beauty.

A slightly different definition of museums' tasks is provided by the Chinese museologist An Laishun. An (1999) puts the emphasis on the social functions of museums:

> Preservation of cultural heritage, and conducting national spirit, and promotion of public's understanding of their cultural origins and development through exhibitions and educational activities, and inspiring the feelings of loving their country and their hometowns. Encouraging local art activities, and improving public's aesthetic standard and knowledge of art appreciation through aesthetic exhibitions and art education. Protection of local traditional folk art and crafts, and developing modern craft productions. Promoting protection of local natural resources and environment, popularising knowledge of putting rescuers to rational use in the modern life, improving people's living environment and health conditions. Encouraging understanding, unity and co-operation among different nationalities who enjoy different clutters [sic] and traditions, through art and cultural activities.

The function of education is here complemented by other tasks, such as supporting local forms of arts and crafts; this is a fresh element in a cultural and museological context that has traditionally privileged high arts (the arts of the court) or propaganda arts. The encouragement of art appreciation – until a few decades ago considered a 'bourgeois' activity – is also a relatively unusual element. References to environmental protection and the improvement of health conditions also point to an attempt to explore and expand the museological field.

Today, one can tell the difference between politically sensitive museums,[14] where the educational function is still conceived as ideological indoctrination, and museums adopting a more innovative approach. The priorities of the most highly politicised museums, such as the National Museum of China and the Military Museum in Beijing, remain to 'serve as an excellent "classroom" to familiarise the general public with the traditions of the revolution' (Museums Department of the State Administrative Bureau of Museums and Archaeological Data 1980, 173). Conversely, in other museums (such as the Shanghai Museum or the Capital Museum in Beijing) different narratives are being put forward – narratives of national pride and beauty. There is a growing emphasis on aesthetics, on the unique and intrinsic characteristics of objects. Exhibits are no longer viewed primarily as tools for education but rather as objects worthy of appreciation *per se*. It has become acceptable for objects to be merely admired, without the need for them to deliver historical, political, ethical or civic lessons.

While education is perceived as one of the most important functions of museums, educational goals are not necessarily attained through boring or patronising texts, lengthy wall charts or outdated dioramas. The views expressed by the chief of the Education Department at the Shanghai Museum, Professor Guo Qingshen (2004, *pers comm*) on museum education shed new light on this area. The first point made by Guo is the link between education and public

---

[14] For example: the National History Museum, the Revolutionary Museum and the Military Museum in Beijing, and the Site of the First Congress of the Communist Party in Shanghai.

relations (interestingly, the Department of Education is also responsible for the museum's public relations). At the Shanghai Museum, Professor Guo explains, education takes the form of initiatives aimed at familiarising audiences not only with the Museum and its exhibits, but also with lesser-known aspects, such as conservation techniques. Professor Guo also reports the example of a very successful public seminar on calligraphic practice. Participants were invited to reproduce famous calligraphy pieces exhibited in the Museum with technical guidance provided by the Museum experts. These initiatives are intended not only to attract a larger public but also to educate through a better knowledge and appreciation of the techniques involved in the making of the art object. Here, the process of learning is pursued through the public's active participation. This approach reflects a relatively recent trend that sees museums in China as loci of socialisation and leisure. The museologist Lu Jinmin (1994, 3) conveys this idea as follows:

> [The] museum is an important sign of measuring social progress and human civilisation [...] In museums there not only should be the activities of propaganda and education, but also public places of entertainment and rest, where visitors can get food, drinks, souvenirs and publicity materials. These are proper ways to strengthen museums' vitality and to serve visitors.

The thread of socialisation, leisure and consumption is taken up by the former director of SACH, Zhang Wenbin (quoted in Xiao 2002, 6): 'museums in China not only serve as institutions for obtaining knowledge and aesthetic enjoyment, but also as attractions for tourism and consumption'. In a later statement featured in an article published in UNESCO's *Museum International* journal, the same Zhang Wenbin (2008, 8) notes: 'Museums contain the history of human civilization; they disseminate knowledge, elevate the nation's cultural calibre, nurture the public's aesthetic taste, and enhance people's mental as well as physical health. Museums have a responsibility to take the pulse of the times [...].' In this definition, references to patriotism have been replaced by emphases on knowledge dissemination, cultivation, taste and well-being. One may wonder to what extent these differences in the formulation of the main functions of museums in China are the result of changed perceptions and conceptualisations of museums' social roles, or are due to the fact that, in the latter quotation, Zhang is addressing an international professional readership, rather than domestic audiences.

These statements cast new light on the old slogan 'museums must serve the people'. The expression can now be read as a turn towards the individual's needs. In the words of the museologist Wang Hongjun, museums are meant to 'help people to develop themselves, bring entertainment and happiness in their life' (Wang 2004, *pers comm*). Considered in a global context, these ideas suggest that the functions museums are called upon to perform are gradually changing. Old-school approaches stressing the centrality of ideological indoctrination remain prominent in official discourse but they are increasingly being sidelined by new priorities – aesthetic appreciation, preservation and leisure – which reveal a novel attention to visitors' needs and expectations. Feng Chengbo (1993, 10) notes that 'the ideological control of exhibition is still there, especially for some of the sensitive themes, but it has been less rigid than in the past'. Elevated to the status of privileged locus for patriotic education several decades ago, the museum has seen its didactic content of Communist ideological indoctrination in the 1950s, 1960s, 1970s and 1980s shift to patriotism impregnated with cultural nationalism in recent years.

TOWARDS A 'NEW CHINESE MUSEOLOGY'?

Chinese museology, like Chinese society, seems to be undergoing a process of transition loaded with inconsistencies and contradictions. On the one hand, Marxism–Leninism imposed a view of history as a succession of phases (primitive, slavery, feudal, capitalist and socialist) where ancient times are associated with a lower level of development and the climax corresponds to an idealised Communist society. According to this perspective, revolutionary relics are the most valuable museum objects since they are tokens of the Communist struggle and victory over other forces – 'bourgeois' classes and foreign 'imperialists'. On the other hand, the decline of Communist ideals and the crisis of legitimacy of the early 1990s triggered a turn to cultural nationalism and a connected re-evaluation of ancient treasures and cultural features now regarded as the 'core' of Chinese culture and civilisation. In museological terms, this movement has been accompanied by and expressed through displays that emphasise the aesthetics of objects.

Having been influenced by different museological traditions (Japanese, Soviet and Western), Chinese museology is today searching for its own path as a way out of the current impasse. According to Professor Song Xiangguang at Peking University (Song 2012, *pers comm*), the 1990s were characterised by the marked influence of Western museum approaches; Europe (notably through the work of supranational institutions such as ICOM and UNESCO) has provided the main reference as far as museum theory is concerned, while the United States has set the standard for museum practices. More broadly, Western museums have provided a model for museums' architecture, interior facilities and technical equipment. In the new millennium and especially since the 2008 Olympic Games, continues Professor Song, one of the priorities of Chinese museums has been to open up to the world and to introduce Chinese culture and civilisation to the widest possible audience. In parallel, more attention is being paid to the celebration, in museums and through museums, of vernacular cultural forms, visible for instance in new museum buildings inspired by local architectural and artistic traditions. Notable examples include the Capital Museum in Beijing, the architecture of which incorporates a traditional bronze vessel; the Shanghai Museum, shaped as a *ding*; and the China Pavilion at the Shanghai 2010 World Expo, turned into a major museum of contemporary art and presenting a traditional architectural style (called *Dougong*) which dates back to the Spring and Autumn Period (770–467 BC). In a similar vein – and corroborating observations made earlier on in the text – Professor Lu Jiansong (2012, *pers comm*) argues that two main features distinguish the museums being created in China today from their predecessors. Firstly, old museums focused on objects, while the new focus on narratives. Secondly, traditional museums focused on research and collection activities, while contemporary museums focus on education and public service, and invest in state-of-the-art technologies and modern architecture.

Museum curators and academics in China emphasise that Chinese museums should import from abroad the best technological implements, but also retain Chinese character. An Laishun (1991, 6) explains:

> the meaning of Chinese characteristics is that museological study should reflect the national conditions of China, and the actual situation of Chinese museums, to link the general principle of museology as academic discipline with the reality of Chinese museums, to seek for a special law of Chinese museum development.

Lu Zhangshen (quoted in Szántó 2011), director of the National Museum of China, commenting on the first international exhibition held at the Museum and devoted to European Enlightenment, noted: 'This exhibition is profoundly significant for China in furthering its understanding of the international world as well as recognising and embracing its own cultural values.' This statement summarises the two directions of contemporary museology in China: on the one hand, the pull towards the outside and the willingness to open up to world cultures and histories, and on the other, the firm focus on national values and the strengthening of a Chinese cultural identity, which also gains definition through encountering other world cultures.

On a more cautious note, Professor Song Xiangguang maintains that China is not yet ready to develop its own museological approach, as it is still in the process of adapting its museums and museum practices to meet the international standards to which it subscribed when it became a member of ICOM. Professor Song (2004a, *pers comm*) expresses reservations about the museological quality of the exhibitions in some Chinese museums. Too much attention, in his opinion, is devoted to 'modernity', associated with the use of technology, and to the appearance, both interior and exterior, of museums. Indeed, discussions with museum curators and academics reveal a primary concern with figures – especially record figures – that not only illustrates the scale (in physical and financial terms) of Chinese museum projects, but also the perceived importance of China's primacy on a global scale. For instance, the architects of the new National Museum of China were concerned with achieving a museum surface area larger than that of the Metropolitan Museum in New York, thereby enabling the National Museum of China to claim to be the largest museum in the world. In the same vein, the number of museums in China (over 3000 in 2010) is judged to be 'not enough' since the United States has the highest number of museums (Lu 2012, *pers comm*). According to Professor Song (2004a, *pers comm*), the emphasis on museum facilities' dimensions works to the detriment of the substance – the quality of items on display and of related information – which fails to transmit a notion of Chinese culture.

This chapter has examined the unique historical trajectory of museums in China and the development of legal provision, governmental bodies and scholarship with the aim of managing, studying and ultimately institutionalising the fields of cultural heritage and museums in China. The next chapter will pursue this line of analysis by taking a closer look at the various actors that operate in the Chinese 'museum world'.

New Actors in the Chinese Museum World

According to Howard Becker (1982, x), the concept of an 'art world' refers to a 'network of people whose cooperative activity, organized via their joint knowledge of conventional means of doing things, produces the kind of art works that art world is noted for'. Despite its tautological definition, 'art world' is a popular and widely used term due to its capacity to capture the fuzzy world that surrounds the production, distribution and consumption of works of art. Drawing on Becker's notion, the concept of the 'museum world' can be taken to represent the group of people involved in museum activities, and the relationships that link them to museums.

In China, the participation of non-governmental actors in the museum world might suggest that the state is loosening its control over museums and their activities. The historian of China James Flath (2002, 57) notes that 'the state is still seeking to divest itself of both the ideological and economic complexities of public history by turning management over to the private sector'. Yet the Chinese state is not so much divesting as *delegating* the management of specific museum categories, with the twofold advantage of continuing to exert indirect supervision over all museums without incurring the related managing costs, while maintaining direct, full control over a selected range of museums of strategic importance, such as those dealing with the representation of history and the nation.

A comprehensive analysis of the actors that, at varying levels, participate in the museum world would exceed the space that can be devoted here to this theme. Analysis will thus be confined to the most prominent actors: the Chinese government and public authorities at large, state-owned and private enterprises, museum professionals, museum donors and museum audiences.

The Chinese Government

Most museums in China are public, or are indirectly financed and controlled by the state. It follows that the Chinese government, together with its operative branches, is the main actor in the museum world. In most countries, the administration of museums falls under the broad competence of the Ministry of Culture, which then delegates it to subordinate designated departments (such as 'cultural heritage departments'), organised within hierarchical levels. The Chinese system, however, presents significant differences. As mentioned, museums in China are organised into three levels – national, provincial and local. Partly mirroring this classification, institutions dealing with the management of museums are structured over four levels: governmental, provincial, prefectural and county.

Governmental is the highest level. The main authority in the field of museum administration is the State Administration of Cultural Heritage (SACH), based in Beijing. This body reports directly to the Ministry of Culture and oversees all the lower levels of management. Its main tasks include approving the construction of new museums and supervising cooperation projects and exchanges between museums, as well as coordinating the training of museum personnel. SACH is also responsible for formulating museum policies and regulations, supervising their implementation, coordinating professionals' activities, selecting the sites (and cities) to be protected, supervising archaeological excavations and offering consultation on the creation of new museums. Moreover, central authorities are responsible for the financing of museums and related activities. Professor Lu Jiansong at Fudan University in Shanghai observed that employees' salaries form the largest share of museums' budgets; the second largest expenditure is on renovation costs; and, finally, most of the remaining funds are allocated to cover everyday maintenance activities and museum research (Lu 2006, *pers comm*). In the case of national museums, the administrative competence of SACH is coupled with that of the different ministry cabinets. In contrast with organisational structures in most European countries, Chinese museums are not automatically placed under the competence of the Ministry of Culture, but are instead attached to a ministerial cabinet according to the museum's nature and content. Each museum is linked to a ministry that is deemed relevant to it. So, for instance, the Ministry of Defence is in charge of the National Military Museum; the Ministry of Telecommunications is responsible for the National Museum of Telecommunications; the Ministry of Education supervises all university museums; the Ministry of Industry is responsible for science and technology (as well as industrial) museums; while the Ministry of Culture is responsible for the National Museum of China, the Palace Museum (Forbidden City) and the Lu Xun Museum (Song 2006, *pers comm*). The subordination of museums to specific ministerial cabinets on the basis of content suggests a vision of museums not so much as cultural institutions *per se*, but rather as 'attributes' of the various governmental branches.

The second level of jurisdiction is the provincial level. Provincial museums are subordinated to provincial authorities, namely the Provincial Cultural Bureau, although for important, non-routine matters (such as the destination of archaeological findings or collection loans), competence falls back to the central SACH. The third level corresponds to prefectures, where an administrative commissioner is responsible for museum-related matters. The fourth is the county level. County museums respond in the first instance to local cultural departments, and in the second instance to provincial and central authorities. One of the major problems encountered by county museums is lack of funds, which, according to James Flath, encroaches on exhibition content and notably on the representation of history. Flath (2002, 54) notes that 'the extent to which they [local museums] support an explicitly state-centred interpretation of the past should also be seen as a consequence of their incapacity to raise independent funds'. Finally, a further level, the city level, may overlap the levels mentioned above; museums of large cities, such as Shanghai, may in some instances report directly to the central authorities in Beijing (Song 2006, *pers comm*).

STATE-OWNED ENTERPRISES

Museums devoted to an industrial sector – or industrial museums – are a relatively new museum category, the development of which is linked to the economic reforms initiated in 1979, and the connected process of opening up to a market economy (H Wang 2004, *pers comm*; Song 2004a and 2004b, *pers comm*; Lu 2004b, *pers comm*). The gradual reduction in state influence is creating room for new actors in domains previously dominated by the public sphere, with museums being one such domain. For almost four decades following its establishment, the Chinese Communist government was the only actor interested, authorised and financially able to manage museums. This situation changed in the early 1990s, however, with the emergence of museums financed indirectly by the state through state-owned enterprises.

In 2000, Zhang Wenbin, former chief of SACH, stated: 'the state will support some key museums which represent the nation's image, while drawing on businesses and individuals to invest in specialized museums' (*China Daily* 2000a). In other words, the Chinese government plans to concentrate on a limited number of museums, selected for their importance in representing the Chinese nation (over which the government wishes to maintain control) while 'specialised' museums will be the domain of other actors, primarily state-owned enterprises and private individuals. This position was confirmed and further defined two years later, in 2002, by the director of SACH at that time, Shan Jixiang:

> the current multi-owner system is to be largely replaced by the state-owned museums and supplemented by private ones, covering the nation and its industries. The country will continue to build national museums as well as provincial ones in municipalities or provinces such as Beijing, Tianjin and Sichuan. China supports the building of special museums for spheres including finance, postal service and railway transportation, as well as museums with different themes, such as international friendship and ethnic groups. (*People's Daily* 2002)

A 'multi-owner system' is foregrounded as a hybrid system where public, semi-public and private museums co-exist. However, as the state is the major stakeholder in state-owned enterprises, the system is actually a disguised state monopoly.

State-owned enterprises owning and managing museums are framed as 'cultural enterprises', that is:

> economic entities formed in the socialist market economic process. They are mainly engaged in the production, circulation, spreading and exchange of cultural products and provide cultural services. They have independent accounts and are responsible for their own profits and losses. […] The work of cultural enterprises is under the supervision of cultural administrative organs.
> (Gao 1999, 117)

Within this new template, the association of enterprises producing tobacco, for instance, is the administrative body legitimised to run the Tobacco Museum in Shanghai; similarly, the Shanghai Automobile Industry Corporation has established the Auto Museum; and the associations of industries of the textile sector are the founding body of the various textile museums (the Textile Museum in Suzhou, the China National Silk Museum in Hangzhou and the Institute of Clothing Technology in Beijing).

The museums set up by state-owned enterprises may also deal with aspects of the tertiary sector (in the cases of the Public Security Museum, Bank Museum or Post Museum) or educational field (such as the Shanghai Science and Technology Museum). For instance, the latter is technically a foundation financially supported by private corporations, such as the Shanghai Science and Technology Investment Cooperation, Shanghai Pudong Development Bank, Beijing Zhijin Venture Capital Co Ltd, Top Group and others.

The Shanghai History Museum provides another example of the ambivalent entanglement of government and business figures in museum work. The museum has long been deprived of

FIG 3.1. THE TOBACCO MUSEUM, SHANGHAI.

FIG 3.2. ENTRANCE OF THE SHANGHAI HISTORY MUSEUM IN THE BASEMENT OF THE ORIENTAL PEARL TOWER, SHANGHAI.

a proper location; the Shanghai municipality has repeatedly asserted that it is unsuccessfully searching for an appropriate site for the new building (Qian 2004a, *pers comm*). In the meantime, the museum's historical collections are being partially displayed in an exhibition located in the basement of the Oriental Pearl TV Tower, a major tourist attraction in Shanghai. Curators at the Shanghai History Museum distance themselves from such an exhibition, which they see as a 'commercial' initiative mainly conceived as entertainment to generate profit[1] and the fruit of personal connections between municipal officers and the managers of the Oriental Pearl Tower (Qian 2004a, *pers comm*).

Not surprisingly, it is the political and economic poles of the country – Beijing, Shanghai and its hinterland – that boast the highest concentrations of industrial museums. The success of industrial museums is partly due to the fact that they do not require direct funding from public bodies, as they are supported by the industrial sector which takes charge of their financing and management. The advantages of this system are twofold. On the one hand, the government is no longer responsible for the financing of museums, while, at the same time, it is able to increase the overall numbers of museums. As mentioned previously, increasing the number of museums is an important objective for local and central authorities; a large number of museums is thought to improve the image of the city (and by extension, of the country), which in turn increases tourism and investment. On the other hand, industrial sectors welcome the creation of museums presenting their activities, as it affords them prestige (formalising their contribution to the process of Chinese modernisation) and increases visibility (through museums they can target new audiences and potential customers).

The process of exhibition set-up in industrial museums – and in many cases the design of the whole museum building – is outsourced to specialised design companies. Designers are responsible for the master plan of the project – that is, the organisation of space and activities within the museum building – and, most importantly, they design the exhibitions. Museums provide design companies with visual and textual documentation about the collections. Based upon this documentation, designers select the objects for display and write labels and texts. A design company may work on museum projects and material as varied as archaeological finds, botanical specimens, local history and folklore, musical instruments or the history of the production and consumption of tobacco in China. The involvement of the design company – hence, the exhibition design process – lasts around six months or in some instances up to one year. The design company will then move on to another project; there is no ongoing relationship with the museum staff and no going back to change, adapt or update exhibition content.[2]

Professor Song Xiangguang at Peking University (Song 2012, *pers comm*) points out that the main purposes of industrial museums are to provide insights into a specific industrial or service sector and at the same time to celebrate the officers and businessmen that contributed to the sector's development. Industrial museums will be further discussed with reference to the politics

---

1   The museum ticket to visit the Exhibition of the Shanghai History Museum (excluding access to the panoramic tower) costs 35 Yuan (around US $6), plus a further 30 Yuan for the audio guide, at the time of visiting (July 2004). Prior to moving to the Oriental Pearl building, the museum offered free entry.
2   This information was provided during an interview in spring 2012 with members of a prominent Shanghai-based museum design company (whose identity shall remain anonymous), responsible for the realisation of dozens of new museums in various provinces of China since the early 2000s.

of identity and the discourses on the efficiency of the Chinese nation in Chapter 8, 'The Politics of Identity'.

Private Museums

Since at least the Song Dynasty (AD 960–1276), there has existed a tradition in China of private collecting as an expression of cultivation, connoisseurship, social status and refined aesthetic taste. This tradition has survived in spite of the massive transfer abroad of art treasures in the years preceding the establishment of the People's Republic in 1949 and the persecution of art collectors during the Cultural Revolution (1966–76). The Nantong Museum, founded in 1905 by industrialist Zhang Qian, can be said to be the first Chinese private museum (Song 2008, 41).

In contemporary China, private collections are once again a widespread phenomenon, fuelled by an increase in wealth of the rapidly growing class of private entrepreneurs (Song 2008, 41). However, ownership of museums by private individuals in China remains a relatively recent phenomenon. In the 1980s, as a result of the liberalisation of the economic system, China experienced a revival of private collecting, though this did not immediately translate into an increase in private museums. It was in the 1990s that the development of private museums started to gain momentum.

The status of private museums in contemporary China is ambiguous. In contrast to the poor official support enjoyed by private museums, national legislation on cultural relics (notably the law of 2002) not only allows private individuals to own cultural relics but also encourages private initiative in the domain of trade in cultural relics. Similarly, in 2006, the Ministry of Culture issued guidelines on Management Methodology in Museums, specifying that 'the nation will aid and develop the museum business and will encourage personal, legal and other organizations to set up museums' (Song 2008, 47).

At the end of 2010, it is estimated that there were approximately 475 private museums in China (Lu 2012, *pers comm*). Estimates are inaccurate since the number of private museums that are officially registered is often considerably lower than the actual number of private museums operating in the country. For instance, in Beijing in 2012 only around 20 private museums were registered, out of a total of approximately 100 private museums in the capital (Song 2012, *pers comm*).

Private museums are unevenly distributed across the Chinese territory. The municipality of Shanghai, for instance, has several private museums; the first private museum in the city, devoted to the abacus and manual calculators, opened in 1981. In the mid-2000s there were around 60 museums in Shanghai, although most of them were reportedly experiencing financial difficulties due to steep real estate prices (Xinhua News Agency 2004). This is a common problem for museums in Shanghai; for example, the first private folk art museum, established in 1990 in the Minzhu Village of Qingpu District, was closed down in July 2003, as a new road was planned to pass through the museum premises. Similarly, two other private museums in Shanghai, the Donghua Porcelain Museum and the much debated Liu Dalin Sex Culture Museum, were forced to relocate to more peripheral locations, away from tourist areas. In other areas of the country, however, private museums are thriving. In the mid-2000s in Chengdu, Sichuan Province, Mr Fan Jiachuan, a private collector and former deputy mayor of Yibin township, set up a private museum complex in Anren town, Dayi county, devoted to modern Chinese history with a special focus on Maoist memorabilia, including badges, posters, photos, etc (*China Heritage Newsletter* 2005a).

Beijing boasts the 'first privately-owned museum of China as an officially approved and regis-tered body corporate' (Ma 2003, 100), the Guanfu Museum of Classic Arts.[3] The Museum, located in the basement of an office building in the suburbs of Beijing, opened its doors in January 1997 on the initiative of Mr Ma Weidu. Mr Ma is an example of what may be termed a 'self-made man': from a modest background, he was first a journalist and later a literary editor, film producer and successful businessman. An art enthusiast, Mr Ma has, through more than 20 years of collection activities, accumulated a remarkable collection of furniture, metal objects and porcelain from the Qing (AD 1644–1911) and Ming (AD 1368–1644) dynasties. In addition to organising exhibitions, the Museum offers advice on buying and selling cultural relics. In an article, Mr Ma (2003, 100) maintains that 'as a social facility with an educational purpose, both public and private museums may play a role to promote knowledge, enlightenment and inspira-tion in the minds of museum-goers'. This position is corroborated by the Museum's curator, Ms Li Xuan, who stresses that Mr Ma's collection does not merely reflect a personal interest in antiq-uities but aspires to be a 'place for educating young people' (Li 2004, *pers comm*). This position dovetails with the idea that visitors can touch and even try out objects in the Guanfu Museum: for example, it is possible to stroke an ancient wood table or sit on a Qing Dynasty chair.

Another private museum in Beijing deserves attention for its unique profile and contrast to the Guanfu Museum of Classic Arts: the Poly Art Museum. The Poly Art Museum is run by a state-owned enterprise. Inaugurated in December 1999 with the blessing of the State Bureau of Cultural Relics (the predecessor of SACH) and the Beijing Cultural Relics Bureau, the Poly Art Museum is located on the first floor of the high-end Poly Plaza Hotel. The Museum is relatively little advertised; this – combined with the relatively high entry price[4] – suggests that the Museum does not really address the general public but rather a select audience, including the clients of the Poly Plaza Hotel, who are mainly wealthy Chinese and overseas businessmen.

Objects are exhibited in large, dimly lit, elegant, air-conditioned exhibition rooms, equipped with state-of-the-art security systems. The Poly Art Museum has opted for a display approach that emphasises the aesthetics of objects, while information on historical and cultural context is reduced to the essential. The objects on display are limited in number (around 100), but of exceptional rarity and beauty; they include mainly bronzes[5] and Buddhist sculptures. The quality of the objects selected is assured by a team of experts:

> only the finest pieces are sought, and a panel of more than thirty specialist consultants, including
> Ma Chengyuan of the Shanghai Museum and Li Xueqin, head of the History Institute under
> the Chinese Academy of Social Sciences (CASS), has been selected to assess and authenticate
> the pieces in the museum and potential purchases. (Dewar 2000)

The institutional profile of the Poly Art Museum is intriguing. The Museum has close ties with the government as it is run by a state corporation, the chemical China Poly Group. Its director, Mr He Ping, is a senior-ranking officer of the People's Liberation Army, and married to the last daughter of Deng Xiaoping. The Poly Group has been described as a 'former weapons dealer linked to the People's Liberation Army (PAL), that plays the patriotic patron in addi-

3   Guanfu Museum of Classic Arts, Beijing. Visited in February 2004.
4   The ticket entrance was 50 Yuan at the time of the visit, in February 2004.
5   The bronzes exhibited range from the Shang (c. 1600–1046 BC) to the Tang Dynasty (AD 618–907).

tion to running successful activities of import-export, real-estate and hotels' (Bobin 2003, my translation). But, most interestingly, the China Poly Group is sponsor of the non-governmental organisation 'China Foundation for the Development of Social Culture', established in 2002 to pursue 'China's Lost Cultural Relics Recovery Program'.[6] The Poly Group purchases valuable Chinese cultural relics through international auctions and makes them available to the public through the Poly Art Museum.[7] In this way, the Poly Group gains public visibility as a patriotic and philanthropic corporation.

The Poly Group enjoys the full favours of the government, to which it offers a mutually profitable relationship, since the Chinese government cannot, as such, take part in international auctions to repatriate cultural relics. The international convention on the smuggling of cultural artefacts (UNESCO 1970), to which China has been a signatory since 1989, recognises the right of a country to claim for the return of objects believed to have been taken out of the country illegally only if the original source of the object – an art dealer or an antiquities shop, for instance – can be verified, which is in most cases impossible. Therefore, the Poly Group is in a privileged position to act as a 'mediator' in the process of the repatriation of relics. The mission statement of the Poly Art Museum is clear: the Museum aims at 'promoting the most excellent traditional art and culture of the Chinese nation, salvaging the finest Chinese works of art in danger of being lost overseas, and pushing forward the building-up of culture in the commercial environment' (Poly Art Museum n.d.). If the goal is to preserve 'traditional art and culture of the Chinese nation', one might legitimately wonder why such relics are not then donated to public museums. Why create a separate museum for this purpose? It is possible that Chinese authorities do not wish to be directly associated with cultural relics of dubious provenance. The Poly Plaza Group acts then as an institutional 'buffer'.

Museum Professionals

In Imperial China, the *shiguan* figure approximates a contemporary curator. The *shiguan* was a 'civil servant in charge of the conservation, writing and study of governmental archives' (Chang 1999, 103). Despite the antiquity of the profession, museum training in China only began in the 1980s (Jisheng 1987, 291). Professor Wang Hongjun is a member of the first generation of Chinese museum professionals and is today one of the most prominent figures in the domain of Chinese museology. Professor Wang started his career in the museum field as an employee of the cultural department of the army, before moving to the National Museum of History in 1959, where he spent the rest of his career. He started working in museums shortly after the creation of the People's Republic, at a time when no museology course existed in China; he had had no previous training in museology, and it was through practical experience that he developed his professional competence (Wang 2004, *pers comm*).

---

6 Further details of this programme, the foundation and the Poly Group can be found in Fiskesjö (2010).
7 In May 2000 at a Hong Kong auction, the group obtained three important sculptures that had been looted by French troops from the Summer Palace, Beijing, in 1860. The event was proclaimed a repatriation of cultural relics that had left the motherland illegitimately, and the act was therefore coloured with strong nationalistic overtones. The affair also provided extensive media coverage for the Poly Group.

Things have since changed. The number of Chinese universities offering museum studies courses is steadily increasing. Peking University, Nankai University in Tianjin and Fudan University in Shanghai all have university departments where museologists and curators are trained at postgraduate level. Museum studies curricula (for instance at the Department of Cultural Relics and Museology, Fudan University, and at the Department of Archaeology and Museums, Peking University) mostly include publications by Chinese authors; the few non-Chinese titles adopted are texts of Japanese museology and the English publication *Museums in the 1980s: A survey of world trends* by Kenneth Hudson, published in 1986. Courses related to museums at undergraduate level[8] are available at universities in Shanghai, Hangzhou, Nankai, Fudan, Wuhan and Jinlin. The government has also established training centres offering three-month courses on museum-related activities (including conservation and exhibition techniques, photography and classification of ancient relics, as well as administrative museum management).

However, in most cases, museum staff receive professional training on the spot, and this is left to the initiative of each museum, where senior and more experienced staff simply teach the less experienced. Lack of appropriate training is an emerging issue in Chinese museums. According to a survey conducted in 2008 and 2009 by Pan Shouyong, Professor of Museum Studies at China Minzu University, 'nearly 90 percent of museum employees in China did not have college degrees and very few of them had studied museum-related subjects' (Yuan 2011).

In 2011, Chinese museums employed around 59,900 staff, of whom only 4.5 per cent were well-trained technical personnel (State Administration of Cultural Heritage).[9] The director of the National Art Museum of China, Feng Yuan, former director of the arts department of the Chinese Ministry of Culture, admits, 'many of the staff members in our museums are not qualified to run a modern public museum' (*China Daily* 2004). Zhang Xiaoming, Deputy Director of the Cultural Research Center of the Chinese Academy of Social Sciences, declares: 'Many major museums have become microcosms of inefficiency in China. If change can't be brought about internally, it will be necessary to bring to bear some outside pressure for reform' (Yuan 2011). The problem is also linked to the system of recruitment of curators. Currently, most curators in top positions are appointed by government authorities and selected from government officials – people not necessarily in possession of museum specialisations or experience. Professor Song (2004a, *pers comm*) explains the permanence of Marxist–Leninist philosophy as the main museological paradigm by pointing out that changing their approach is difficult for the people who were working in museums during the Maoist era, and thus suggesting that a new generation of museum staff might bring about a deeper change in museological paradigms. In addition, there is a chronic paucity of personnel. He Shuzhong (2000) notes:

> The ratio of people to protect the range of cultural property is one per 20,000 people, only about one museum for one million people and one professional is responsible for looking after 20 sites, which include protected sites and registered sites. Almost every day there are properties

---

8 Such courses include: 'museology, history and theory of foreign museums, revolutionary commemorative museums, archaeology, ancient cultural and material history of China, study and identification of ancient relics, cataloguing and conservation of museum collections, artistic design of displays, audience psychology' (Jisheng 1987, 294).

9 Quoted in several newspaper and online articles, including *People's Daily Online* (see Yuan 2011) and *China Daily* (2011).

lost or damaged because they are unprotected, and valuable information are [sic] lost because of the absence of the relevant professional on site.

The issue of inappropriate training of museum staff emerged during the course of 2011, when a series of thefts and accidents at the Palace Museum in Beijing (see, for example, Yuan 2011) called into question the competence of curators at the Museum. Conditions for the exhibition and preservation of ancient relics at the Palace Museum are not of the highest standards. Anthropologist Tamara Hamlish (2000, 137, 147) notes:

> few visitors notice the peeling vermilion paint or the weeds that grow wild among the bricks that pave the immense courtyards [...] Vitrines that bear the smudged imprint of a prior visitor's hand and nose pressed against the glass in an effort to view an object despite poorly placed and inadequate lighting constitute a sharp contrast to the elaborately renovated period rooms.

The crowded, old glass cases of the Palace Museum not only hinder full appreciation of objects but also fail to offer appropriate protection from the dramatic variations in temperature and humidity that characterise Beijing's climate.

These considerations might be extended to several other ancient temples and historical buildings that have been transformed into exhibition spaces. Another infamous case of curatorial incompetence occurred in Shandong Province, where the company China Confucius International Tourism Co Ltd, responsible for the management of Confucian sites in Qufu, undertook unauthorised 'restoration' of ancient stelae, wooden plaques and murals, 'using water and scrub brushes to accomplish the task, which caused extensive damage to the delicate artifacts' (Flath 2002, 56).

Nevertheless, a generational change is gradually bringing young, skilled, enthusiastic museum curators into Chinese museums. Many have studied abroad and extensively visited museums outside China. Fully aware of the need to preserve Chinese heritage, they are eager to renovate their museums, to introduce more advanced display technologies, to experiment with new exhibition techniques, to further the study of objects and to engage in new research activities. These young museum professionals are extremely interested in museum developments abroad and are becoming more and more involved in collaborative projects with foreign museums. In particular, the main areas of interest are technologies (notably, with reference to display techniques and the digitalisation of museum collections), museum architecture and museum management (especially marketing) (Lu 2004a). As Feng Chengbo (1991, 16) notes:

> Chinese museum professionals are undergoing two kinds of mental emancipation. One is trying to free themselves from the narrowness of political orientation. [...] The second type of emancipation is the transition from a closed to an open orientation – open not only to museum visitors but also to the international museum community.

Museum Donors

The participation of individuals in museum work takes essentially two forms: ownership of museums and, more commonly, financial support and/or the donation of objects. While the

FIG 3.3. DONORS ARE ACKNOWLEDGED IN THE LOBBY OF THE SHANGHAI MUSEUM.

rise in donations to museums from private individuals in China is linked to increasing levels of wealth, various considerations may motivate a donation to a museum. In addition to the philanthropic aspect, donations to public museums also bear a social dimension. As Carol Duncan (1995, 54) notes, 'art museums and the high-cultural products they contained also conferred social distinction on those who possessed them'. This consideration could be extended to the donors of those same 'high-cultural products'; not only does donation to a museum confer social distinction, it also contributes to 'immortalise' the donor, especially when a museum hall, gallery or library is named after the donor. At the Shanghai Museum, for instance, donors have been acknowledged spectacularly in the form of large gold inscriptions in the entrance hall.

Donating to public museums may also be framed as a patriotic gesture. As Lisa Claypool (2005, 589) points out, 'within the recent context of looting and plundering, the donation of objects glorified patriotic attachment and sentiment (even if – or perhaps especially because – some of the objects at one time might have been a part of the imperial collection)'. Many art objects that had been taken out of the country illegally by colonial powers are being repatriated through purchase in international auctions, as discussed in reference to the Poly Art Museum. Repatriation through this channel may successfully avoid issues of repatriation law, since the purchase is made primarily at a personal level, with the collector only later donating the art object to a museum. Furthermore, since Western auction houses are not allowed to operate in

China, wealthy businessmen and collectors (including those of the Chinese diaspora) are ideally positioned to participate in such auctions and subsequently act as museum donors.

The link between the donor/collector and the object donated can be overemphasised in instances where the donor is a particularly prominent personality. This was the case for example with Mr Sunny Yip, a Hong Kong-based tycoon and well-known art collector. In 1997, Mr Yip donated to the Shanghai Museum a bronze vessel, known as Pan of Zi Zhong Jiang, dating from the Zhou Dynasty, 7th century BC. The relic – a unique water vessel featuring elaborate relief decorative motifs – is extremely valuable due to its age, and its artistic and technical features, and it is also well preserved and rare. The vessel is on permanent display in the bronzes gallery of the Shanghai Museum in an individual glass box situated in the centre of the exhibition room, superbly illuminated and complemented by a label indicating that the object was donated to the museum by Mr Yip. The rich cultural and social biographies of such an object would allow for a range of alternative display methods and interpretative approaches. For instance, its historical value could be emphasised, explaining how it was used, or its origins (it is known that Zi Zhong Jiang was the wife of a Head Musician of the State of the Zhou Dynasty for whom the vessel was commissioned). However, such interpretations have been put aside in favour of the sole association with its donor – an association that is perpetuated through labels, brochures and media advertisements. The donation received wide media coverage and the Shanghai Museum published an elegant brochure to celebrate the event. The brochure, on sale at the Museum bookshop, bears a full-page picture of Mr Yip, accompanied by a short section of text in which the Museum thanks Mr Yip for the donation, described as 'a generous contribution to our motherland' (Shanghai Museum 1997).

Abroad, the Hong Kongese Hotung and T T Tsui families sponsored two major redisplays of Chinese objects in national museums in Britain in the early 1990s: the T T Tsui Gallery at the Victoria and Albert Museum (1991) and the Joseph Hotung Gallery of Oriental Antiquities at the British Museum (1992) (Barringer and Flynn 1998, 7). The same families financed the establishment of two of the main galleries of the Shanghai Museum, which have been named after their sponsors: the T T Tsui Gallery of Ceramics and the Hotung Gallery of Jade. Donations of this kind not only confer visibility to donors but also, and crucially, they establish a long-term association between the donor, the donated object and the museum.

MUSEUM AUDIENCES

> The audience's reception is as creative and constructivist a process as [museum] representation.
>
> (Perin 1992, 192)

Chinese museums are also changing as a result of the changes affecting – and provoked by – their audiences. As the sociologist Pierre Bourdieu has authoritatively argued (1984; Bourdieu and Darbel 1966), museum-going can be a tool of social distinction, a way to situate the self within the social framework. However, in addressing audiences as the actors of the museum world, the focus is not so much on the social meanings of museum-visiting, as on museums' efforts to reach their target audiences and meet visitors' expectations.

Museums do not merely 'receive' visitors; they can actively reach out for them. In setting up an exhibition, for example, museum professionals work with the profile of the ideal museum visitor in mind; the public is 'segmented' in order to offer to each category of visitor the most satisfying product. Audience segmentation is a function of various factors (age, class, education, etc), but, according to Professor Song Xiangguang, it may also be related to geography. Professor Song argues that the most successful exhibitions in Shanghai tend to be those that stress the leisure and entertainment aspects of the museum experience. By contrast, in Beijing, museum audiences tend to value the didactic dimension, preferring exhibitions that prioritise cultural edification. In Shanghai, the average length of a museum visit is 50 minutes, while, in Beijing, visits tend to last more than an hour (Song 2004a, *pers comm*).

Museums may employ various strategies in order to attract a specific audience; the use of particular promotional methods, materials and location is one such example. Advertising exhibitions within a university department rather than at a Rotary Club or at a local supermarket is likely to reach different audiences. Other audience determiners may be the price of entry tickets or the language used in the presentation of collections (for instance using technical or specialised rather than popular language). In terms of exhibition advertising, major museums in China rely on newspaper advertisements and television announcements (mostly as part of a news report); minor museums may use street hoardings and posters, and advertisements on tourism leaflets.

The transformation of the Chinese museum system is accompanied and reflected by a transformation of visitors' profiles and preferences. In 2006, a small survey was conducted among museum audiences in three museums in Shanghai: the Shanghai Museum, the Site of the First Congress of the Communist Party of China and the Shanghai Natural History Museum.[10] These were chosen for their diversity of scale, political relevance and thematic content (historical-artistic, political and scientific respectively).

The results of the survey suggest a correlation between museum category and visitors' profiles and interests. So, for instance, the Natural History Museum was, as expected, a typical destination for local school groups (mainly pupils of primary and middle schools), representing the majority of the Museum's visitors. In the case of the Site of the First Congress of the Communist Party, most visitors at the time of the survey were women. There were also a significant number of middle school students. It appears that visits were often prompted by teachers requesting that students write essays about the Site of the First Congress of the Communist Party as part of their 'political' education. Younger visitors were often accompanied by an adult (usually a relative) who guided them in the visit. During the survey period at the Site, almost all visitors were Chinese. This is not surprising considering the subject of the museum, despite the museum's location in the heart of Xintiandi, a tourist area in downtown Shanghai.

Conversely (and predictably), in the case of the Shanghai Museum, audiences were more international and varied. With regard to the purpose of the museum visit, the 'quest for refinement' was a recurrent theme in visitors' answers. The appreciation of museum exhibits is perceived as

---

[10] The survey was conducted in April 2006 in collaboration with the Department of Cultural Relics and Museums of Fudan University, Shanghai. I designed the questionnaire; it was composed of 17 questions (some of them open-ended) and included questions on visitors' profile (origin, age, education and profession), frequency of museum visits, type of interest in the exhibits (artistic, historical, patriotic, educative, scientific, curiosity or other), and expectations (education, leisure, specific services or other). The questionnaires were submitted over a period of four weeks, both on weekdays and weekends, to capture feedback from a variety of visitors. At the time of the survey, the entry price was 20 Yuan for the Shanghai Museum and 5 Yuan for both the Site of the First Congress of the Communist Party and the Shanghai Natural History Museum.

an elevating experience, a way to improve one's taste and cultivation. A few visitors commented that in the Shanghai Museum they could 'get in contact with the past', an assertion that might suggest a hint of nostalgia for past times. Some visitors, especially the middle-aged, claimed that the education they received did not cover the arts (today's middle-aged were students during the Cultural Revolution) and as a result they felt somewhat limited in their abilities to appreciate works of art.

For visitors to the Natural History Museum, education was understood in quite conservative and passive terms: students found it helpful to memorise names and categories of flora and fauna. The educational function of the Site of the First Congress of the Communist Party was predictably imbued with patriotism and Communist ideology. Roughly half of the Site's visitors at the time of the survey were members of the Chinese Communist Party, for whom a visit to the Site – a high point in the history of the Communist Party – is a form of pilgrimage. In terms of how the exhibits were received, some visitors at the Site of the First Congress of the Communist Party reported that they would have appreciated staff or volunteers explaining the exhibits, despite the presence of extensive texts and panels. This may suggest limited familiarity with the historical events presented by the Site, but may also highlight an interest in learning more about that specific historical event. Some visitors also would have welcomed facilities such as a bookshop, library or audiovisual room. At the Shanghai Museum, visitors (some of whom were non-Chinese) were more forthright in lamenting the insufficient explanations illustrating the exhibits. This was particularly the case in the painting and calligraphy galleries: one-third of interviewees stated that the captions were too 'essential' – including only author and date details – thereby not allowing them to 'understand' the exhibit. Although visitors to the Shanghai Museum tended to request more information, they were not willing to pay extra for it: the audio guide made available at the Museum entrance was refused by the majority as it was considered too expensive (at the time of the survey it cost 20 Yuan).

As for the features perceived as problematic or unpleasant, in general, visitors pointed out a lack of interaction and the passive, pedagogical, non-compelling structure of exhibitions. In many instances, visitors would have welcomed the opportunity to touch samples; this was particularly the case among younger audiences at the Natural History Museum. The glass box was perceived as an obstacle to direct appreciation. Some visitors also expressed dismay at the quality of some exhibits: at the Natural History Museum and at the Site of the First Congress of the Communist Party objects were considered to be not of significant interest, too 'ordinary' and not very attractive. Some visitors to the Natural History Museum claimed that the scientific information supplied by the exhibitions (notably with reference to biological classification) was out of date. Visitors also expressed the desire to see temporary exhibitions at the Natural History Museum (which features only permanent exhibitions) and, more generally, to be stimulated by new, fresh items and ideas. Many regretted the lack of a bookshop or souvenir shop. The fact that visitors expected and requested such additions is indicative of their willingness to expand the museum experience by either deepening their knowledge of the exhibits through books and museum catalogues, and/or by bringing home a souvenir. However, a few visitors were against the creation of bookshops and other facilities, arguing that these would jeopardise the authenticity of the museum and of its exhibits. Such criticisms and requests suggest that, in Shanghai, museum audiences' tastes and preferences are changing as a result of the socio-economic transition. Improved levels of education and greater earning power draw an informed, demanding, curious and diversified audience.

Having discussed the main actors within the realm of museums in China, it is now time to take a closer look at the objects to be found inside museums and examine their importance. The next chapter will thus focus on museum objects – their relevance and meanings – and their association with the Chinese nation.

Museum Objects and the Chinese Nation

This chapter explores how museums interpret objects in order to create and disseminate specific narratives of the Chinese nation. Since the process of representation begins with the interpretation of objects, it seems fitting to consider object biographies, and how these influence the ways in which objects are interpreted. How have specific objects endured over time and what contexts have they encountered during their 'social life'? How have museum practices (documentation, research, conservation, exhibition) affected their meanings and values, and to what extent are new meanings created in the museum?

One can think of museum displays as assemblages 'of people, things, ideas, texts, spaces, and different media' (Macdonald and Basu 2007, 9) which bear the 'capacity, through the studied manipulation of the relations between people and things in a custom-built environment, to produce new entities that can be mobilized – both within the museum and outside it – in social and civic programmes of varied kinds' (Bennett 2005, 525). By removing objects from their original contexts and placing them in an artificial, *ad hoc* environment, museums alter the perception and meaning of objects, as well as changing interrelations among objects, and between objects and persons (Bennett 2005, 523ff). By putting specific objects on display and by linking them through narratives, museums contribute to shaping individual and collective understandings of identities, the past, present and future. This implies that museums can also inform visitors' perceptions through those objects, facts and ideas they do *not* exhibit: in the framework of museum exhibitions, omissions become approximations of oblivion (Varutti 2010d).

To a large extent, these processes – that remain mostly implicit and invisible – are an inevitable component of museum practice. Museums provide new epistemological frameworks for their objects that reflect institutional authority and agendas. The ability of museums to confer upon (or deny) an object the status of art, scientific specimen or cultural or historical relic is in itself an exercise of authority.

Objects in a museum collection are alike in having been alienated from their contexts of creation and use. Their links with daily life will have been mostly severed and their circulation inevitably slowed down, if not arrested. Their original functions may at times be re-evoked, but their accumulated layers of cultural, personal and emotional meanings are mostly compressed and contained within their glass box. Many museum objects lie silently in the obscurity of the museum storeroom. Museum practices such as conservation contribute to a conceptual transformation: the object has entered a realm of immobility, where change is perceived not only as undesirable but as detrimental – the ultimate aim being preservation of the object for as long as possible.

The combined processes of de-contextualisation and subsequent re-contextualisation of objects in the collections and displays may be described as the 'museum effect'. The museum effect can be understood as the performative capacity of museums to create value: once an object has entered a museum collection it gains a different status, shifting from commodity to historical, scientific, cultural or artistic specimen. Svetlana Alpers (1991, 26–7) suggests that the museum effect – which she defines as 'turning all objects into works of art' – is basically a 'way of seeing'.

The museum effect endows objects with an aura of significance and value. The enchantment that objects may hold for viewers has been explored by the anthropologist Alfred Gell. Gell's seminal theory – developed in his book *Art and Agency: An Anthropological Theory* (1998) – argues that objects are invested with agency and thus able to affect people's thoughts and behaviour. This theory has the potential to shed new light on the system of social relations created and sustained through museum objects. Gell's insights, and the scholarly literature they have inspired, contribute to framing the relationship between museums and the nation in a novel way, making it possible to view museum objects as material evidence of the nation.

THE MUSEUM OBJECT REINTERPRETED

Although the meanings of objects on display may be presented as definitive and 'objective', an exhibit can be interpreted in many ways. As Michael Ames (1992, 4) notes, 'what some call appropriation, others see as inspiration; while some view glass boxes as a form of cultural imprisonment, others see them as a way of preserving heritage for future generations; and what some call the channelling of consciousness, others term consciousness-raising'.

In Chinese museums, the notion of the museum object can be stretched to include unusual object categories. The Site of the First National Congress of the Communist Party illustrates this point. Exhibited alongside historic documents (such as maps, letters and photos) are the personal belongings (some authentic, others reproductions) (Qian 2004b, *pers comm*) of the 13 attendants at the founding meeting of the Chinese Communist Party. Exhibits include items of clothing, such as uniforms, as well as personal seals, visiting cards, a typewriter, a wall clock, jade ornaments and also more unusual objects, such as the tea set that was purportedly used to serve tea to the attendants, and the ashtray and matches used on that occasion – even the lamp switches are presented as cultural relics, silent witnesses to a historic moment. The aim of the exhibition is not so much to provide information on the historic event as to provoke an emotional response and create within the visitor a fictional sense of participation in the event.

The same kind of museological approach – creating an aura around mundane, ordinary objects – is employed at the Military Museum in Beijing. Here, the worn clothes and shoes of anonymous soldiers of the Red Army are exhibited next to water flasks and old, creased geographic maps. Similarly, at the Tobacco Museum, in the section devoted to 'tobacco culture', the smoking implements of famous people such as Song Qingling, Deng Xiaoping and Mao Zedong are exhibited; in the context of the Tobacco Museum, Mao's pipe is regarded as a first-class cultural relic. Further examples of this approach can be found at the former residences of famous people such as Song Qingling or Sun Yat-Sen in Shanghai.

Recalling the concepts elaborated by Stephen Greenblatt (1991), these exhibitions adopt a resonance approach, emphasising the objects' associations and references. They are mostly everyday items which, by virtue of association with famous people or historic events, have been transformed into emotionally powerful objects. These items are exhibited for their evocative effect rather than their inherent historical value; from a Marxist–Leninist perspective, it is an

FIG 4.1. SOIL WITH FRAGMENTS OF PROJECTILE BECOME 'WITNESSES OF HISTORY' AT THE NATIONAL MUSEUM OF CHINA, BEIJING.

object's status as 'witness' of history that provides its worth.[1] In this museological approach, emphasis is placed not so much on the singular object as on the narrative. It is the narrative of struggle, sacrifice, martyrdom and, ultimately, the narrative of the nation, conveyed by the emotional weight attached to the object, that takes priority over the historical significance of the singular item on display. This perspective helps to explain the extensive use in historical exhibitions of contextualising display techniques such as dioramas (where individual objects acquire meaning when viewed in relation to each other). The prominent narrative also clarifies the presence of replicas, which are not necessarily perceived as problematic within historical exhibitions if they contribute to upholding an overarching narrative.

DISPLAY TECHNIQUES

A narrative may be created from a set of objects by making connections between them, establishing a sequence or a hierarchy, creating associations and oppositions, highlighting analogies and contrasts, 'telling a story' through figurative structures such as metaphors, using a particular

---

[1] The use of everyday objects in Chinese museums is reminiscent of the concept of 'objet-témoin', literally 'witnessing object', developed by Jean Gabus (1975) to convey that every object is a witness of something or someone, and can thus become a scientific document.

linguistic tone such as irony or provocation, or employing textual tools such as diagrams, panels, labels, maps, timelines or dioramas. These elements may be seen as the building blocks of the 'museum language' – that is, the set of tools, techniques and narratives that museums employ to disseminate a message and/or to forge an image.

The degree of visitors' familiarity with Chinese symbolism, history and culture are likely to affect their perception and interpretation of displays. While this applies to all cultures, it is especially true for China. For instance, a porcelain bowl decorated with peaches will be appreciated by a Chinese visitor not only on an artistic level (for the quality of the porcelain, technical skill, the precision of the drawing, the delicacy of its colours, the calligraphic traits and the overall sense of harmony and balance, etc) but also on a metaphorical level, as peaches are considered symbols of longevity and immortality in China. In most museum exhibitions, the visitor's familiarity with an object's symbolic meanings is taken for granted (or not considered relevant); only rarely do labels or panels make their meanings explicit, almost as if the symbolic appreciation of the object were a private matter, or too obvious to state for Chinese audiences.

Among exhibition techniques, dioramas (especially those including wax figures) deserve a special mention. Dioramas are so commonplace that it seems fair to say that they are a characteristic trait of museum displays in China. These life-like, life-size, three-dimensional figures are intended to surprise visitors and impress them with the realism of the scene reproduced. The guidebook to the Memorial Museum of the Chinese People's War of Resistance to Japan goes as far as stating: 'Dioramas are a new display method [they] exemplif[y] the level of development of our construction projects and museums' (quoted in Mitter 2000, 288).[2] The popularity of dioramas may be ascribed to a number of reasons. First and foremost, they allow the visitor a form of 'participation' in the event portrayed. At the Site of the First Congress of the Communist Party in Shanghai, for example, the visitor is faced with life-size wax reproductions of the 13 founding members of the Communist Party engaged in an animated discussion, giving a hyper-realistic and vibrant depiction of the historical event. Similarly, dioramas feature in the Bank Museum in Shanghai (recreating the interiors of a bank of the Qing Dynasty), at the Shanghai History Museum (depicting a street scene in a 1930s avenue in the French Concession), as well as in memorial halls and former residences of personalities (as in the cases of Song Qingling and Sun Yat-Sen), where they enhance and 'immortalise' the charismatic aura of these figures. Dioramas allow a unique form of proximity with the subject of the representation. Dioramas are also used extensively in displays of ethnic minority groups, as will be discussed later, in Chapter 10.

CONSTRUCTING VALUE AND MEANING

Anthony Shelton (1990, 98) provides an incisive introduction to the discussion of the construction of value: '"value" is an arbitrary category, having no natural innate residency within objects, but having its origin within a social classification that hides behind the object'. Value can thus be a function of infinite variables: aesthetic, historical, scientific, political and social, as well as subjective criteria; moreover, these criteria change over time. Nevertheless, it is possible to

---

2   Dioramas are not, in fact, a new display method, having been used in natural history exhibits from the mid-19th century, and in folk museums in the UK from the 1930s.

identify a set of factors that contribute to making objects 'valuable' in museums. The following considerations are based on observations in Chinese museums, but can be extended to other museums.

Rarity is a source of value. The example of the so-called 'Ru ware' Chinese ceramics illustrates this point. The term 'Ru ware' comes from Ruzhou, the Chinese town where these kind of ceramics were produced. The exceptional value that is today attributed to the objects made from this particular material is to a lesser extent linked to their historical importance, age or artistic value, and is more concerned with their rarity. These ceramics, created exclusively for the imperial Song court, were only produced over a period of 40 years, around AD 1100. Today, only 100 complete pieces survive (Clunas 1997a, 58), hence their high value. 'Ru ware' ceramics appear in the ceramics collections of the Shanghai Museum. However, they are rarely included in loans due to their extremely high insurance costs – another measure of value.

Singularisation (that is, the selection of a specific object, so as to make it conspicuous or noteworthy) is another source of value. The scholar Igor Kopytoff (1986, 67) maintains that 'power often asserts itself symbolically by insisting on its right to singularise an object'. Paraphrasing Kopytoff, the power of museums over objects is also expressed through their authority to singularise objects and to exclude them from exchange circuits and fossilise them in a timeless dimension. Chinese imperial collections provide a good example of singularisation. Here, the emperor's persona is made sacred through the sacralisation of his accoutrements. In turn, the singularisation of imperial paraphernalia through their crystallisation in imperial collections points to the prestige and authority of their holder, the Chinese government. Distance is a further source of value. The creation of value in the museum relies on the imposition of distance between the object and the viewer. Such distance expresses the transformation that the museum operates on the object, changing it from a commodity into an entity that has no market.

Value creation is also the outcome of curatorial research and effective display. Eilean Hooper-Greenhill (1992, 124) captures the complexity of these processes: 'the curatorial meanings of objects in museums are produced through complex and multilayered museological processes where museum objectives, collecting policies, classification methods, display styles, artefactual grouping and textual framework come together in articulation'. Value is thus a function of display techniques. For instance, ritual bronzes – food and water ritual vessels dating back to the Shang (c. 1600–1046 BC) and Zhou (1046–256 BC) dynasties – are among the most prestigious items in collections of ancient Chinese art. Considered masterpieces of bronze-casting techniques, Chinese bronzes also carry ritual and symbolic meaning, as they were used in ceremonies devoted to the cult of the ancestors and later came to embody wealth and political authority. Bronzes may be appreciated as museum objects on several different levels. The displays might, for instance, emphasise the skills and the difficulties of the casting techniques employed, as part of discourses on technological development that aim to compare the trajectories of different centres of human settlement in Ancient China. This is the approach favoured by the Sanxingdui Museum, an archaeological museum located in the Sichuan Province which holds archaeological finds of the ancient Shu civilisation, estimated to date back to 1300–1200 BC. Here, the display compares ancient bronzes of the Shu civilisation of south-west China to the Shang and Zhou bronzes unearthed in the northern provinces of Hebei, Henan and Shandong, considered the cradle of Chinese civilisation. In other exhibitions, museums may choose to stress the ritual importance of the bronzes and their association with political authority, as in the case of the National Museum of China in Beijing, where the exhibition highlights how the accumulation and transmission of bronzes followed dynastic lineage. In other instances, such as in the case of the Shanghai Museum, the technical and historical significance of bronzes is not prioritised; instead, the aesthetics of the artefacts are accentuated. Yet another approach to the study and display of bronzes is provided by Louise Tythacott's (2011) reconstruction of the biographies of five Buddhist sculptures originating from the island of Putuo, on the eastern coast of China, and currently in the collections of the Museum of Liverpool.

Resonance and Wonder in Chinese Museums

Visiting the Shanghai Museum is an experience designed to please the senses. Softly lit exhibition rooms host arrays of glass cases and crystal pedestals where objects sit silently in the eloquence of their beauty. The dark, velvet-covered interiors create a quiet and elegant (if formal and almost reverential) atmosphere from which the objects emerge to catch the gaze of the visitor. Labels are discreet – their texts reduced to the essential – as are introductory panels. Iridescent spotlights drown the object in waves of light, almost as if light emanated from the object itself. Their aesthetics thus sublimated, objects appear isolated from their setting and singularised: no distractions, no stimuli from the background disturb the encounter with the masterpiece. The display seems designed not so much to educate as to seduce, appealing primarily to aesthetic sensitivity, rather than to intellectual curiosity. The exhibitions of the Shanghai Museum speak a language of beauty, aestheticism and refinement.

Stephen Greenblatt's (1991) concepts of 'resonance' and 'wonder' are useful tools for disentangling the mechanisms through which the museum's displaying of an object may affect the visitor's perception. Resonance has been defined as 'the power of the displayed object to reach out beyond its formal boundaries to a larger world, to evoke in the viewer the complex, dynamic forces from which it has emerged and for which it may be taken by a viewer to stand'. Wonder, on the other hand, indicates 'the power of the displayed object to stop the viewer in his or her tracks, to convey an arresting sense of uniqueness, to evoke an exalted attention' (Greenblatt 1991, 42). An exhibition that focuses on the 'wonder effect' tends to isolate the object, which is meant to be admired for its material, technical or aesthetic characteristics. In other words, a wonder effect emphasises 'the masterpiece', stressing its uniqueness and charismatic aura. As Greenblatt (ibid, 49) puts it, in the wonder gaze 'the act of attention draws a circle around itself from which everything but the object is excluded'.

Wonder is precisely the kind of response that the Shanghai Museum aims to generate in the visitor. Here, objects – bronzes, calligraphy texts, paintings, porcelains, coins and suchlike – are exhibited in ways that underline their 'singularity', their 'artfulness'. Each object, before consideration is made of its contribution to the understanding of Chinese culture, is presented as a masterpiece of technique, art and civilisation. With regard to display techniques, 'singularisation' is mainly achieved through the use of individual exhibition boxes and special lighting. The kind of lighting adopted by the Shanghai Museum corresponds to what Greenblatt calls 'boutique lighting': one or two spots illuminate the object from different angles, separating it from the background and stressing its individuality.

For instance, among its collections, the Shanghai Museum boasts a bronze vessel – the Pan of Zi Zhong Jiang – of extreme rarity for the bronze-casting techniques employed as well as for its beauty and refinement. As is also the case for the Shanghai Museum's other masterpieces, the vessel is exhibited in an individual glass box located in the centre of the exhibition room; it

FIG 4.2. EXAMPLE OF 'WONDER' APPROACH TO DISPLAYS AT THE SHANGHAI MUSEUM.

FIG 4.3. EXAMPLE OF 'RESONANCE' APPROACH AT THE NATIONAL MUSEUM OF CHINA, BEIJING.

is illuminated by powerful spotlights pointing at each side of the object, allowing an all-round appreciation of its details. Despite the item's historical and artistic relevance, the label reports only its name, approximate date of production and the name of the donor. The visitor is invited to admire the object in its materiality, but is left with scant information with which to contextualise it and appreciate its historical, cultural and technical importance.

In contrast to the wonder effect, exhibitions that emphasise the resonance of objects tend to highlight their social history. The original context in which the object was created, as well as the set of relations that were knitted around it, tell the story of 'the negotiations, exchanges, swerves, and exclusions' that have punctuated its social life (Greenblatt 1991, 45). Instead of evoking admiration, the resonance mode aims to sensitise the viewer to issues around the social life of the object, emphasising contexts of production and use, and supplying information that is not immediately apparent to the mere gaze.

Following in the footsteps of the Shanghai Museum, a growing number of recently built or refurbished museums (including the Poly Art Museum and the Capital Museum in Beijing, as well as the Sichuan University Museum in Chengdu) have embraced the wonder effect paradigm, the singularisation and aesthetisation of objects being a major trend in exhibition practices in China, notably in museums devoted to art and history. However, display techniques adopting a resonance approach remain widespread, especially in museums created during the first decades following 1949. The Military Museum in Beijing is a case in point.

One of the most visited museums in China, as well as one of the largest, the Military Museum houses collections of weapons and military paraphernalia. Its exhibitions illustrate the accomplishments of the Red Army in the years preceding and following the creation of the New China (the Long March epic is one of the highlights). The objects exhibited evoke the Red Army soldiers' spirit of sacrifice and devotion to the revolutionary cause. This eulogy to the military power of the country is in tune with the nationalistic tone of the museum.[3] Exhibits are organised over four floors; most relate to the Communist Revolution and the establishment of Communist rule through the armed struggle. Objects bear little aesthetic or scientific significance: the visitor is presented with the personal belongings of anonymous soldiers (shoes, over-worn clothes, water containers, maps, etc). These items are meant to impress, to generate an emotive reaction by evoking a past experience and by enforcing (or creating?) an association with ideals of sacrifice and martyrdom. In so doing, the exhibits tell a story that emphasises some aspects of the Revolution while neglecting others (such as despair, poverty and hunger). Displays at the Military Museum illustrate an approach to exhibition based on the idea of resonance: the 'communication power' of the objects is used to project an idea, a message that the exhibition is meant to convey.

The National Art Museum of China in Beijing provides an example of exhibitions mixing 'resonance' and 'wonder' effects. The Museum mostly exhibits Chinese paintings of the 20th century, with a special focus on the artistic production of Communist propaganda. Exhibition rooms are extraordinarily large and, likewise, hold paintings of remarkably large dimensions, mostly portraying working 'comrades' in factories, rural areas, and science and technology labo-

---

[3]   A number of Chinese flags hang from the museum's façade and at the entrance. In the main hall, the visitor is greeted by huge portraits of the great men of China: Mao Zedong, Deng Xiaoping, Jiang Zemin. Most of the museum attendants are members of various army bodies (Military Museum, Beijing, last visited in November 2004).

ratories, soldiers in the battlefield and portraits of 'Chairman Mao' reproduced on canvasses that are metres long. The wonder effect is achieved through the large dimensions of the paintings. At the same time, more subtly, the size of both the exhibition spaces and paintings also creates the resonance effect, as the physical dimensions of paintings suggest other forms of metaphoric 'greatness': morality, dignity, pride and authority.

AESTHETICS AND THE NEW NARRATIVES OF THE NATION

As remarked upon earlier, a visit to the Shanghai Museum is an experience designed to please the senses. Situated on one side of Shanghai's majestic People's Square, its stunning architecture symbolising the round sky over the square earth of Chinese cosmology, the Shanghai Museum is as distinctive as any of the world's great museums. Inside, one enters a marble hall filled with light and marked by sharp architectural lines. Beyond this, shadowy, intimate and almost secretive, the galleries entice the visitor. In these exhibition rooms the soft light is complemented by velvet furnishings and carefully placed arrays of crystal cases, their treasures disclosed in an atmosphere that is still and sumptuous, almost sacred. The objects themselves are positioned in pools of light, which sculpt their forms. Against muted backdrops, the objects emerge as absolute and discrete, possessing a material potency that seems to owe little to time and space. The objects are silent, eloquent only in their beauty, with nothing to distract visitors' attention away from this encounter with the masterpiece. By these means, the museum seduces the senses and forces the visitor to suspend any remnant of disbelief. By these means, exhibitions at the Shanghai Museum use the wordless language of beauty to communicate the magnificence of Chinese civilisation.

Although the Shanghai Museum is likely to remain unsurpassed among Chinese museums for its architectural grandeur and the quality of its collections, it is by no means alone in its choice of a museological model which emphasises and invites an aesthetic approach to objects. Since its opening in 1996, an increasing number of national museums in China have followed its lead by reorganising their displays in ways that give a renewed importance to aesthetics. While this is a trend seen in other parts of the world, its presence in a country which only a few decades ago framed its collections in the rhetoric of Marxist–Leninist social theory deserves closer investigation (see Varutti 2010c).

An increased focus on the aesthetic dimension of objects in exhibitions is achieved through particular display techniques that pursue both the singularisation and the decontextualisation of objects. Increasingly, the celebration of the aesthetic dimension of objects is embraced by Chinese museums as a trademark of 'modernity'. The focus here is not so much on beautiful things, as on the act of bringing out the aesthetic qualities of objects by using specific display techniques which draw the viewer's attention to the object's formal characteristics by inviting an appreciative and contemplative approach. If one accepts that the aesthetics of objects are historically and culturally specific (Descola 2007), then there is good reason to examine systems of representation and viewing which exploit aesthetics in order to create meaning and deploy it within narrative (Shanks and Tilley 1987, 68). The aesthetics of a museum exhibition can, in these circumstances, be understood to arise not from the intrinsic properties of objects but from institutional discourse (Vickery 2007, 227). As such, aesthetics constitute a mode of representation that cuts through different epistemological registers. The aesthetic gaze is allegedly 'neutral' vis-à-vis different cultural and disciplinary constructions (historical, ethnographic, scientific or artistic). Its application means that museums can dispense with object meanings and instead substitute aesthetics. Deborah Root (1996, 111) notes, 'once an object is named as art either by the relevant specialists or by the market, it tends to be exhibited alone, displayed as an aesthetic form rather than a source of cultural information [...] Art universalizes the object and places it beyond culture.'

However, aesthetics can also be used to place objects within a culture, even one that is mythological and unspecific. In China, that cultural setting might be understood as 'the nation', defined by beauty, craftsmanship and longevity. For instance, at the National Museum of Chinese History – prior to its refurbishment and transfiguration into the current National Museum of China – visitors could admire a selection of masterpieces including ceramics, bronzes, sculptures, jewellery and lacquer items. Museum panels stated that 'people find themselves overflown by pride when they walk around the exhibition hall and feel the aesthetic rhythm from precious relics'.[4] The nation is here celebrated as a masterpiece. As to the intentions of such exhibitionary acts, Donald Preziosi (2010, 82) is in no doubt: 'museums exist in the first place to manufacture belief'. What beliefs, then, are being manufactured in the aesthetics of Chinese museums?

One particular implication of the approach has been the ability to transcend historical, cultural and technical specificities. For example, in the temporary exhibition *Imperial Treasures from China*, held at the China Millennium Monument in Beijing in November 2004 to promote the 2008 Olympic Games, bronzes from the Shang Dynasty (c. 1600–1046 BC) were displayed next to calligraphy from the Qing Dynasty (AD 1644–1911). Aesthetic display creates a sense of coherence and continuity out of the heterogeneous and fragmentary. In museum exhibitions, this interlinking and conflation of time produces an abstract sense of antiquity, beauty and craftsmanship which projects a nation defined by longevity, refinement and ingenuity.

Chinese artistic traditions are known for their refined and elaborate aesthetic canons which draw on ideas such as balance, harmony, liveliness, spontaneity and propriety. Karl-Heinz Pohl (2008, 90) has remarked that 'these features served, well into the modern period, as fundamental elements of a Chinese cultural identity'. It seems then plausible that the display and reception of Chinese material culture in modern-day museums is informed by these aesthetic principles, deeply embedded in Chinese culture.

In the mid-1990s, a new category of national museum – of which the Shanghai Museum is the most iconic example – was established in China. These museums used aesthetic approaches to display that served to uphold a very specific political discourse, which had its roots in the ideological crisis of the early 1990s. In these new museums, Ancient China is no longer presented as belonging to a dark era of oppression. On the contrary, it is considered of pivotal importance in supplying Chinese civilisation with its roots. This re-evaluation of Chinese history and heritage provided a platform for the revival of traditional Chinese aesthetics in what became known as the 'culture craze' or 'culture fever' (*wenhua re*) (Lin and Galikowski 1999, 54; Pohl 2008, 93; Wang 1996). This rhetoric of national pride and cultural prestige is translated in national museums into the aestheticisation of the material culture of Ancient China (Su 1995). This same aesthetic approach is also affecting relics of the Revolution: the most recent displays of the revolutionary past strive to revitalise Chinese patriotism through 'attractive' displays that enable visitors to perceive history 'directly through the senses' (Denton 2005, 568). This movement towards the aestheticisation of the ancient and revolutionary past can be seen in the two permanent galleries

---

[4]   National Museum of Chinese History, Beijing, May 2006.

of the new National Museum of China specifically devoted to Ancient China and the revolutionary past.[5]

The transition to aesthetic displays is accompanied by – and expressed through – a shift from chronological to thematic approaches. These thematic displays reshuffle object associations, distancing them from the historical, cultural and socio-economic conditions of their production. Such remodelling may, however, result positively in new and unexpected connections between diverse types of object. In this way, visitors could enjoy new pleasurable experiences rather than simply enduring an education in ideology. As Guo Qingshen, an educator at the Shanghai Museum, remarked, the museum had become customer oriented and attuned to individual needs, desires and expectations (Guo 2004, *pers comm*). In the mid-1990s, national museums were well placed to transform themselves in this way, since they had high public visibility and could attract considerable funding and government endorsement.

In these new types of museums, explanatory panels, photographs, charts, video screens and other information devices tend to be physically separate from the object, as if not to encroach upon its aura. At the Shanghai Museum, for example, panels introducing the content of the exhibition galleries are located in the entrance to the gallery and at the start of each gallery section, so as not to interrupt the visual flow of objects. The most spectacular exhibits (bronzes, ceramics and sculptures) are displayed in individual cases situated at the centre of the exhibition space. Information pertaining to these objects is provided by the optional audio guide which is limited to the highlights of the collection.

Intriguingly, in some instances, display techniques vary according to the type of material on display. At the Sanxingdui Museum in Sichuan, for example, which displays artefacts of the ancient Shu civilisation, the galleries devoted to ceramics, pottery and gold artefacts are highly contextualised, with panels and charts providing information on their archaeological significance. In contrast, the bronzes tend to be accompanied by minimalist labels, but set dramatically – almost theatrically – against huge panels decorated with large reproductions of bronze masks. The Shu bronzes are given this kind of prominence because they are radically different from those of the Shang Dynasty excavated in northern China, yet they also demonstrate advanced casting techniques (Clunas 1997a, 19). The Shu remain a relatively mysterious and enigmatic people – a perception enhanced by the museum's displays, which portray the civilisation as a 'controversial legend' and 'a rare treasure of ancient humanity' that provides a 'missing link in the evolution of Chinese culture'.[6] In this way, the museum amplifies the charismatic aura of the objects, increasing their significance. Here, aesthetic impact is in part used to address a deficiency of historical information, but one also senses that this lack of data has been romantically deployed to connect history to legend.

Objects – such as bronzes – which possess important ritual, mythical, historical, political and social meanings receive minimal historical and cultural interpretation, as if their relevance and meanings were self-evident. Other more functional objects do receive interpretation. The distinction is deeply rooted in the realms of connoisseurship. Outside China, displays of Chinese material culture, which mainly focus on the art of the court, tend to be deeply influenced by aesthetic approaches (see Varutti 2008b). Chinese material culture is labelled as 'Asian Art', 'Oriental Arts'

---

[5] For more on these two galleries of the new National Museum of China, see page 113.
[6] From the museum panels of the Sanxingdui Museum. Visited in May 2006.

or 'Far-East Asian Antiquities'; it is 'high art', the province of connoisseurs and art experts, rather than ethnographers (Fiskesjö 2007). This aesthetic approach also reflects the market in cultural artefacts which favours aesthetics and intrinsic decorative elements over context and data, and which has fuelled illicit trade in artefacts. These aesthetic values – of high art and the art economy – have undoubtedly been imported back into China, but they are clearly not the only reason behind Chinese museums adopting an aesthetic approach.

The framing of objects as masterpieces, rather than as cultural relics, leads to a flattening of history, in stark contrast with the historical materialism that informed museum displays during the Maoist era. Visitors are no longer invited to appraise, for instance, the ritual and political roles of bronze vessels in Ancient China, or to appreciate the meaning of the various inscriptions and seals on paintings and scrolls. Instead, the objects are dehistoricised (Jewsiewicki 2007). As Shanks and Tilley (1987, 73) remark, 'the aesthetic artefact is an escape from the nightmare of history'. The past is thus reactualised in an aseptic, unproblematic form, and the museum can distance itself from the object's historicity and obviate potentially contentious issues that might undermine or threaten authoritative narratives, such as those centred on the unity of the Chinese nation. And because of its aesthetic emphasis, creating objects and notions which are absolute and universal, this exhibitionary mode reinforces the myth of a similarly absolute and universal entity – the nation. Indeed, the absence of significant hiatuses over 5000 years of history is one of the grand narratives of the present Chinese government. China's glorious past is celebrated, while historical discontinuities and cultural differences are shunned.

The Chinese situation is not unconnected from a broader worldwide emphasis on aesthetics in museums. Indeed, there are grounds for arguing that, in the new millennium, aesthetics have become a mainstream mode of display, and that this is especially the case for the representation of national identity and national past. Engagement with the consequences of colonialism and a new social mobility has resulted both in collaborative practices and a retreat into aesthetics, permitting a disengagement from contestations of the past (Clifford 1997; Errington 1998; Price 2007). As Donald Preziosi (2010, 9) remarks, 'great national museums exist precisely in order to foster and perpetuate the belief in the truth of abstractions such as national identity, character, mentality, or ethnicity'. The popularity of aesthetics as a mode of exhibition of the nation, in China if not elsewhere, can be explained at least in part by the fact that aesthetics work as a 'belief enhancer' by seducing the viewer, by pleasing the senses and by reaching for the individual, the personal and the intimate – even if, ultimately, a collective goal is desired.

MUSEUMS AS ARTEFACTS: THE IMPORTANCE OF ARCHITECTURE AND LOCATION

The most stunning facet of the transformation of Chinese museums is probably their architecture. Anthropologist Michael Ames (1986, 1) considers museums as 'artefacts of society [...] exhibits in their own right'. Can one then look at museums as cultural artefacts? Museums are indeed a composite cultural product, mirrors of the societies that created them, and vehicles, through collective representations, of shared values.

Through their architecture, museums make a statement: from the exterior, their architecture sets the tone; inside, the visitor's experience is shaped by architecture, influencing visitor perception and contributing to the museum's narratives (see MacLeod et al 2012). Neo-classical buildings with colonnades, ascending steps and imposing doorways, for instance, imply a formal, respectful, almost reverential attitude. At the same time, the reference to ancient civilisations such as the Greeks and the Romans upholds the idea of continuity with that past and its values: beauty, symmetry, harmony, purity of forms, rationality and rigour are metaphorically translated into political, intellectual and moral authority. As Carol Duncan and Alan Wallach (2004, 52) note, 'Roman-derived architectural rhetoric [...] has been used in public buildings since the Renaissance to symbolise state authority'. More trenchantly, Michaela Giebelhausen (2003, 4) argues that museums are 'monuments to the idealised power of civilisation and the paternalistic concerns of the nation state'. While some museums strive to be user-friendly and informal, others emphasise their official, authoritative, even intimidating potential. For instance, the newly built National Museum of China receives its visitors with a platoon of armed guards performing an impressive security check. Beyond the threshold, the visitor is dwarfed by an overwhelmingly large entrance hall designed to exude authority and grandeur.

Stunning futuristic architecture is instrumental in creating a city's image. The Guggenheim Museum in Bilbao, for instance, was crucial in enhancing the city's natural profile. This iconic institution exemplifies the role that museums can play in triggering forms of urban regeneration and enhancing the cultural appeal of a city. In this perspective, '"culture" [...] is seen as a focal point, from which radiate not only opportunities in economic terms, but also – and maybe more importantly – the hope for a change of identity of the transforming societies' (Baniotopoulou 2001, 1).

Architecture is to a museum what a frame is to an art object. Marc Maure (1995, 164) details the role of the frame as a physical and symbolic element of the exhibit:

> The frame demarcates the line between two different worlds, in the sense of categories or groups of messages. It indicates that what is within the frame has another meaning than that what [sic] is outside it. The frame expresses a commentary on the framed, creates a message over and above the main message. It meta-communicates values and expresses a relationship to what is communicated. The frame gives us an idea of how we should understand the framed message. It initiates and organizes certain patterns of feelings, reasonings and behaviour.

Extending this metaphor, if we compare the museum to an object, the architecture can be seen as its 'packaging', its presentation to the outside world. No one knows better than museum directors how important architecture is for the visibility of the museum and its positioning, not only within local artistic or intellectual circles but within the community at large. Increasingly, architectural forms are assigned the task of attracting visitors, while also making a precise statement about the character of the institution.

An example of this is the New Zealand National Museum, Te Papa Tongarewa, in Wellington, inaugurated in 1998. The architecture of Te Papa aims to combine modern design with elements of traditional Maori architecture: the Museum represents both the colonial and postcolonial history of New Zealand as well as its multi-ethnic present (Legget 1995, 29). Another illustration of the importance of architecture is provided by the South Korea National Museum in Seoul (McKillop 1995, 27). Prior to the creation of the new building in 2005, the South Korea National Museum was based in the Capitol building, formerly the headquarters of the Japanese government during its occupation of Korea between 1910 and 1945. The South Korean government was anxious to end the association of the National Museum with such history. The demolition of the old building, together with the creation of a new museum were intended to distance modern South Korea from its colonial past, as well as providing a spectacular assertion

FIG 4.4. THE UNIQUE ARCHITECTURAL STYLE OF THE SHANGHAI MUSEUM.

of South Korea's contemporary cultural and national identity. These examples illustrate that museum architecture can be a powerful tool of expression, especially when museums are involved in the construction or renegotiation of national identity.

Among Chinese museums, one finds a large number of unique architectural styles that have made museums iconic. Examples include the Shanghai Museum and the Tobacco Museum in Shanghai, as well as the China Millennium Monument and the Capital Museum, both in Beijing. A significant number of museums retain the distinctive features of imperial architecture, especially of the Ming (AD 1368–1644) and Qing (AD 1644–1911) dynasties. This is the case not only for historical buildings now transformed into museums (such as the Palace Museum, the Summer Palace and the Temple of Heaven in Beijing, or the Shenyang Palace Museum in Liaoning Province); it is also true of more recent museums, for which drawing inspiration from imperial architecture has become a trademark. For instance, the structure of the Nanjing Museum, created in 1947, is inspired by the architectural style of the Ming Dynasty, as are the National Art Museum of China (NAMOC) in Beijing, opened in 1963, and the Arthur Sackler Museum of Art and Archaeology, inaugurated in 1993. In these cases, reference to imperial architectural styles acts to validate the authenticity of the museums' collections and assert their institutional legitimacy as heirs to the imperial legacy.

In quite a different way, the 'museumification' of the former residences of political personalities, such as Song Qingling or Sun Yat-Sen, whose dwelling styles reflect personal taste, can be framed as a form of cultural and political (re)appropriation: by transforming these private, intimate and formerly inaccessible spaces into public loci, the government is appropriating, interpreting and crystallising the image of these figures, their open houses becoming a metaphor of their eternal role as public personae. Similarly evocative in terms of reappropriation is the case of the Shanghai Arts and Crafts Museum, located in a French-style building created in 1905 to host the Chamber of Commerce during the French occupation of Shanghai.

Most museums created in 1950s China are easily recognisable by their Soviet architectural styles, of which the buildings on Tian An Men Square, including the Museum of National History, the Military Museum and the Mao Zedong Mausoleum are among the most representative examples. As the Chinese museologist Hung Chang-Tai (2012, 574) notes, 'In Communist nations, an imposing government building is hardly just a representation of architectural artistry. It is often a fusion of technology, art and, most importantly, state policies.'

In the creation of the most recent museums, the imposing, austere, monolithic structures of Soviet architecture have been abandoned in favour of individuality and originality; old forms have given way to new architectural paradigms combining geometric, futuristic forms and references to traditional Chinese architecture and symbolism. The Shanghai Museum is representative of these new paradigms. Its emblematic architecture is meant to embody the idea of continuity between past and present, echoing classic elements of Chinese cosmology: the round roof with a square base is said to refer to 'the ancient Chinese philosophy that the square earth is under the round sky' (Shanghai Museum n.d., 3). The Tobacco Museum, opened in September 2004 in Shanghai, is another example of evocative and futuristic architecture. This five-storey building of asymmetric forms and pure lines has a concrete façade bearing a large engraved representation of a ship, in homage to Christopher Columbus who, on discovering the Americas, introduced tobacco to the Western world and eventually to China. Also, the cylindrical construction that welcomes the visitor at the entrance is said to symbolise a Mayan temple, as the Maya allegedly attached particular importance to tobacco (*China Daily* 2003).

The Sanxingdui Museum in Sichuan offers a further example of spectacular architecture highly charged with symbolic meaning. The main building bears the shape of a rising spiral, representing 'the development of society: from primitive to civilized; from inferior to advanced. It tells us the surging and winding course of the history' (Xiao 2000, 23). In the same vein, the roof of the Shanghai Urban Planning Exhibition Center has been built to resemble the four petals of the white magnolia, the flower emblem of the city.

In the more conservative Beijing, the National Museum of China, built in 2010 and designed by German architects, sets itself in a line of continuity with the imposing, rigorous Soviet-inspired architecture of the other (mostly governmental) buildings on Tian An Men Square. Yet, although the architecture of the National Museum may seem to run counter to the trend in museums elsewhere, examples of museums exhibiting futuristic and evocative architecture are plentiful in Beijing.

The China Millennium Monument (actually a museum) was created to celebrate the new millennium. This futuristic building boasts evocative architecture: an arrow pointing skywards is located high at the end of a concrete path representing the timeline of Chinese history. The visitor, walking along the path, metaphorically walks through the whole course of Chinese history, moving towards the future, which is represented by the arrow at the far end of the path. At the base of the monument burns a perpetual flame. Each architectural element is charged with symbolic significance. As reported in an inscription at the base of the monument, 'the gentle centripetal slope of the ground suggests the rise of the Chinese nation'. The flame represents the spirit of China: 'the ever burning flame in the middle of the plaza is the Holy fire of China. It originated at the site of the Peking Man at Zoukoudian. The flame is a token of the unceasing creativity of Chinese civilisation.' The small flow of water surrounding the flame symbolises 'the mother rivers of the Chinese civilisation: the Yangtze and the Yellow Rivers'.[7] The message of this highly visible heritage site in downtown Beijing could hardly be more imbued with nationalistic tones. In sharp contrast to the monumental Soviet style of the nearby Military Museum, the Millennium Monument has been designed to suggest the idea of modernity, rendered through a physical projection towards the sky and, metaphorically, towards the future.

More recently, the Capital Museum, inaugurated in May 2006, has secured a place at the forefront of the Beijing museum scene. With its curved lines recalling the arched roofs of traditional Chinese architecture, the Capital Museum stands out among the city's panorama and has become one of Beijing's main attractions. Here again, the architecture of the museum suggests a 'harmonious integration of past and present, history and modernism, art and nature' bearing 'distinct national characteristics on one hand and obvious modern feeling on the other' (Capital Museum n.d.).

In addition to stunning architecture, the most successful museums share another feature: a strategic location. In China, the most central and prestigious locations were, until recently, reserved for the more 'political' museums (such as the former National Revolutionary Museum, on Tian An Men Square, and the Military Museum, located along one of the main arteries crossing Beijing, or the Site of the First Communist Party in the touristy compound of Xintiandi, downtown Shanghai). Interestingly, these museums are now gradually being displaced by a new generation of museums of art and antiquities which, in the style of the new National Museum of China in Beijing or the Shanghai Museum, are stealing the spotlight from Revolutionary museums. Location is one of the contributing elements that most immediately 'defines' a museum; as Kirk Denton (2005) remarks, central or strategic locations are *per se* expressions of power and, increasingly, of substantial funds. So, for instance, the futuristic architecture and content of the Shanghai Science and Technology Museum fit perfectly into the concrete landscape of skyscrapers and large avenues of Pudong, the financial hub created in the early 1990s on the west banks of the Huang Pu river.

The case of the new Shanghai Museum, built in 1996, demonstrates how important a museum's location can be: the directors waited for years to obtain governmental authorisation to build the new museum in the main, central square in Shanghai, where all the other 'important' cultural institutions would be established: the new theatre and concert hall, the new Urban Planning Museum and the Museum of Modern Art, as well as government offices. The Shanghai Museum directors were fully aware of the dramatic impact that the spectacular museum architecture would have once it was located in the frame of the square, and with good reason: the Shanghai Museum has become one of the symbols of the city.

The Site of the First National Congress of the Communist Party provides further proof that location is key. The Site was declared a memorial in 1952 and has been open to the public since. The buildings were renovated in 1996 as part of a major real estate project of urban regeneration that led to the creation of a downtown commercial and tourist area called Xintiandi. There is a certain irony in the fact that one of the most iconic sites of China's Communist past is now

---

[7]   China Millennium Monument, Beijing. Last visited May 2006.

nested in the most commercial neighbourhood of China's most capitalist city. This has led some observers to note that the Site is an illustration of how, in contemporary China, 'ideological pedagogy and leisure consumption can be fused into one project' (L Pan 2012, 131). Yet this might be only an apparent paradox, as the location of the Communist stronghold at Shanghai's modern and cosmopolitan core contributes to a reframing of the role of the Communist Party as the maker of modern China. References to the more austere Communist principles of martyrdom, self-sacrifice and collective struggle are downplayed in favour of a new narrative of revolutionary spirit presented as avant-garde thinking and thus compatible with the capitalist venture (see L Pan 2012, 131ff). Through this renewed association between the Site and Shanghai's thriving commercial present, the Communist Party is actually recasting its past in order to continue to play a significant role in China's present.

The architectural style of a museum is also an exhibition topic in its own right. For instance, in late spring 2012, the new National Museum of China in Beijing hosted a temporary exhibition entitled *The Architectural Design Exhibition of the National Museum of China*, which provided visitors with an in-depth understanding of the process of reconstruction of the Museum.

In a cultural context that tends to emphasise form over content, the growing importance of architecture is almost a truism. However, one may wish to reflect on the words of Andrew Sayers (Humanities Research 2001), director of the National Portrait Gallery of Australia: 'museums are about collections and ideas – buildings are important, too, but it is essential that the right balance is maintained and the core values which sustain museums are not put under impossible pressures by over-investment in bricks and mortar'.

This chapter has considered the many ways in which museum displays and practices can impact the values and meanings of objects, ultimately affecting viewers' perceptions and interpretations. The next chapter builds on these points to consider the larger implications of the association of museum objects with the Chinese nation. What happens when museums operate on the meanings and values of museum objects in order to put forward a specific narrative or image of the nation?

The Nation in the Museum

Each country uses its museums to represent and reconstitute itself anew in each generation. (Kaplan 1994, 4)

Museums are privileged loci for the representation of the nation: 'museums are major apparatuses in the creation of national identities. They illustrate the nation as cultured, as elevated in taste, as inclusive and as paternal' (Hooper-Greenhill 2000, 25). Museums are the warrants for national identity as they are 'the site of a symbolic transaction between the visitor and the state. In exchange for the state's spiritual wealth, the individual intensifies his attachment to the state' (Duncan and Wallach 2004, 59). To this, one should add the temporal dimension: the museum 'confers unity to the past, a unity of place and time' (Ditchev 2001, 330).

The representation of national identity implies the selection and (re)interpretation of its components (ethnic, historical, territorial, linguistic, cultural, artistic and symbolic, among others). As Prasenjit Duara (1993, 19–20) remarks:

the manner in which a nation is created [...] is the imposition of a historical narrative or a myth of descent/dissent [...] When a mytho-historical narrative is imposed upon cultural materials, the relevant community is formed not primarily by the creation of new cultural forms [...] but by transforming the perception of the boundaries of the community.

Museum representations (and particularly those in national museums) supply 'miniatures' of culture (Lévi-Strauss 1966, 22–30): history, language, literature, art, cultural production, technological achievements – all the major defining features of a culture find representation in the museum.

These considerations apply especially to China. As Craig Clunas (1998, 42) notes, 'the National Museum acts as a key site of promotion of the existence and validity of the state formation [...] the discursive practices at the heart of the museum lay claim to scientific objectivity, to a transcendental mimesis of what is "out there"'. Archaeological and ethnographic material, continues Clunas, supports the nation's claims of sovereignty, independence and unity. Notions of unity and continuity, in particular, are central to representations of the nation in Chinese museums, since it is precisely on the basis of historical unity and continuity that political legitimacy is claimed.

This serves as a reminder that museum representations are the result of a specific interpretation and understanding of the nation that is dictated by a given political stance and by a specific cultural and historical setting. The concept of 'nation' is not universal, but a culturally, historically and socially determined construction. So what does this concept mean in China? How have understandings of the Chinese nation evolved within 20th-century China? And how have they been translated in museums?

The Chinese Nation: A Concept in Transition

The concept of 'nation' (in Chinese, *guojia*) has been the object of a range of interpretations in 20th-century China. Interestingly however, the notion of 'state' in China has consistently occupied a position of centrality in relation to the conceptualisation of the Chinese nation. The concept of nation started to form in China towards the end of the 19th century. It had its roots in the crisis of the imperial system – a crisis triggered by, among other factors, the colonial experience. In this sense, the idea of nation may be understood as a response to the colonial encounter and the ensuing perception of China's relatively outdated political, military and technological systems. Social cohesion, which until then had been (at least formally) provided by dynastic rule, was dramatically brought into question by the collapse of the imperial system. After 1911, social cohesion was remoulded around new notions of citizenship and modernity. For their conceptualisation, Chinese intellectuals looked to the West, considered a source of inspiration and, though not unconditionally, a model of reference (this was especially the case in Chinese literature and philosophy). The nation in early 20th-century China was essentially an intellectual project centred on the modernisation of Chinese culture and the formulation of a Chinese citizenship based on the rejection of Confucian principles – their 'traditional' and conservative character now being associated with China's main problem, 'backwardness'.

The formation of a discourse on the Chinese nation has occurred in parallel to the development of another central theme in the politics of Chinese national identity: Han nationality. The notion of Han nationality is relatively recent, appearing with the dissolution of the imperial system and the surge in discourses on the Chinese nation. According to Dru Gladney (1994, 98), the idea of a Han nationality was mainly fostered by Sun Yat-Sen – the first president of the Republic of China and leader of the Kuomintang, the Nationalist government – as a tool to engage the masses in the insurrection against the Qing rulers. The growing emphasis placed on the Han component of the nation led, during the first decades of the century, to a reformulation of this concept in racial terms. The sociologist and historian of China Frank Dikötter (1996, 593) points out that the notions of race and nation in the political philosophy of Sun Yat-Sen can be seen as mutually constitutive, the Chinese nation being essentially based on the idea of a shared descent from the mythical 'Yellow Emperor' – whence the formulation of Chinese national identity in terms of the 'Yellow race'. In the political philosophy of the Kuomintang, the notion of the Chinese nation encompassed the four main national minorities (Mongolians, Tibetans, Manchu and Muslim Chinese). In Sun Yat-Sen's Nationalist government's approach to the question of nationality, the centrality of the Han race was not displaced. Rather, now on a 'civilising mission' with regard to the four ethnic minorities, the Han race continued to constitute the backbone of the theory of the Chinese nation.

In the post-1949 era, the establishment of the Communist government led to a reformulation of the concept of the Chinese nation, this time focused on the notion of social class. In the Communist political philosophy, the Chinese nation was seen as composed of the working class (including both peasants and urban workers) and the army. This class-based approach served as a springboard for the elaboration of a Chinese nationalism centred on patriotism and fostering idealised images of a society of labour, equality, order and harmony. During the first decades following the creation of the 'New China', patriotism was fuelled by anti-imperialist propaganda, which portrayed Western imperialists and colonisers as the source of China's problems. Over time, the anti-imperialist vehemence tempered, in part replaced by xenophobia directed at Japan. This suggests that the Chinese nation and national identity are also defined by contrast with other countries. It has been noted, however, that references to patriotism help to downplay the xenophobic components of nationalism in favour of a more general definition of the nation that is more easily associated with the state and the Chinese Communist Party (L Pan 2012, 125–6). Today, patriotism and national pride are the main tenets of the nationalist discourse.

The Chinese Nation in Museums

Craig Clunas (1997a, 9) famously stated that there is no such thing as Chinese art, only art in China. In other words, one cannot bundle together a composite set of objects under the title 'Chinese art' when the only thing they have in common is the fact of having been produced in a territory that is today known as China. Yet museums in China (and elsewhere) are doing precisely this: they are creating, through the act of labelling and juxtaposing objects, the idea of a coherent whole, known as 'Chinese art' and associated with the Chinese nation.

Building on this assumption, it makes sense to consider: how are the links between museum objects and the Chinese nation instantiated? How do museums create the concept of a coherent national whole out of the heterogeneity of their collections? One perspective is provided by Alfred Gell's (1998) theory of art and agency. Gell's seminal theory casts light on the relationships between (art) objects, museums and the nation. In this case, the analysis refers to museums in China, but the theory behind it can be extended to other countries.

The core of Gell's argument is based on the concept of metonymy – that is, 'a figure of speech based on the substitution of either a part for a whole, or an associated thing for the thing itself' (Barnard and Spencer 1996, 614). Susan Pearce (1994, 27) adds that 'objects (and other messages) operate as a *sign* when they stand for the whole of which they are an intrinsic part [...] and in this case the relationship between the different parts of the whole is said to be metonymic'. Metonymy can also be seen as a 'strategy of "reduction" used to bring some higher or more complex realms of being (down) to the terms of a lower or less complex realm of being' (Burke 1969, 506). The basic assumption of Gell's theory is that, in some instances, art objects, rather than merely representing, can become *substitutes* for people in a metonymic sense.

The extension of this theory to museums implies that it is possible to conceptualise museum objects as substitutes for the 'person' that is the Chinese nation. To use Gell's (1998, 12) terms, as 'objects merge with people', so one might say that museum objects merge with the nation. These hypothetical constructions rely on two assumptions: firstly, that a nation can be thought of as a person, and secondly, that the Chinese government is the legitimate proprietor of objects in public museums and the subject entitled to represent and speak for the Chinese nation. This last implies a form of state nationalism that 'portrays the state as the embodiment of the nation's will' (Suresh 2002, 15).

The parallel person–nation gains substance in the specific case of China. The development of concepts of the person in China has been deeply influenced by Confucianism (King 1991). Confucian principles inform social relationships through their emphasis on filial piety, respect for the superior, the parents, the elderly and the ancestors. These principles extend to the relationship between the citizen and the sovereign. As a result, the individual in China has been defined with reference to social relations (mainly, although not exclusively, of kinship) and their related obligations (although more recent scholarship places an increasing emphasis on individual agency and self-identity construction through self-cultivation: see Brindley 2010; Hansen and Svarverud 2010; Kleinman *et al* 2011). Confucian principles outline a personified vision of the state. In Confucian terms, the ideal statesman is a model person whose government is imbued with virtue – honesty, equanimity, respect for elders and, overall, filial piety. According to Confucian principles, a demeanour in line with these virtues is not only due by and to government officials, but it is also to be directed towards the state, constructed as a superseding, almost paternal entity. The relationship between the state and government officials – and by extension, all citizens – is framed by the father–son relationship. Nationalism has partially appropriated and reinterpreted this approach: 'in nationalist rhetoric the nation is personified, treated as a living creature with soul, history, and destiny, and above all, attributes that make it uniquely itself' (Handler 1984, 59). In this nationalist perspective, the government acts as if the nation were not a social and political construction but, rather, an entity that merely needs to be acknowledged. Museums are one of the channels through which such notions of the nation can be disseminated.

The personification of the nation becomes apparent if one considers that nationalism fosters the use of terms such as 'motherland'. So, for instance, the Chinese nation is seen as the 'mother' of the large 'family' composed of the Chinese provinces, where Taiwan and Tibet are depicted as the 'rebel sons'. The Chinese nation is often depicted as female, and associated with female characteristics. Prasenjit Duara (1993, 16) notes, 'Historically in China, the purity of the woman's body has served both as metaphor and metonymy of the purity of the nation. The bodies of Chinese women raped by foreign invaders – Mongol, Manchu or Japanese – were both symbol and part of the national body violated by these foreigners.'

If one agrees that the Chinese nation can be thought of as a person, then it is possible to imagine museum objects becoming substitutes for the Chinese person–nation. Precisely because it is a construction, an abstract entity, the nation has to be made concrete, real, apprehensible through the senses. Objects, and notably museum objects, contribute to the materialisation of this abstract concept. Webb Keane (2001, 75) usefully points out that the capacity of an object to represent a person 'is not an inherent property of objects themselves but requires human efforts and interactions to sustain'. Museums play a key role here.

In museums, a link is established between objects and the nation. This is achieved through two complementary processes: the objectification of the nation and its distribution through loans, exchanges and travelling exhibitions. This theoretical perspective also sheds new light on the issue of repatriation, discussed below, which can thus be understood as a way to reconstitute the nation.

Objectification can be understood as a mode of creation of the person–nation. Objectification implies 'the dual process by means of which a subject externalises itself in a creative act of differentiation, and in return reappropriates this externalisation through an act (of) sublation' (Miller 1987, 28). In the case of China, the Chinese government creates through museums a world of objects that define national identity. The importance of objects in contemporary China can be appreciated through the influence that historical materialism – the search for evidence of theoretical constructions in concrete things – has for decades exerted over scientific thought. Using the 'evidence' supplied by museum objects, the government is forging a discourse on the nation's unity, continuity and 'borders' (determining who and what is, and is not, 'Chinese').

The objectification of the nation is attained through discourses that construct museum objects as tokens of the nation. As a result, museum objects are made to stand for the Chinese nation in a metonymic relationship, that is, as if they *were* the Chinese nation. It follows that museum objects (and, in a larger sense, cultural heritage) do not merely *represent* a country's cultural capital in Pierre Bourdieu's terms, but they *materialise* the nation itself.

For instance, Shang and Zhou bronzes, porcelain vessels, calligraphy scrolls and jade carvings are only a few material culture items that have come to epitomise Ancient China. They are agents insofar as they make Ancient China real, tangible, apprehensible. But they are also agents to the extent that they create an image of Ancient China – as a refined, cultivated, elitist, male-focused society revolving around the imperial court.

TRAVELLING EXHIBITIONS AS DIPLOMATIC TOOLS

Museum loans, exchanges and travelling exhibitions, more so than other museum activities, bring to the fore the link between a nation and its cultural treasures. Exhibitions of 'national treasures' travelling abroad are not only symbols of the country's cultural richness but they also *stand for* that country. To illustrate this point, one might look at the Chinese nation through Alfred Gell's idea of a 'corpus' of art objects. Discussing Marquesan art, Gell defines a '"corpus" of artworks as a kind of spatio-temporally dispersed "population". Marquesan art, considered as a whole, can be conceptualized, macroscopically, as a "distributed object" in time and space.' Within such a corpus of art objects, Gell continues, exists a certain coherence, an organic order: 'each piece, each motif, each line or groove, speaks to every other one' (1998, 221). Building on Gell's predicate, the Chinese nation can be seen as a corpus of art that can be distributed. Conceptualising the nation as a compositional, fragmented yet consistent 'corpus' of objects clarifies the high political and symbolic importance of the movement of cultural heritage abroad – as object loans to foreign museums, travelling exhibitions, illicit traffic or colonial booty.

For instance, since the 1970s, China has used heavily advertised exhibitions of Chinese art abroad as a tool of 'cultural diplomacy', designed to establish, reinforce or restore diplomatic and cultural relations with the recipient country. In addition, they help sponsor tourism, improve business relations and more generally introduce Chinese civilisation to foreign audiences. These processes are, however, strictly controlled by the government. Until well into the 1980s, China was a closed country. The few foreigners who were granted access were mainly journalists or leftist intellectuals. The gradual implementation of 'open door' policies brought tourism and a growing interest in 'Chinese things'. Since the 1990s, the Chinese authorities have allowed an increasing number of cultural relic loans with a view to establishing exhibitions of Chinese art and antiquities in foreign museums. Museum object loans are subject to quantity and quality restrictions. The number of objects on loan cannot exceed a total of 120 items (Michaelson 2007, *pers comm*) and those classified as 'first class' or 'grade one' cultural relics are usually not allowed to leave the country. A grade one cultural relic is a highly valuable piece and as such, wherever found, it must be sent to the State Administration of Cultural Heritage (SACH) in Beijing, where its final destination will be decided.

This suggests that a core of objects are perceived as pivotal for the nation and that their dissociation from national territory is simply not acceptable. This core of objects may be described as what Annette Weiner (1992) has labelled 'inalienable possessions'. Weiner (1994, 395) notes that 'symbolically dense possessions are politically salient because keeping a highly prized object against all the demands for its exchange defines and even entrenches the owner's difference' and authority. Weiner explains:

> there are [...] possessions that are imbued with the intrinsic and ineffable identities of their owners which are not easy to give away. Ideally, these inalienable possessions are kept by their owners from one generation to the next within the closed context of family, descent group, or dynasty. The loss of such an inalienable possession diminishes the self and by extension the group to which the person belongs. (1992, 6)

Crucially to our discussion, 'the right to control inalienable possessions can be used as the means to effect control over others' (Weiner 1992, 39). Thus, ownership and possession of 'first class' cultural relics, due to their highly symbolic meaning, embody a form of authority. In this sense, imperial collections are the ultimate inalienable possessions.

Restrictions on the circulation of valuable cultural relics are also driven by concerns of over-exposing Chinese art. Discussing a loan request presented to SACH, Mr Xiaoneng Yang, curator of Chinese art at the Nelson-Atkins Museum of Art of Kansas City, reveals, 'because I selected all the pearls of the Chinese art, they [SACH] worried that if the exhibition were realised there would be no more overseas exhibitions' (Dewar 1999, 62). This comment suggests that by keeping the number of loans offered inferior to demand, a scarcity is created and interest in a culture may be sustained over time; preventing the movement of items helps a culture to retain its interest and therefore its value (see, for example, Appadurai 1986, 25). Cultural heritage is here being treated like a commodity.

The use of travelling exhibitions as diplomatic tools may be illustrated by the following examples. The first exhibition of Chinese art in the United States took place in 1974. Cultural heritage played a key role in the normalisation of China's international relations in the 1970s, as part of what has been called 'the cultural relics diplomacy'. In the 1950s, the international political climate led China to a position of isolation. The war in Korea brought American troops close to the Chinese frontier and relations with the old ally, the USSR, were compromised in 1959. Later, the Cultural Revolution exacerbated China's isolation. It was Chairman Zhou Enlai in the early 1970s who put forward the idea of using cultural heritage as a tool to establish (or re-establish) relationships with foreign countries. In 1974, following the historic 1972 visit of American President Richard Nixon to Beijing (the first US president to visit China), an exhibition of Chinese cultural relics travelled to several museums in the United States (Lu 2004b, *pers comm*), followed by many similar initiatives between 1974 and 1977. In 1980, the re-establishment of regular Sino-American diplomatic relations was accompanied by a tour of the United States of the exhibition *Treasures from the Bronze Age of China*. The exhibition presented 105 objects (including not only bronzes, but also jades and iron tools) which documented the origins of Chinese civilisation and its technological achievements; the exhibition was meant to introduce not only some of the best pieces of the Chinese Bronze Age, but also Chinese culture and China as a whole.

The Olympic Games have proved to be another forum at which national exhibitions have played eminently political roles. The exhibition *Imperial Treasures from China*, held at the China Millennium Monument in Beijing in November 2004, was meant to showcase Chinese culture and herald the 2008 Olympics in Beijing. The exhibition was originally on show at the National Gallery of Greece, Athens, to mark the 2004 Olympic Games. As stated in the catalogue, the exhibition was 'a concentrated and ample display of Chinese culture, the cradle of Eastern civilisation, in Greece, the cradle of Western civilisation' (Beijing Administrative Bureau of Cultural Relics 2004, 2). The exhibition displayed over 100 pieces, selected from the collections of the Beijing Capital Museum, Beijing Art Museum and the Ming Tomb Museum. Exhibits included bronzes, gold and silver jewellery, jades, porcelains, paintings, calligraphy and textiles.

The objects' layout was minimalist, with few captions and little or no background information and contextualisation. Objects were presented as art pieces, in individual glass cases. Despite the varied range of materials and epochs, the exhibits shared a relevant feature: they were all ceremonial, ornamental and prestige items. They spoke of the refinement and exquisite charms of life at the emperor's court, a world of elegance, cultivation and wealth. This image of China contrasted sharply with the austerity and spirit of sacrifice of Communist China celebrated in the Military Museum, just a few metres from the Millennium Monument. In a successful exercise of objectification, the wealthy, urban, cultivated art of the imperial court was here made to embody 'China' and 'Chineseness' for the eyes of the world.

This leads to a final example. The exhibition *China: The Three Emperors, 1622–1795*, held at the Royal Academy of Arts in London, was a major event in winter 2005–06. Considered to be the largest exhibition of court art ever shown outside of China, the exhibition displayed almost 400 items, including paintings, jades, bronzes, porcelain and lacquer ware, textiles, furniture, weapons, and scientific and ritual items dating back to the three Qing Dynasty emperors: Kangxi (1662–1722), Yongzheng (1723–35) and Qianlong (1736–95). Most objects, taken from the collections of the Palace Museum in Beijing, were claimed to be unique pieces that had never before been exhibited abroad. The exhibition was part of a series of events and ceremonies to celebrate London's successful bid to host the Olympic Games in 2012. The passage of the Olympic torch from Beijing to London was the occasion for a grand celebration of Chinese culture in London entitled *China in London* which continued over several months.[1] The exhibition at the Royal Academy was instrumental in the promotion of bilateral economic links between the UK and China. In the celebration's inaugural discourse, the Mayor of London, Ken Livingstone, could hardly have been more explicit: 'I want to see these links [between the UK and China] develop in all fields, investment and business, visits and stays by tourists and students, cultural exchange and creative links' (Greater London Authority 2006). Museums were among the first to implement the mayor's dictum. Early in 2004, the British Museum initiated a programme of collaboration with Chinese museums, resulting in a major loan of objects from the British Museum's Ancient Egypt collections to the Capital Museum in Beijing. In 2005, an agreement between the British Museum and the National Museum of China established a loan of British Museum collections for the occasion of the 2008 Olympic Games. In return, the British Museum received loans for the blockbuster exhibition *The First Emperor: China's Terracotta Army*, held in 2007–08. In a similar vein, the Victoria and Albert Museum (V&A) made arrangements for loans of its collections to Chinese museums (including the Shanghai Museum) in return for loans of a major exhibition on Chinese contemporary art, *China Design Now*, held in 2008. Collaborative initiatives between museums in Europe and Shanghai were also planned as part of the 2010 World Expo.

---

[1] Celebrations also included the Chinese New Year festivities and parade, a photography exhibition introducing the Beijing Olympics 2008, a festival of Shanghainese films and a number of parallel events organised by other organisations, including the British Museum, British Library, Victoria and Albert Museum, National Portrait Gallery, Museum in Docklands, Asia House and Natural History Museum.

Collaborations with foreign museums also increasingly include partners from the private sector. Since its reopening in 2011, the National Museum of China has displayed an unprecedented number of large-scale exhibitions resulting from collaboration with foreign museums and private corporations. For instance, *The Art of the Enlightenment*, a major exhibition opened in April 2011, was the fruit of collaboration with German museums and was financed by BMW, the automotive company. Other similar initiatives include a collaboration with the luxury goods conglomerate LVMH for the exhibition *Louis Vuitton Voyages* (May 2011) and the *BVLGARI Retrospective Exhibition* (September 2011).

Collaborative projects between Chinese and international museums have been steadily increasing over the last two decades. Some observers talk of a governmental cultural strategy labelled 'Going Out, Inviting In', whereby exchanges between Chinese and foreign museums are being actively promoted by the central government (Perlez 2012). Professor Lu Jiansong (2004a, *pers comm*) anticipates that the phenomenon of travelling exhibitions is likely to increase in the future, for at least three reasons. Firstly, there is an increasing demand abroad for exhibitions that introduce Chinese art, history, culture, civilisation, aesthetics and philosophical thought. Secondly, in contrast to the 1980s, today China has the financial means necessary to host important exhibitions abroad. Thirdly, and most importantly, the Chinese government wishes to strengthen its position on the international scene by establishing closer cultural links with foreign countries and by making Chinese culture more visible internationally. This desire was stated explicitly by Chinese president Hu Jintao in a 2007 speech: 'We must enhance culture as part of the soft power of our country' and 'strengthen international cultural exchanges to enhance the influence of Chinese culture worldwide' (quoted in Szántó 2011).

China is also increasingly hosting exhibitions devoted to non-Chinese cultures and civilisations (see, for example, Holden Platt 2012). Such initiatives may be inspired by different agendas. In some cases, they may have political undertones. For instance, in spring 2012 the National Museum of China hosted the exhibition *The Yellow River – Exhibition of Nakamura Sadao's Oil Paintings*, sponsored by the China International Culture Association and devoted to the works of a contemporary Japanese painter. The exhibition was intended to 'commemorate the fortieth anniversary of the normalization of Sino-Japanese diplomatic relations and promote the cultural exchanges between peoples from China and Japan' (National Museum of China 2012a). In parallel with this exhibition, and running counter to its stated goals, the same museum devoted a special exhibition to photographic material taken by a war correspondent and photographer of the Communist Party during the Sino-Japanese war (referred to in the exhibition as the 'Anti-Japanese War' and 'War of Liberation').

More often, special exhibitions devoted to non-Chinese cultures aim to promote trade, investment and business relationships. This has been particularly apparent with respect to African countries. The exponential increase in Chinese investment in Africa since 2000 (Brautigam 2009) has been reflected by an increased focus on African cultures in Chinese museums. In spring 2012, the National Museum of China inaugurated a special exhibition entitled *African Cultures in Focus*. The text introducing the exhibition on the museum's website (National Museum of China 2012b) is candid about the exhibition's aims:

> Since the fourth ministerial meeting of the Forum on China-Africa Cooperation which was held at the end of 2009, China and Africa have cooperated closely and paid more attention to promoting the cultural exchanges between the two sides, and a new strategic partnership

featuring political equality and mutual trust, economic win-win cooperation and cultural exchanges has been developed. This exhibition is to review the cooperation achievements between China and Africa in culture, public diplomacy, broadcasting and television, press and publication, sports, cultural heritage and so on. The sponsor hopes to help visitors understand the general situation of the cultural exchanges between China and Africa over the recent years, raise their awareness and enhance initiatives for consolidating the cultural relations in the new era, and make contributions to improving the understanding, deepening the friendship and expanding the cooperation between the two sides.

In parallel with this exhibition, the same National Museum of China presented *Selected African Sculptures in the Collection of the National Museum of China*, including over 500 artefacts which 'will impress the audience with a touching primitive and rugged beauty' while aiming to 'deepen Chinese people's understanding of this art form that combines different African tribes' diligence and intelligence and the mysterious time-honored African customs and culture, and will promote the cultural exchanges between China and Africa and the development of the two cultures' (National Museum of China 2012c).

The enhanced internationalisation of Chinese museums and the circulation of Chinese heritage in non-Chinese contexts can be understood as a facet of cultural and institutional globalisation, as well as an index of the ongoing process of harmonisation of museum practices at international level. Nevertheless, it would be misleading to think of such international collaborations as smooth, unproblematic processes; in most cases, collaborations between Western and Chinese museums involve extensive negotiations, delays, misunderstandings and compromises that highlight divergent museum practices and philosophies. As the French Sinologist Geremie Barmé (2010) notes:

> Museums, galleries, curators and art historians are regularly faced with the dilemmas of working with China's state institutions. These are bodies that impose a particular politico-cultural scheme on the selection and exhibition of the cultural properties in their trust. Although the latitude of the Chinese state has increased in recent years in keeping with its own changed and evolving priorities, those who would collaborate with the party-state are forced to submit to complex forms of censorship and self-censorship in presenting the complex realities of China's past and present to international audiences.

REPATRIATION

The relationship between museums, cultural heritage and the nation is made manifest in claims for the repatriation of lost national cultural treasures. This relationship has been spelled out clearly by Li Xueqin, an eminent Chinese historian politically engaged in the return of plundered artefacts: 'culture is the spirit of a nation and relics are the purveyors of culture' (quoted in Fiskesjö 2010, 231). China's attachment to what are considered 'national treasures' is further exemplified by the director of China's Lost Cultural Relics Recovery Program, who commented, 'the loss of these treasures [...] is that of the blood of a nation' (Bobin 2003). The programme is an initiative of the China Foundation for the Development of Social Culture, an NGO sponsored by the China Poly Group – the corporation behind the Poly Art Museum. The foundation was established in 2002 under the aegis of the Ministry of Culture with the aim of recovering cultural treasures from abroad. The foundation, described as a 'semi-official patriotic vanguard' (Fiskesjö 2010, 231), mainly addresses wealthy Chinese elites willing to purchase and donate items of Chinese art in return for public praise of their patriotic gesture.

Most of the items claimed back by the Chinese government were looted from imperial palaces during the Opium Wars. In the second half of the 19th century, army soldiers, colonial officers, missionaries, traders and seafarers increasingly forced their way into new Chinese territories; their ventures were often accompanied by plunder and forced sales of ancient cultural relics. The appropriation of art treasures was legitimised by the victory of British and French troops in the Second Opium War, which reframed plunder as legitimate war booty and colonial trophies.

One of the most debated instances of repatriation pertains to a set of sculptures looted from the Summer Palace (*Yuanming Yuan*) in Beijing, during the Second Opium War, in 1860. In May 2000, the Poly Art Museum in Beijing – as previously mentioned, a prominent actor in the repatriation of art objects through international auctions – bought three bronze animal heads (ox, monkey and tiger) at auctions in Hong Kong. A bronze boar head was also purchased and donated to the Poly Art Museum in 2003. The sculptures now form part of the Poly Art Museum collections. The sculptures had been part of a zodiac fountain at the Summer Palace and were looted by French and English troops when they razed the estate in 1860. Another two sculptures from the same fountain (a rabbit and a mouse) formed part of the Yves Saint Laurent art collection which was auctioned in Paris in 2009. The Chinese government tried unsuccessfully to stop the auction, but following an attempt by a Chinese bidder (said to be linked to China's Lost Cultural Relics Recovery Program) to halt the auction, the sculptures were finally withdrawn from sale (Kraus 2009, 837–8). Rather than simply being icons of Chinese art aesthetics – the zodiac fountain was actually designed by the Italian Jesuit Giuseppe Castiglione, as part of a European-style garden – the sculptures are imbued with symbolic significance, since they were part of the imperial personal treasures and, most importantly, there is historical evidence that they were looted (Kraus 2009, 839).

While the repatriation of the zodiac sculptures has received ample media coverage, the repatriation of items of higher artistic or historical value may go almost unnoticed outside of China because they are less recognisable, or because they are only known within circles of experts and art connoisseurs. This is the case for the ancient calligraphy texts known as *Chunhua ge tie*. In 2003, the Shanghai Museum acquired these ancient texts through international auctions. The return of these calligraphic masterpieces to China was accompanied by great celebrations. The wording that appeared on the Shanghai Museum leaflet advertising the celebrations illustrates the symbolic resonance of these works: 'A series of activities of the exhibition, competition and forum on the *Chunhua ge tie* – To promote Chinese culture and national spirits, Shanghai Museum, 24 September–31 October 2003'. The leaflet (which is in English) continues:

> In spring 2003, the Shanghai Museum successfully rescued one of our national treasures, the best rubbings of the *Chunhua ge tie* [...] from the United States. [...] To celebrate the return of the *Chunhua ge tie* a series of important activities will be held in Shanghai. It is believed that these activities will help to raise the level of citizen's quality, build up the cultural image of Shanghai, enrich the artistic connotation of our city's spirits, and even promote Chinese culture and national spirits.

China's position vis-à-vis the issue of repatriation remains ambivalent. China is a signatory to the 1970 UNESCO *Convention on the Means of Prohibiting and Preventing the Illicit Import, Export and Transfer of Ownership of Cultural Property* (UNESCO 1970); however, the Chinese government has, to date, failed to introduce domestic laws that adequately protect national heritage sites and prevent theft and archaeological looting (Cuno 2008, 88ff; Kraus 2004, 205). While the Chinese government rightly highlights its status as a victim of imperialist plunder, China is also one of the world's major exporters of recently plundered artefacts, thereby fuelling the international market in illicit art and antiquities (Kraus 2004, 196). These unresolved issues are likely to continue contributing to heated debates on the overall question of repatriation.

China Seen from the West

Until the mid-19th century, the UK's image of China was that of a model society, albeit one that was 'exotic and unusual' (Pagani 1998, 28). However, the outbreak of the First Opium War in 1839 led to a sharp drop in China's esteem in the eyes of the British, to whom victory gave a sense of cultural and technological superiority. In the second half of the 19th century, 'China was regarded as a marketable commodity just as were her products' (Pagani 1998, 29). The increasing demand for *chinoiseries* signalled the decline of China's artistic lead 'at the very period when the West, in particular Britain, was enforcing its political and economic hegemony in the Far East' (Clunas 1987, 20). Things changed with the turn of the century, when interest in Chinese arte-facts was enhanced by a series of extraordinary archaeological findings, gradually bringing to light the cultures of Ancient China.[2] Early Chinese art provided a source of inspiration (echoing the role that primitive art had played for Cubist and Surrealist artists) – a 'novelty' that refreshed the image of Chinese art and material culture, notably superscribing the static and decadent qualities of late imperial art, no longer able to arouse collectors' interest (cf Clunas 1998).

Over the course of the 19th century, a split gradually formed between a worsening perception of the Chinese people and relatively high esteem for Chinese art and material culture. In this division, one might perceive the seeds of a dissociation between China's artistic production and its socio-political context – a dissociation that persists in today's museum representations, though in a different form. Indeed, Craig Clunas aptly reminds us that the very notion of 'Chinese art' is a creation of 19th-century Europe and North America. This concept allowed the grouping of a corpus of artistic production spanning over two millennia and including a heterogeneous ensemble of materials, techniques, styles, references, values and meanings. Therefore, in line with Orientalist discursive practices, the notion of 'Chinese art' allowed for an emphasis of the differences between Chinese and Western art, and the contextual blurring of diversity *within* Chinese art (Clunas 1997a, 9). However, with time, fissures developed along the lines of what was considered art by the Chinese versus what was considered art by the British coloniser. Clunas (1997b, 418) remarks that 'Chinese elite categorizations of art, as expressed in texts, as well as in the practices of the art and craft markets, excluded much of the Chinese material subsequently displayed in the museum context in Britain'. Such a discrepancy between Chinese and British concepts of art is intriguingly mirrored by Chinese collections in museums.

---

[2] Findings included, for example, those at the Anyang site, Henan (1928); followed by, among others, exca-vations in Mawangdui, Hunan (1972); the discovery of the Terracotta Army, Xi'an, Shaanxi (1974); Shang funerary complexes in Anyang and Shaanxi (1976); the tomb of Yi Marquis of Zeng, Hupei (1978); and the Ancient Shu civilisation, Guanghan, Sichuan (1986).

Let us take the examples of bronze vessels, jade carvings and calligraphy. Although iconically Chinese, these items are rarely 'highlights' in Chinese collections of British (and for that matter, Western) museums, which tend rather to focus on ceramics, silks and furniture (cf Clunas 1987). By contrast, these same items feature almost invariably at the core of collections and exhibitions in China. In partial explanation of this, it could be said that the appreciation of these artefacts tends to require a 'skilled vision' (Grasseni 2007): these items (and associated artistic practices and traditions) embody and convey a system of references that is firmly enshrined in the Chinese cultural universe. Thus, their full appreciation requires some knowledge of, and sensitivity to, their cultural importance. So for instance, Chinese audiences will normally be familiar with the historical ritual use of bronzes to symbolise the legitimate retention of political authority, or the historical associations between calligraphy and the literati class.

For centuries, China and Chinese art have attracted (with varying degrees of success) the interest of Western audiences and this movement of interest extends to the present day. Indeed, since the 1990s, Western museums have demonstrated a renewed interest in Chinese art and culture. An indicator of this phenomenon might be the total refurbishment, in the early 1990s, of the Chinese galleries of two major museums in the UK: the V&A and the British Museum. This was accompanied by a sequence of major exhibitions devoted to Chinese art: *Gilded Dragons. Buried Treasures from China's Golden Ages* at the British Museum in 1999; *China: The Three Emperors, 1662–1795* at the Royal Academy of Arts in 2005–06; *The First Emperor: China's Terra-cotta Army* in 2007–08 at the British Museum; and *China Design Now* at the V&A in March–July 2008 – to mention but a few.

In France, the distribution of Chinese collections within the network of national museums reveals implicit categorisations of Chinese objects (cf Fiskesjö 2007, 8). Chinese objects are displayed at venues including the Musée du Quai Branly (an art and ethnographic museum where one can find exhibited Chinese ethnic minorities' costumes) and the Musée Guimet (the French national museum of Asian art). Displays at the Musée Guimet focus on the arts of the court and present China as a 'high civilisation', while Chinese ethnic minority artefacts are framed as ethnographic material at the Quai Branly. In what respects do the Miao skirt on display in the Quai Branly and the Tang Dynasty ceramic sculpture in the Musée Guimet differ? What images and narratives of China do they uphold? Who and what presides over this compartmentalisation of objects and knowledge? In China, as in other countries, the representation and interpretation of Chinese objects are influenced by ideological, historical, cultural and political considerations.

This chapter has looked at the relationships between museums and the nation in China through the lens of Alfred Gell's anthropological theory on art and agency. As we have seen, this theoretical approach sheds new light on the movement of museum objects (eg in travelling exhibitions) and its surrounding controversy (as evidenced by repatriation claims). The next chapter will focus analysis on the ties between the Chinese nation and museums in a historical perspective, examining how museums have dealt with the representation of the past, and how such representations and narratives have evolved over time as a result of changing political ideologies.

6

The Politics of the Past

This chapter explores the complex relationship that links the Chinese political present to its recent and ancient past. The Chinese political system fits Michel Foucault's definition of 'discursive regimes' as 'systems for managing and policing discourse (who produces or evaluates what will count as true or valid knowledge and what will not, and the conditions of such truth)' (Hodge and Louie 1998, 10). Within such 'regimes', museums are assigned the function of shaping the image of the nation and its past. Yet, while Tony Bennett's (1995) Foucault-inspired paradigm of museums as political tools is not inappropriate in explaining the relationship between the state, museums and society in China, Foucault's approach to museums as disciplinary tools is not entirely satisfactory in the case of China. In China, museums serve more as tools to *legitimise* political authority, rather than to exercise it. In other words, museums act more as media to promote the government's ideology rather than as an apparatus of control.

The modalities through which museums disseminate official ideology have changed over time. Post-1949, museums aided the spread of Communist ideology and actively participated in the nation-building project. They did so by providing a unified, government-approved vision of Chinese identity, culture and history (notably, revolutionary history), by illustrating the sacrifice of martyrs to the revolutionary cause and by celebrating the accomplishments of the Communist government. Thus, the aim was for museums to forge the people's consciousness by developing and strengthening a sense of loyalty towards Communist ideals and, by extension, towards the Communist government. Instilling a sense of belonging and loyalty to the Communist government and assuring social support – more than exerting control – have been the priorities of Chinese museums in the second half of the 20th century. The scholar Kirk Denton (2005, 581) has summarised one of the main conundrums at the heart of China's relationship with its past, namely 'how can revolutionary history, grounded in martyrdom and self-sacrifice, be made to relate to a globalizing market economy that has self-interest as its primary motivating force?'

As previously mentioned, the events of 1989 – in China, the former USSR and Eastern European countries – generated a shockwave that deeply affected the Chinese Communist system. As a result, providing political legitimation to the government became a priority. One method used was to shift attention away from China's troubled present by emphasising its millennial and glorious past. The attitude of the post-1989 government towards China's ancient and recent past may be described as an effort to inscribe the government's legitimacy in a line of continuity with the imperial tradition by claiming a historically uninterrupted link to that source of authority.

Indeed, the rulers' appropriation of cultural and artistic treasures – of which the imperial collections are the emblem – has always represented a powerful legitimating tool. As Tamara Hamlish argues (2000, 155), 'the institution of the museum legitimises the State's appropriation of the luxurious accoutrements of imperial power, while the appropriation of these accoutrements legitimises the political authority of the State'. Museums play a key role in these processes since governmental claims to political legitimacy – based on a direct, continuous link with ancient imperial dynasties – are substantiated in museums' representations of national history and identity. As Hamlish (2000, 139) notes, 'all [museum] visitors become part of re-membering a Chinese past that legitimises – both locally and globally – the political, cultural, and historical authority of a modern Chinese state'.

Ever since the early years of the People's Republic, providing political legitimation has been a prime function of museums. However, museums are no longer passive channels of political indoctrination, as they were after 1949, but have become full agents in the dissemination of cultural nationalist discourses. The narratives through which such discourses are substantiated in museums are the topic of the following sections.

POLITICAL USES OF THE PAST

The relevance of the past to political matters is well illustrated by David Lowenthal's observation (1985, 213): 'Just as memory validates personal identity, history perpetuates collective self-aware-ness'. Collective self-awareness is, however, a construction, the ever-changing result of a process of selection, of remembering and amnesia, determined by highly subjective criteria. Crucially, the way we relate to our past affects our perception of the present and our vision of the future. Vera Schwarcz (1991, 90) appropriately notes that 'to commemorate the past is an act of repossession'.

While these considerations may apply to any country,[1] they are particularly salient in the case of China. 'Traditionally for the Chinese, the past has always been in part a morality tale providing precepts for a proper behaviour and thought in the present' (Fowler 1987, 238). Remembrance, collective memory and historical evocation play a central role in the Chinese political and social present. Chinese society has been compared to the Jewish community for their common mission to 'remember'. As with Jewish culture, Chinese culture is strictly linked to its history, memory and traditions. Schwarcz (1991, 90) notes, 'from Confucius onward, the moral imperative of seeking the past (*giugu*) has been the heart of China's spiritual continuity over time'. However, not all of the past is equally worth remembering: if some aspects of Chinese history are celebrated, others are disregarded and forgotten. Historical features that serve the rhetoric of unity, longevity, continuity and the splendour of Chinese civilisation are extolled. In particular, the notion of continuity constitutes one of the major axes of Chinese political discourse on the past: the history of Chinese civilisation is seen as an uninterrupted chain of events. So, for instance, although the dating of ancient Chinese cultures such as the Xia, Long-shan, Liangzhu and Yanshao neolithic cultures is still subject to debate among historians and archaeologists, the historians Li Xueqin and Jiang Linchang (2003, 187) maintain that:

> a cultural lineage can be traced from the culture of Yin Ruins of the late Shang, to the Erligang culture of the early Shang, to the Erlitou culture of the Xia, and up to the Longshan culture of the era of the Five Lords, and up to the late period of the Yangshao culture.

In the same vein, the permanent exhibition of the National Museum of China in Beijing devoted to Ancient China promises that it 'give[s] a complete picture of the long Chinese history from

---

[1]   For a comparative analysis of uses of the past and representations of national history in Chinese and Norwe-gian museums, see Varutti (2010a).

the prehistoric times to the late Qing Dynasty and shows in a comprehensive way the vitality and continuous evolution of Chinese civilization' (National Museum of China n.d.a).

Despite claims of historical continuity, the trajectory of Chinese history has not been devoid of interruption. Craig Clunas (1991, 62) explains:

> At least as many radical disjunctions in society and culture may have taken place between the China of the Han Dynasty (220 BC–AD 200) and that of the Ming, but they were not felt by the majority of the elite to involve a rupture of the connections between themselves and their equivalents, as bearers of a continuous cultural tradition.

Clunas raises a key issue: ruptures are undeniable, but they may be deliberately overlooked. This strategy has served rulers of the ancient and recent past in their legitimation claims. During the imperial era, the line of continuity was assured by the 'Mandate of Heaven' concept. Once the imperial system was discarded, the reinstatement of political authority required different strategies; the cult of personality and instilling feelings of guilt or pride, patriotism and nationalism became prominent themes.

One of the issues that most clearly illustrates the political relevance of the past – and is also, unsurprisingly, a highly politicised issue that has engaged both ancient and modern rulers in endless debate – is the question of the origins of Chinese civilisation.

THE ORIGINS OF CHINESE CIVILISATION

One of the ways through which political authority legitimises itself is by establishing a genealogical link with the symbolic figures associated with the origins of the community, or its founding myths (Fowler 1987, 230); hence the considerable political relevance of the origins of Chinese civilisation. The origins of Chinese civilisation are far from historically evident. Mystery surrounding the genesis of Chinese civilisation has led to diverse interpretations and theories. Until the late 1970s, the dominant theory suggested a single settlement of civilisation situated along the Yellow River, from which the population then spread out across the rest of China. This theory is relatively recent: 'it was not until the late Qing, when racist ideas spread from Europe, that a story was put together of a Han race descended from the Yellow Emperor defending a northern sacred plain, the Middle Kingdom, against barbarians' (Friedman 1994, 72). This first Han settlement is usually identified as 'Huaxia'. This term – often used in museum exhibitions to indicate the ancestors of the Han – was created by the Chinese scholar Zhang Taiyan in the early Republican era. Huaxia 'could be used interchangeably to mean China the nation-state, Chinese the race (or tribe), and China the geographic location […] Hua, Xia or Han formed a unity – an undifferentiated race originating in North China' (Wu 1991, 161). Moreover Huaxia:

> indicates more of a cultural space than a geographic designation, and also implies a historical lineage. 'Xia' is the name of the first-known dynasty of what later came to be 'China', dating to some three millennia ago. The term 'Hua' includes both overseas Chinese as well as non-ethnic Chinese under the overarching umbrella of China. (Li and Luo 2004, 123)

The Huaxia nationality is described as 'the people inhabiting the Central Plains of the Yellow River [...] they had a highly developed economy and culture and were the first to enter class society and establish primitive states' (National Museum of Chinese History 2002, 57). This interpretative model also attributed a supposed superiority to the Han group:

> [During the Slave Society period] an advanced culture crystallized, and the Central Plains truly became the Center of Chinese civilisation, the crucible and cradle of the Han-Chinese people. With their strong tendency to absorb and fuse valuable elements from other less-advanced peoples around them, the great family of the modern Chinese people was created.
>
> (Thorp 1988, 22)

This interpretation was strongly backed by the Republican government: the archaeological excavations of 1928 in Anyang – providing 'evidence' of the Yellow River theory – were in fact heavily supported by the Republican government. As Craig Clunas (1997a, 18) notes, 'the picture of an early Chinese polity which was geographically and culturally united, with a strong and prosperous centre extending its influence outwards [...] suited the needs of the new and often fragile Republic for a usable past'.

Subsequently, the Communist Party also approved the Yellow River theory. Indeed, the theory became one of the main arguments of Mao's anti-imperialist rhetoric (Friedman 1994, 68) and remained a reference for historians and archaeologists for more than three decades. The Communist government used reference to the Han Dynasty to create an image of itself as the heir of the Han, supposedly at the origin of Chinese civilisation. Thus the 'Museum of History [National Museum of China] displayed this nationalist history as an ascent from Peking man through an expansionist, amalgamating and unifying Han culture to the founding of the People's Republic' (Friedman 1994, 70). Since the 1980s, the Yellow River theory has been abandoned in favour of an alternative interpretation based on a plurality of settlements that, through interaction, led to population spread within the territory. This is known as the theory of the 'interactions spheres' (Von Falkenhausen 1995, 199).

The Museum of Sanxingdui, near Chengdu in Sichuan Province, provides an example of how archaeological theories and archaeological finds are woven together in exhibitions to form 'appropriate' narratives of Chinese civilisation. Inaugurated in October 1997, the Sanxingdui Museum hosts cultural relics of extraordinary historical value. The objects exhibited in this museum – including bronzes, jades, gold objects and pottery – were unearthed during archaeological excavations in 1986, following their discovery in 1929. The finds are attributed to the Shu culture, estimated to date back to 1300–1200 BC. The artistic style of these objects is radically different to that of any other excavated artefacts in China. They are the tokens of a civilisation contemporary to the Shang Dynasty (c. 1600–1046 BC) that had bronze-casting techniques that were at least as advanced as the dynasty's.

This archaeological discovery represents a turning point in the interpretation of Chinese ancient history. Prior to the excavations, the settlements in Anyang, in northern China, had been thought to be the 'cradle' of Chinese civilisation. The discovery of an advanced and culturally refined civilisation in the south-west of the country, totally independent from the northern settlements, wholly discredited the Yellow River theory. As mentioned earlier, the Central Plains theory was strategically promoted by the Republican and Communist governments, who relied upon it to support their discourses on the unity, homogeneity and continuity of Chinese civilisation.

The archaeological finds in Sanxingdui disproved the Central Plains theory and provided

Fig 6.1. Cultural relic of the ancient Shu culture, Sanxingdui Museum, Sichuan Province.

evidence in support of a multicentred interpretation of the origins of Chinese civilisation. The panels at the Sanxingdui Museum acknowledge the multicentred theory ('the Sanxingdui civilisation definitively confirms the multiple and widespread origins of Chinese civilisation'),[2] and present the development of Chinese civilisation as a process of integration ('the Sanxingdui culture, as a major part appearing in the upper reaches of the Yangtze River of brilliant Chinese civilisation, supports the conclusion that the Chinese civilisation is of pluralistic *integration*'). A slightly different interpretation is given on the Museum's CD-ROM guide, where the Shu civilisation is said to be a 'different branch of Chinese Civilisation', 'a member of the multinational Chinese family', and consequently, 'the Chinese nation did grow up along the Yellow River Valley only, but the Yangtze Valley is an equally important place of the Chinese civilisation'.[3] In this statement, the expression 'Chinese nation' is used in exclusive reference to the Yellow River Valley (hence reinforcing the Central Plains theory), whilst the Yangtze Valley cultures are defined by the term 'civilisation'. This use of the terms 'nation' and 'civilisation' might suggest that the concept of the Chinese nation is understood as geographically, historically and ethnically defined, while the notion of Chinese civilisation allows for the inclusion of different cultural forms, marginal and peculiar, such as the Shu of Sichuan.

The thesis of multiple independent sources of civilisation has been accepted as part of official historical narratives, yet it remains in the background, overshadowed by the old monolithic vision focused on the Central Plains and Yellow River cultures. Although the province of Sichuan and, to a larger extent, its capital, Chengdu, rely on the Sanxingdui Museum and on the mystery of the Shu civilisation as main tourist attractions, references to this civilisation are scant outside the Sichuan Province. Sanxingdui archaeological finds are afforded relatively little importance in the context of displays in national-level museums – notably in the National Museum of China and the Arthur Sackler Museum of Art and Archaeology, both in Beijing, and the Shanghai Museum. When the ancient Shu civilisation is mentioned, it is usually in terms that extol its uniqueness, yet link it in a subordinate manner to the civilisation of the Central Plains. For instance, the panels of the Sanxingdui Museum read, 'the ancient state of Shu at Sanxingdui represents one of the many distinct regional cultures that surround the Central Plain in ancient China'. Similarly, in the catalogue of the National Museum of Chinese History, the only mention of the Sanxingdui finds appears in a paragraph on ethnic minorities inhabiting the peripheral areas of the country. The reference to the Sanxingdui civilisation does not appear in the main text of the catalogue, but in a caption. The picture in question shows a bronze human head and the catalogue entry reports 'sacrificial object […] it is the image of a sorcerer' (National Museum of Chinese History 2002, 58).[4] The term 'sorcerer' evokes notions of superstitious practices, which in Communist rhetoric are associated with the primitive phase of development. In a similar vein, the catalogue of the exhibition *The treasures of a nation: China's cultural heritage 1949–99*, celebrating the 50th anniversary of the founding of the People's Republic, describes Shu relics in terms of 'remains of ethnic minority states of the Shang Dynasty' (State Cultural Relics Bureau

---

[2]   All quotes in this section, unless otherwise indicated, are taken from the Sanxingdui Museum. Visited in May 2006.

[3]   These statements are made on the CD-ROM introducing the Sanxingdui Museum.

[4]   The art historian Craig Clunas (1997a, 19), commenting on a similar bronze figure, suggests a different interpretation: 'these pits are not the tombs of human beings, nor do they contain the human sacrifices found at Anyang'.

1999, 61). Consistently, museum descriptions of the Shu civilisation highlight its 'mysterious', 'enigmatic' character, depicting it as a 'controversial legend', 'a rare treasure of ancient humanity' that provides a 'missing link in the evolution of Chinese culture' and 'reveals the infinite fascination of ancient Chinese civilisation'.[5] The narratives woven around the archaeological finds of the Sanxingdui civilisation place it in a subordinate position compared to the main culture of the Central Plains, in relation to which Shu culture is seen as 'peripheral'. In this way, Sanxingdui is inscribed in the official version of history, as narrated from the Han centre.

Political Legitimation in Imperial China

According to Max Weber (quoted in Wechsler 1985, 10), political legitimacy can be based on:

> *rational* grounds – on the belief that the rules and laws are 'legal', and that the authorities have the right under such rules to issue commands; *traditional* grounds – on the belief in the historical sanctity of timeworn traditions and the legitimacy of the status of those exercising authority under those traditions; *charismatic* grounds – on the devotion to the holiness, heroism, or exemplary character of some person, and on the moral values and order revealed or prescribed by that individual.

If the cult of personality of Mao is an example of legitimation on charismatic grounds, in Imperial China, political legitimacy was mainly sought on traditional grounds, namely political ancestry. Political ancestry was originally determined by familial or dynastic lineage, but the concept later expanded, referring more broadly to 'the line of orthodox political succession' (Wechsler 1985, 229). As a result, political ancestry could be traced back to several dynasties, continuity being assured not so much by direct dynastic descent, but rather by the legitimate *transfer* of imperial authority, in turn based on the manifestation of moral and political virtues (*te*). Thus, in Imperial China, sources of political authority relied on a set of interrelated factors: kinship, hierarchy, moral authority of the rule, military power and exclusive access to gods and ancestors (through rituals, art and calligraphy). Moral authority was embodied by the 'Mandate of Heaven' (*Tian Ming*) – that is, the positive judgement of the gods ensuing from the virtuous conduct, morality and wisdom of the ruler. A failure within the government or in war, or a natural disaster were seen as Heaven's punishment for misconduct (this concept was introduced during the Zhou Dynasty).

The Mandate of Heaven concept constitutes a key reference in the realm of Chinese political philosophy, as it was crucial in regulating legitimacy and continuity in the transmission of power. The Mandate was transferred through linear male descent and could be revoked in cases of immoral rule. Natural disasters, such as earthquakes or famines, were considered signs of disapproval from Heaven; conversely, the reported appearances of mythical creatures, such as the unicorn, were interpreted as auspicious symbols. The Mandate of Heaven served to justify both long dynastic periods – long-lasting dynasties being associated with 'good' rule – and discontinuities in dynastic succession over the centuries.

The ruler was not deprived of means to improve his conduct. The observance of a set of rules,

---

[5] Sanxingdui Museum, extracts from panels. Visited in May 2006.

including social and moral obligations, respect for tradition and self-cultivation, formed the core of a complex ritual. Adherence to ritual became not only the *conditio sine qua non* for 'good government' but also the tool through which Heaven's benevolence could be secured. Political support could be gained through 'the employment of rites and symbols that arouse a deep sense of identification with the regime and its authorities' (Wechsler 1985, 4) – a point that was to be fully incorporated in Communist political theory.

Legitimation Strategies of the Chinese Communist Party

The sources of political legitimation of the Chinese Communist Party have changed over time. If one considers in particular the time during which Mao dominated the political scene – roughly between 1949 and 1976 – from the perspective of the government's relationship with the past, it is possible to identify two distinct periods. The first covered the years between 1949 and 1959. This decade was marked by strong Soviet Union influences in most areas of political, economic and social life. The second period began in 1959. After this date, the fracture in diplomatic relations with the USSR led the Chinese government to abandon Soviet references and replace them with a combination of nationalism and Communist utopia. During this second phase, the search for sources of legitimation became a pressing issue. Political slogans of this period illustrate attitudes towards the past: 'stress the present, not the past' and 'make the past serve the present'. Disregard for the past reached a peak during the Cultural Revolution (1966–76), when even academia lost its prestige: 'the supposedly academic research conducted in China did not constitute true scholarship, but rather merely served the political power struggle, reaffirming political authority' (Tong 1995, 178).

One of the Communist government's main strategies of legitimation has been the manipulation of history. Official history has not only forced some figures and events to be remembered while others are neglected, but has also superscribed symbols (Duara 1988). The superscription of symbols aims to 'adapt' the characters of historical or mythical figures; an emblematic example is provided by the Emperor Qin Shihuangdi. Qin Shihuangdi is a semi-mythical figure who unified China around 221 BC and commissioned the impressive 'Terracotta Army'. He was salvaged from collective amnesia by the Communist government, reinterpreted, and cast as a national hero to support narratives on the longevity, continuity and unity of the Chinese nation. These narratives are successfully exported to other countries, as illustrated by the success of the temporary exhibition *The First Emperor: China's Terracotta Army*, held at the British Museum in 2007–08. As Duara (1988, 780) notes, through miraculous stories and anecdotal tales, 'cultural symbols are able to lend continuity at one level to changing social groups and interests even as the symbols themselves undergo transformations'.

Another strategy of legitimation deployed by the Communist Party is what the historian Ci Jiwei calls 'the technology of guilt'. Vera Schwarcz (1994, 55), elaborating on Ci's thought, explains that 'the Communist Party presents itself as the "archcreditor" while everyone else stands in a "debtor" relationship to it. Anyone who lacks a sense of indebtedness to the party is forced to undertake a "ritualised confession".' This strategy was largely used during the Cultural Revolution, a historical period over which the Communist Party maintains a deep silence.

A radically different strategy of legitimation involves the use of art as a tool of redemption, of reparation and of indemnification for past events. Fred Myers (2001, 60) explains that 'to "redeem" is literally to take or buy back, but it is extended to notions of repurchasing, clearing, and restoring – of freeing from what distresses or harms, to change for the better, to free from the consequences of sin, to offset the bad effect of, and so on'. In this sense, art treasures of the past are used by the Chinese government with the aim of redeeming its current image. The use of art as a redemptive tool may take the form of commemoration in museum exhibitions (Coombes 2001, 236). The archaeological discovery of the Terracotta Army provides an example of the use of art as a redemptive tool. In Xi'an, the site of the discovery, it has not been possible to create a proper museum given the dimensions of the archaeological pit and the ongoing process of excavation. Instead, large hangars have been built above the archaeological site. Given the lack of contextualisation of the Terracotta Army in its original site in Xi'an, it is interesting to see how these archaeological finds are interpreted and presented when they enter the context of a museum exhibition.

Although the museum texts and display choices for *The First Emperor: China's Terracotta Army* were those of the British Museum curators, the exhibition was set up in collaboration with Chinese archaeologists and curators. In the British Museum exhibition, the status of Emperor Qin Shihuangdi is elevated to founder of the Chinese nation – his authority, power and charisma are indexed by the materiality of the thousands of terracotta sculptures that he commissioned, and by implication, by the level of resources that he was able to mobilise for his majestic project. The exhibition's display emphasises the beauty of the sculptures, as well as the technical skills and refinement attained. Conversely, less pleasant aspects, unsuitable for the emperor's hagiography, are banished from the display. For instance, suggestions that the emperor was a tyrant, that he suppressed freedom of expression, burnt books and, in an attempt to eradicate Confucianism, had hundreds of Confucian scholars killed, are omitted from the exhibition.[6] Nevertheless, as the anthropologist Stephen Feuchtwang (2011, 76) notes, 'the First Emperor's spirit is sacred in the way the nation is sacred. China is an empire that has become a nation, like other land empires. The so-called First Emperor is part of the government-sponsored preservation of Chinese histo-ricity and its direction of political ambition.'

The creation of new slogans is another way in which the Communist Party has imparted its ideology and legitimised its authority. 'Socialism with Chinese characteristics' is one example. The formula, which has become omnipresent in official discourse, was originally introduced by Deng Xiaoping at the XIIth Congress of the Communist Party, in 1982. The slogan aims to overcome a problematic dualism at the heart of the current political system: Communist ideology on the one hand and the capitalism of the socio-economic system on the other. This dualism has been described as 'China's peculiar situation of the coexistence of incommensurable forces, of a market-oriented economy and a bureaucracy founded on the past command economy and Maoist ideology' (Liu 2000, 126). The scholar Roderick MacFarquhar has pointed out that the 'leadership seems ready to shift from the goal of "Building Socialism With Chinese Character-istics" to that of "building China with socialist characteristics"' (quoted in Pye 1996, 109). This reformulation might suggest that the Chinese government's focus is moving away from political ideology in favour of socio-economic development.

The current climate of heightened economic and social transformation demands political stability, as the government needs to be able to guide the country through the rapids of acceler-

---

[6]   For a more thorough discussion of the British Museum exhibition *The First Emperor: China's Terracotta Army*, see Varutti (2008b).

ated economic growth. The Communist Party is focused on tackling the legitimisation crisis through the reconstitution of the Party's symbolic legitimacy, achieved through a growing emphasis on nationalism and, specifically, through the re-evaluation of China's ancient past.

THE GROWTH OF NATIONALISM

Despite the economic reforms introduced by Deng Xiaoping, since Maoism the loss of faith in the values of the Chinese Communist Party has been tangible. As Gries and Rosen note (2004, 16), 'in this new environment, traditional ideological appeals to implement Marxism–Leninisim–MaoZedong Thoughts and build a socialist China find little resonance among the public'. Myron Cohen (1991, 130–1) argues that 'the absence of cultural links between China's population and its political elites at all levels of government and party organization has led to the ironic consequence that the State has had little or no success in realizing the ideological or cultural goals of its policies'. Other scholars note that the post-socialist political system tends to 'keep alive a vague vision of future socialism as a common goal of humankind while denying to it any immanent role in the determination of present social policy' (Dirlik and Meisner 1989, 364). The divide between the government and its citizens is amplified by the rapid pace of social change triggered by economic development, namely the industrialisation and urbanisation of coastal southern provinces (such as Guandong) and internal migration towards these areas. Impressive growth rates and the associated promise of an increase in life quality are certainly strong arguments of political legitimacy. However, they do not erase the basic contradiction of a political system promoting a market economy while still retaining the socialist model as its ideological base.

Despite economic growth, the Communist Party is constantly faced with the challenge of ensuring its own endurance and the perpetuation of the status quo. On 19 September 2004, the 78-year-old Jiang Zemin withdrew from his post as director of military affairs, making way for President Hu Jintao. This enabled the latter to head the three main state functions (state president, head of the Communist Party and head of the army) and thus to become the true leader of China. Hu Jintao's early efforts to reform the political system and improve the image of the government – including a 'tolerant' attitude towards the media, open condemnation of corruption and cuts to Communist leaders' luxury expenses – led some observers to think that a transition from an authoritarian to a democratic system might not be too far away. However, the pace of political reform slowed considerably in the face of rampant economic liberalisation. Rather than reforming its core, the Communist Party reformulated its political rhetoric: if the form remains Communist in style, the content is becoming increasingly nationalistic since 'nationalism remains the one bedrock of political belief shared by most Chinese' (Unger 1996, xi).

China has been described as an empire attempting to become a nation, and Chinese nationalism as 'state nationalism', where 'an existing state strives to become a unified nation' (Unger 1996, 7). Culture plays a central role in these strategies. As Guo Yingjie (2004, 2) explains:

> having shifted away from its traditional Marxist–Maoist basis of legitimization, the CCP is compelled to reposition itself in relation to the 'people' and 'nation'. [...] As state nationalism is embraced as a supplement ideology, it has opened up considerable space for cultural nationalism [...] culture, rather than loyalty to the party-State or the concept of class, has become the most essential criterion for defining the national community.

Frank Dikötter (1996, 590) specifies that cultural nationalism 'imagines the nation to have a distinctive civilisation based on a unique history, culture and territory. Nations, according to cultural nationalists, are not merely rational political units, but organic beings that have been endowed with a unique individuality which should be treasured by all its members.'

State and cultural nationalism have been mainly fuelled and justified by the colonial experience. Colonialism and imperialism have been held mainly responsible for China's technological backwardness and identity crisis. The importance of culture in the framework of nationalism is expressed by Professor Qiu Mingzhen, director of the Institute of Literature of the Shanghai Academy of Social Sciences. Professor Qiu (2000, 315) estimates that:

> a nation with an advanced economy and powerful politics has not only an economic and political strength that play an important and even decisive role in the international society, but also a culture that stands above other national cultures with its exceptional superiority and lofty image, and becomes an important index of comprehensive national power.

The re-evaluation of ancient Chinese culture can be better understood in the light of such statements. As Ann Anagnost (1997, 2) notes, 'the gaps bridged by narrative always bear the potential to reappear at moments of crisis, producing a "double time" of the nation whereby the nation's impossible unity in the present rests on its (re)narrativization of the past'.

Confucianism is one of the aspects of Chinese 'traditional' culture and China's past that has received the most attention; indeed, in the 1990s, China experienced a revival of Confucianism. Elisabeth Croll (2006, 68) explains this phenomenon as:

> an uprooting of Confucian precepts that was seen to underlie loss of uniqueness and continuity. [...] In terms of sheer longevity, the Confucian inheritance was seen to have served China well and was therefore more than capable of healing any scar or rupture. To this end Confucius himself was rehabilitated.

The revival of Confucianism was marked by spectacular political acts, such as high-profile visits by political leaders to Confucian temples. The 'Confucian renaissance' had essentially two aims. On the one hand, it was meant to 'moralise' and correct the '"money worship" associated with Western capitalism' (Ong 1997, 179). It was thought that Confucianism would bring morality back into economic practices, with a focus on patriotism rather than on sheer profit. On the other hand, the emphasis that Confucianism places on the long uninterrupted history of ancient Chinese civilisation (*wenming*)[7] has been used 'to inculcate a new sense of belonging to the nation among Chinese students' (Ong and Nonini 1997, 21). This has led to a new form of nationalism centred on patriotism: 'since June 1989, the Chinese government has renewed the slogan "aiguo zhuyi" (patriotism) with such unprecedented fervour that the slogan appears on almost every important political occasion' (Wang 1996, 309).

---

[7] As underlined by Anagnost, *wenming* has to be understood as 'civilisation' in terms of 'an advanced stage of historical development' (1997, 75).

In the aftermath of the crisis following the events at Tian An Men in 1989, considerable resources were mobilised for patriotic campaigns as the government sought to stabilise the situation. Measures included a vast project involving the major Chinese cities, aimed at dusting off and renovating museums, memorial halls and revolutionary sites, reframed as 'bases for patriotic education' (Y Guo 2004, 25). According to Jonathan Unger (1996, xiii), Chinese patriotism is a mixture of 'political nationalism, ethnic Han identity and a culturalist pride'.

A revealing feature of patriotic discourses is the use of the kinship metaphor. Barbara Saunders (2001, 19) notes that museums 'create [...] historic kinship of myths, symbols, memories and values carried by the artifacts'. The kinship metaphor is used to describe diverse kinds of relationships, between the Communist Party and Chinese citizens; between the central government and its provinces; and between the government and national cultural heritage. Thus, museum displays become tools to instil and strengthen the notion of kinship, linking the government (metaphorically the 'mother') and its citizens (the 'sons'). Ni Xingxiang (2001, 7), curator at the Site of the First Congress of the Communist Party of China, in Shanghai, explains that the Site is 'an important place for publicizing in a vivid way the glorious history and revolutionary traditions of the CPC and for conducting patriotic education among masses in general and the young people in particular'. This approach aims to create a common corpus of ideological, historical and cultural references which contribute to the visitor's construction as a citizen. Similarly, the 'provinces' of Tibet and Taiwan are pictured as rebellious sons in the family of Chinese provinces, expected to be loyal to the 'motherland'.

Patriotism may also take the form of historical revisionism, as in the case of the Sino-Japanese war, for instance. Humiliation and retaliation are heightened by the representation of the atrocities perpetuated by the Japanese during the 1937 war at the Memorial Museum of the Chinese People's War of Resistance to Japan, in Beijing (Mitter 2000, 279), and the Memorial Museum of the War Against Japan, in Nanjing (see also Denton 2007).

In the same vein, a revision of school programmes promoted by Jiang Zemin in 1991 was aimed at celebrating the ancient splendour of China, ultimately fomenting what has been labelled 'culturalist pride'. The expression 'fever over traditional culture' (*wenhua re*) has been used (Lin and Galikowski 1999, 54) to describe the re-evaluation of Chinese history which gained impetus in the 1990s.

The past, and notably ancient Chinese history, is believed to embody the Chinese 'spiritual heritage' which present-day China should turn to as an antidote to its spiritual weakness. At the same time, the grand narratives of utopian grandeur that marked the Maoist era are fading, in favour of a different, more pragmatic discourse based on material wealth and the legitimacy of its quest. During Maoism, nationalism was imbued with patriotism centred on the newly created nation and its symbols – the effigy of Mao, the red flag, the national day, Tian An Men Square – and militant songs. Today, the focus is on economic development coupled with heavy doses of patriotism. The ideological elements put forward by the Party's leaders are a combination of 'faith in economic development, residual dogmatic communist historiography, nationalist sentiments, and an emphasis of social harmony that echoes selected traditional Confucian teachings' (Hwang and Schneider 2011, 30). Contemporary Chinese nationalism is no longer based on passive indoctrination, but on a two-pillar system: on the one hand, high growth rates and economic development; on the other, a diffused patriotism of which the re-evaluation of Chinese history is a major tenet.

Through discussion of the origins of Chinese civilisation and of the ideologies invoked by rulers to legitimise the exercise of political authority over time, this chapter has demonstrated the crucial importance of the past as a source of legitimacy throughout Chinese history. In the next chapter, analysis will again focus on museums, examining how such political ideologies have influenced museum narratives and representations of the past.

The Representation of the Past in China's Museums

National history and national heritage are often juxtaposed to complement and support each other: the former provides a cohesive narrative and a context for the heritage, while the latter materialises an otherwise abstract past. In museums, the past is transformed into heritage through processes of selection, interpretation and memorialisation. Museums are sites where collective ideas are formed, nurtured, validated, disrupted and contested. In other words, they act as sites of both memory and counter-memory (Zemon Davis and Starn 1989). What makes museums special repositories of memory is the presence of objects. Objects transform museums into treasure houses preserving stories and remembrances, evoking emotions and dreams. Museum objects have the potential to act as sensory, cognitive and emotional catalysts. Susan Crane (2000, 2) notes that 'being collected means being valued and remembered institutionally; being displayed means being incorporated into the extra-institutional memory of the museum visitors'.

If history, as the historian Bo Stråth (2005, 256) puts it, 'is a translation of the past into our time, an act of interpretation', then museum representations of history embody yet another layer of interpretation and can be understood as sites of meta-translation. While memories are highly subjective, 'history usually depends on someone else's eyes and voice: we see it through an interpreter who stands between past events and our apprehension of them' (Lowenthal 1985, 216). The interest in focusing on the museum representations of historical events rests precisely in the aptitude of museums to act as media and interpreters. From a corpus of historical data and objects, some elements are omitted and others are emphasised, while yet others are altered and reassembled to form a coherent visual and narrative ensemble. Museums are key sites where such selective and transformative processes take place and are validated. Thus, in examining how the past is represented in museums, one is dealing not simply with past events, but also with the series of choices, selections and transformations that have occurred along the way and influence the present.

Remembrance is one of the most important functions attributed to museums in China (H Wang 2001). One might speak of an imperative of memorialisation which frames Chinese museums as 'lieux de mémoire' *par excellence* (Nora and Kritzman 1996). This combines with tight state control of the interpretation of the past in general, and in museums specifically. Professor Hung Chang-tai, historian of China based at the Hong Kong University of Science and Technology, has provided one of the most incisive commentaries on the way museums represent the past in China: 'A public museum in China is seldom about the past. It is about the current image of the party and how the party wants itself to be seen' (quoted in Johnson 2011). Similarly, Rubie Watson (1994, 2) notes, 'Mao Zedong created the terms of political discourse – created correct thought – by transforming his reading of the past into the only possible reading.' But remembering in China has also been framed as a ritualistic collective activity whereby:

inspiration, especially at the collective level, invariably carries normative expectations for the individual. In China, where the state has been the main arbiter of communal remembrance, these normative expectations have been particularly obvious. Both imperial and communist China bore the burden of such didactic manipulations of the past. (Schwarcz 1994, 52)

Museums have been instrumental in such manipulations. From imperial collections to revolutionary memorabilia, Chinese material culture has been used time and again to uphold and strengthen the legitimacy of political authority.

Representations of the past in Chinese museums reveal the tension between the remnants of Marxist and socialist ideology – with the past portrayed as a dark era of oppression – and the more recent renewed attention paid to ancient history. As Tamara Hamlish (2000, 138) puts it:

> the museum embodies a central paradox of the construction of the past in the modern [Chinese] State: the need to sever the (post imperial) present from the imperial past while maintaining a sense of connection to and continuity with the ancient culture and civilization from which a modern identity is derived.

The outcome of such a paradox is a mixture of Marxist evolutionary theory and re-evaluation of the past, coated in discourses glorifying the Communist Party. Three main themes inform museum narratives and representations of the past. The first is Marxist–Leninist theory and philosophy; through references to the evolutionary theory and historical materialism, Marxism has been influencing museum representations since at least 1949. The second theme, which gained momentum in the early 1990s, revolves around a revival of the past – especially of Ancient China and the mid imperial periods of the Tang (AD 618–906) and Song (AD 960–1279) dynasties, seen as the 'Golden Ages' of Chinese civilisation. In this approach to the past, linked to the legitimacy crisis, the aesthetics of ancient cultural relics are emphasised and used as a platform to support discourses on the longevity, unity and continuity of Chinese civilisation. The third and most recent theme is a sense of nostalgia for an undetermined past. These themes overlap and mix to create varying, often contrasting, depictions of the Chinese past. The incongruous narratives of the past emerging from contemporary museums demonstrate the ongoing negotiation of China's relationship with its past and with modernity.

THE REPRESENTATION OF THE PAST DURING MAOISM

During the Maoist era (from 1949 to 1976), representation of the past in museums was deeply influenced by Soviet museology and Marxist–Leninist principles. A brief digression on museums in the former Soviet Union thus offers an interesting comparative perspective on Chinese museums. After gaining power following the Bolshevik Revolution of 1917, the Soviet government was faced with the issue of what to do with the immensely rich collections of the tsars. To revolutionaries, these collections were symbols of the elite class that they had just subverted: the collections spoke of luxury, contemplation of beauty, wealth, high culture and social distinction. For the new regime, state maintenance of the collections would have contradicted their revolutionary ideals. On the other hand, the new government could not simply dismiss the importance of imperial collections: they were the material remnants of centuries of history and culture that many saw as the core of the new nation's cultural heritage. The reappropriation of imperial collections – as was the case for China's Republican government after 1911 – was therefore of highly symbolic importance for the Bolshevik government. The Soviet government devised an interesting solution to this dilemma: the aesthetic dimension of objects was ignored in full and exclusive favour of utilitarian, educational and propagandistic functions. As Boris Groys (1994, 146) explains:

> The goal of this newly conceived museum became not to present objects and artifacts that might be considered original, characteristic, and specific in the historical development of art; rather, it was to present only those elements that appeared useful from a didactic point of view. This new museum was oriented not toward the heterogeneity of historical artistic styles or the representation of the historically original in art, but toward homogeneity, the establishment of common ground.

Such 'homogeneity' and 'common ground' encapsulate the ideology of the socialist political system. In Communist countries, 'historical museums were to document and prove the irrefutability of Marx's historical materialism, particularly his principles of class struggle, the disintegration of capitalism, and the inevitability of the victory of Socialism and Communism' (Stransky 1992, 176).

In the 1950s, Soviet museums were a source of inspiration to Chinese Party officials engaged in the creation of new Chinese museums. For instance, in 1950, the visit of a Chinese delegation to museums in Moscow, including the National Museum of the Revolution, provided the impetus for the organisation of collections in the Museum of the Chinese Revolution, which would open in Beijing in 1961 (Hung 2005, 917ff). It should be noted, however, that the Soviet approach to Marxism–Leninism differed from that of China, as the latter 'developed a strong nationalistic feeling, embracing with equal strength China's past and present history' (Lengyel 1991, 1). Indeed, the museums created in China during the first decades of Communist rule were meant to put forward the Party's vision of history, while projecting an image of the country's future.

Representations of the past in these museums were characterised by a vision of history infused with Marxist–Leninist evolutionary theory and historical materialism. Through the lens of Marxist–Leninist evolutionary theory – grounded in the linear evolutionary theory developed by Lewis Henry Morgan in 1877 (1985 [1877]) and later by Friedrich Engels – Chinese history was seen as a succession of phases leading from primitive to slave to feudal society. After 1840, as a consequence of capitalism and imperialism following the First Opium War (1839–42), China was said to have entered a phase of 'semi-colonial' and 'semi-feudal' society. The climax of the feudal period was associated with Western colonisation and the decadence of the Qing Dynasty. Conversely, the establishment of the People's Republic in 1949 was thought to mark China's entry into 'modernity'.

The museums created during the first decades of the People's Republic largely adopted Marxist terminology in their labels and panels. For instance, museum labels employ the terms 'semi-feudal' and 'semi-colonial' to describe the period that corresponds to modern history – from 1840 to 1949. This lapse of time is further sub-divided into the 'old democratic revolution' (from 1911 to 1919, corresponding to the Republican era) and the 'new democratic revolution' (between 1921 and 1949, corresponding to the ascent of the Communist Party and its fight against 'imperialist forces').[1]

Among the museums established in the early years of Communist China was the Museum of the Chinese Revolution, which opened in Beijing in 1961 and subsequently merged with the National Museum of Chinese History to create the current National Museum of China. The Museum of the Chinese Revolution constituted the first and most significant effort by Party officials and curators to present the history of the Communist Party, its ideology, and its place and relevance in modern China. High-ranking Party officials exerted tight control over the Museum's exhibitions, holding decisional power at the expense of museum staff (Hung 2005). In the words of the former premier Zhou Enlai (quoted in Hung 2005, 927), 'The exhibitions in the two museums [the Museum of the Chinese Revolution and the Military Museum] must show that politics is in command, using Chairman Mao's correct thought and revolutionary line as the guiding principle.' In its founders' minds, the Museum of the Chinese Revolution was intended to mark a departure from previous museums, considered to be either tokens of 'foreign imperialists' or outdated 'antique display places' with little or no relevance to modern society (ibid, 915). Thus, the collections of the new museum were gathered through repeated nationwide collection campaigns in which citizens were invited to donate documents and artefacts relevant to the making of modern China, specifically the period from the First Opium War (1839–42) to the post-1949 era.

This method of collecting historical material was not new. In October 1949, just a few days after the investiture of the Communist government, the Propaganda Department of the Central Committee of the Chinese Communist Party issued a 'Notice for the collection of Revolutionary Relics', followed in 1951 by a 'Circular calling for the collection of materials concerning the history of the party' (Murowchick 2013, 20–1). These initiatives testify to a political will to crystallise and historicise coeval events. This mode of acquiring collections also explains the mundane, everyday character of many objects exhibited in revolutionary museums in contemporary China.

In addition to donations, the staff working on the preparation of the Museum of the Chinese Revolution also commissioned prominent painters to capture key moments in the history of the Communist Party. Such paintings played a crucial role in creating and sustaining a collective imagery of the Party and its heroes (see Andrews 1994). Tellingly, many of these paintings are still exhibited in contemporary museums such as the National Art Museum of China (NAMOC) and the National Museum of China (see Hung 2007).

The Museum of the Chinese Revolution was one of the main 'sites of Communist memory' – that is, sites where Communist ideals, key events and figures are remembered and celebrated (they include museums but also memorials, parks and residences of former Party members). These sites continue to be prominent in contemporary China, as illustrated by the government's decision to designate these sites 'bases for patriotic education' (see Vickers 2007, 366).

The Zhejiang Provincial Museum, in Hangzhou, provides an effective illustration of the Marxist–Leninist partition of history. The Museum's permanent exhibition is organised over three floors, each devoted to a different period in the history of Zhejiang Province. The ground

---

[1]   Museum texts, Site of the First Congress of the Communist Party, Shanghai.

floor is devoted to prehistory, and in particular to the Humudu and Liangzhu cultures, dating back 7000 and 5000 years respectively. Museum texts explain that 'the Liangzhu culture existed in the period of transition from primitiveness to civilisation'.[2] The first floor focuses on the dynastic period; it highlights crucial events such as the introduction of irrigation works and the improvements in agriculture under the government of the Wuyue State (late Tang Dynasty, AD 618–906). The second floor, entitled 'Resistance against foreign aggression', illustrates the colonial experience, the Communist rise and the contribution of the 'martyrs' of Zhejiang Province to its political triumph. Underlying such display choices – and manifested in museum panels – is the Marxist–Leninist vision of history as a chronological succession of events and periods, to indicate a linear ascent from prehistory to the Maoist period.

As exemplified by displays at the Zhejiang Provincial Museum, narratives of the past inspired by Marxism–Leninism emphasise the oppression and injustice intrinsic to primitive and feudal social systems. As a result, in Mao's era, antiquity was comparatively far less important than the recent past. As the scholar Theodore De Bary (De Bary *et al* 1960, 941) presciently noted:

> Mao's style of writing, his political vocabulary, his sources of authority, and his whole frame of reference are in most respects so foreign to Chinese tradition as to suggest an altogether different orientation of mind. More significant, therefore, than the explicit rejection of the past is the very small place it has occupied in Communist thinking. As Mao himself puts it, the past is of little concern; the important thing for Chinese Communists is to look to the future.

Drawing on Marxism–Leninism, the Maoist view of the past focuses on historical events and figures that suit the Communist social project, such as the struggle to create an 'equal' society, the annihilation of oppressive and exploitative classes and the establishment of a 'dictatorship of the people'. As a result, museum contents had to be 'reinterpreted' in order to become educational tools for the 'masses'. In the words of the anthropologist Don Fowler (1987, 238), 'the evil, pre-1949 past is contrasted with the glory of the present and the future. The past was evil, not in itself, but because those who ruled China in the past were evil.' This interpretation of the past was adopted by the most important Chinese museums, including the former National Museum of Chinese History, prior to its refurbishment and reopening as the National Museum of China in spring 2011.[3]

The historical narrative of the Chinese nation projected by the National Museum of Chinese History was thoroughly embedded in the Marxist–Leninist paradigm. The rise of Chinese civilisation, for instance, was linked to the accumulation of wealth by a small elite. In the introductory and explicative panels, as well as in the catalogue illustrating the permanent exhibition, social changes were seen through the lens of the Marxist–Leninist theory of evolution. Thus, human development was divided into phases: 'primitive' society (from Peking Man to the Xia Dynasty, 2000 BC); 'slave society' (covering the Shang Dynasty, 1500 BC); 'feudal society' (from the 3rd century BC to the end of the Qing Dynasty in 1911); and capitalist-bourgeois society and socialism, leading to the final realisation of a Communist society. Drawing on Marxist–Leninist theory, the National Museum of Chinese History exhibitions suggested that the shift from the

---

2   Zhejiang Provincial Museum, Hangzhou. Last visited in April 2006.
3   Interestingly, as will be discussed, the narratives of the national past – and notably of Ancient China – in the refurbished National Museum of China have lost their Marxist–Leninist references.

'primitive' to 'feudal' phase was linked to the food surplus created by agriculture. The surplus thus obtained supposedly led to the division of labour, so that handicraft workshops could develop. In turn, increased productivity led to the development of social classes and, with that, a patriarchal system, private ownership and slavery. To illustrate the formation of an aristocracy, the Museum catalogue drew attention to the luxury and sophistication of cultural relics such as funerary sets, presented as evidence of the disparity between the wealthy and indigent. Private ownership allegedly transformed clan conflicts into wars for property. Peasant revolts were interpreted in terms of class struggle and represented, from a Marxist–Leninist perspective, the main force of social change (National Museum of Chinese History 2002, 26ff).

The Marxist–Leninist approach also informs narratives in natural history museums. In both the Museum of Natural History in Beijing and its equivalent in Shanghai, exhibitions aim to provide evidence of the evolutionary theory. Museum texts such as 'humanoids evolved to humanity by mutation, heredity and natural selection under the function of labour' and 'with the emergence of private ownership and social classes, the clan system of the primitive society disintegrated' bear witness to Marxist–Leninist influences.[4]

Marxist–Leninist principles inform not only museum texts but also the way in which objects are presented in exhibitions. In most instances, visitors are faced with a linear visiting path whereby objects are exhibited in chronological order to illustrate the various stages of development. Accordingly, the items in the first exhibition rooms are almost invariably pottery artefacts (pottery being defined as a 'primitive activity, in the earliest stage of human development' (L Li 2004, 4)), followed, in order, by jade, bronzes, rock sculptures and carvings, porcelain, paintings and furniture.

Continuity across the different phases and exhibition rooms is rendered through display techniques emphasising constancy in the use of symbols. For instance, at the Nanjing Museum, the visitor will learn that the black crow and the toad have symbolised respectively the sun and the moon since antiquity and that they appear on ancient pottery as well as on Ming furniture; similarly, pine trees, bats and deer carved on a Qing Dynasty lacquer box are established symbols of longevity, wealth and happiness respectively.[5]

Another display technique that stresses continuity consists of juxtaposing variants of the same kind of object to create a sequence suggesting an evolution in style devoid of hiatus. For instance, in the bronze gallery of the Shanghai Museum, one can observe the evolution and the various interpretations of the mysterious motif of *taotieh*, which is featured on many Zhou and Shang bronze vessels. Similarly, at the Tobacco Museum in Shanghai, cigarette lighters from different periods are displayed side-by-side to show variety and evolution of form.

In addition to the reference to evolutionary theories, exhibitions imprinted with Marxist–Leninist philosophy are characterised by an emphasis on the scientific value of objects. In a historical materialist view, objects are seen as scientific evidence, material traces of the past and carriers of 'objective' memory (Su 1995, 71–2). Historical materialism created a philosophical background favourable to the development of museums since, in tune with the Maoist slogan 'seek truth through facts', museums were and are considered shrines of authenticity insofar as they are the keepers of material evidence. It follows that history, science and art can be 'experi-

---

[4]   Both quotes from the Museum of Natural History, Shanghai. Visited in April 2006.
[5]   Nanjing Museum, Jiangsu Province, last visited in September 2004.

enced' through the senses and in that way 'verified': 'these original objects and materials are the survivors of history, they are able to verify it. Also, as they are the fossils of history and reflect it in materialised forms, they undoubtedly possess an objectivity and reality, which give them a very special value' (Su 1995, 71–2).

This approach to museum objects as 'evidence' helps to explain the importance attributed to personal items in historical exhibitions. For example, the permanent exhibition at the Military Museum in Beijing includes items such as binoculars, lanterns, water flasks and the fabric labels attached to soldiers' uniforms to indicate the army corps to which they belonged.[6] Similarly, the exhibition at the Site of the First Congress of the Communist Party, in Shanghai, features personal belongings of attendants to the congress, such as badges, uniforms, tea sets, typewriters, wall clocks and even lamp switches, here presented as historical evidence.[7] There is a risk of historical objectification and even fetishism in such approaches. Ann Anagnost (1994, 150) cautions, 'in the discourse of historical materialism as spoken by the post-Maoist state, history itself becomes the fetishized object'. Inevitably, this understanding of materiality and of the past is charged with political implications: 'Communist leaders grounded their claims to legitimacy in their special understanding of the principles of scientific socialism. [...] a mastery of the objective laws of social evolution justified the right of the party faithful to direct society' (Watson 1994, 1).

In almost ironic contrast to the idea of objects as verifiers of history, during Maoism, museums often produced distorted representations of the past. During the Cultural Revolution (1966–76):

> some museums went so far as to fabricate history and remould the cultural relics at will for the purpose of meeting the demands of the political struggles. In result, they did win over the high estimation of the then value subjects [political authorities] and thus had a better chance for their survival and development. (Su 1994, 3)

Ma Chengyuan, former director of the Shanghai Museum and an authority in the domain of Chinese antiquities, provides a vivid example of the kind of historic representations expected by museums during the Cultural Revolution. In an interview with the *South China Morning Post*, Mr Ma reported: 'We were supposed to illustrate class struggle, to condemn the life of the rulers, but I thought we can do it in a different way, to show the creativity of the masses because all these works were created by the people.' The article continues:

> Finally, he was allowed to organise four exhibitions – bronzes, pottery, sculpture and painting – to demonstrate the craftsmanship of the Chinese people. A major ideological breakthrough, this meant that the exhibits need not be mounted in any chronological order and thus avoid demonstrating the Marxist view of history as an inevitable progression through stages leading to a classless society. (Becker 2001)

Things were deemed to change as the end of the Cultural Revolution and the country's opening up to economic reform brought new wind to the sails of Chinese museums.

The meaning of the Maoist principle 'the past must serve the present', a principle that has

---

6   Military Museum, Beijing. Visited in November 2004.
7   Site of the First Congress of the Communist Party, Shanghai.

FIG 7.1. ENCOUNTERING MAO AT THE NATIONAL MUSEUM OF CHINA, BEIJING.

informed museum activities for over five decades since 1949, is now changing. As seen in the decades following the creation of Communist China, the vision of history was deeply rooted in Marxist–Leninist theory. These terms have been reversed during the last two decades. As the scholar Feng Chengbo (1993, 10) explains: 'the history museums' exhibitions start to break through the stereotyped five stages of social development pattern, [and they] pay more attention to the daily life and folklore of common people'. Marxist–Leninist principles have gradually lost their influence on Chinese museology, since the 'attempt to replace culture with ideology largely failed' (Duke 1989, 31).

It would, however, be misleading to suggest that Marxism–Leninism and evolutionary theories have been completely edited from museums. Exhibitions in the main national museums created in the decades following the establishment of the People's Republic – as well as in most contemporary museums addressing political topics – continue to adhere to the Marxist–Leninist interpretation of history and social organisation. Revolutionary museums in particular – that is, museums devoted to the revolutionary period and Communist ideals – have proved to be relatively resilient to change.[8]

A peripheral location and lack of funds may also contribute to a museum's stagnation. As Flath explains, referring to local museums in Shandong Province:

> These locations are far from the present economic and cultural center of the province, and so have few opportunities to attract a share of the burgeoning tourist market. As a consequence, the exhibits continue to rely on government support, and so are also the most likely to support the increasingly obsolete state narratives based on patriotism, historical materialism, socialism, and revolution. (Flath 2002, 54)

In other instances, revolutionary museums maintain a rather conservative approach to their permanent galleries, but adopt more dynamic, innovative approaches to their temporary exhibitions. This is the case at the Zhejiang Provincial Museum in Hangzhou. As mentioned, historical material in the Museum's permanent exhibition is organised according to evolutionary theory, and representation of the more recent past is imbued with revolutionary propaganda. However, since at least the early 2000s, the Museum has been actively involved in the organisation of a conspicuous number of temporary exhibitions, the fruit of exchanges with other Chinese and international museums. For instance, in spring 2006, the Museum hosted a temporary exhibition devoted to Yunnan bronzes of the Warring States (475–221 BC) and Western Han periods (206 BC–AD 8). Despite their historic relevance, their high craftsmanship and aesthetic refinement, these bronzes seldom feature in exhibitions of Chinese art, which tendentiously focus on the more famous Shang and Zhou bronzes of the Central Plains. To some extent, the dynamism of the Zhejiang Provincial Museum is linked to the rapid development of the city of Hangzhou and the growth of its tourism industry.

---

[8]   These considerations do not apply to university museums, many of which are of a relatively high museological standard, employing sophisticated technologies and facilities (such as the Anthropology Museum of Yunnan University in Kunming, the Sichuan University Museum in Chengdu, and the Museum of the Central University of Nationalities in Beijing). Indeed, according to Professor Song Xiangguang at Peking University (Song 2012, *pers comm*), university museums are rapidly increasing; in 2012, he estimated that there were around 280 university museums in China.

THE RE-EVALUATION OF ANTIQUITY

Over the last two decades, the decline in Marxism–Leninism's influence on museums has been accompanied by a growing interest in new historical perspectives, in particular on China's ancient past. The early 1990s crisis of political legitimation engendered a process of re-evaluation of the past charged with nationalistic connotations. Cultural nationalism brought China's ancient past to the forefront. Ancient China is no longer synonymous with a dark era of oppression but with the birth of Chinese civilisation.

The ideological vacuum created by the decline of Communist ideals has led to the emergence of a discourse on Chinese identity based on ancient Chinese history and civilisation. The renewed interest in ancient history that spread in China from the 1990s (see Lin and Galikowski 1999, 54) is also a consequence of the partial lifting of censure on Chinese traditions, customs and popular culture. At least one generation of Chinese – those who experienced the tragedy of the Cultural Revolution (1966–76) – has been deprived of the possibility to learn about ancient history and traditional culture; today's revival of interest in those topics can be seen as a form of reappropriation of a 'stolen' past. Thus 'minor' forms of craftsmanship such as jade-carving, lacquer, ceramics, jewellery and bronze-casting, previously dismissed during Maoism as 'bourgeois' or 'remnants of feudal, superstitious practices', are now acknowledged as important traditions of Chinese culture. The Shanghai Museum of Arts and Crafts, for instance, has regained its appeal over the last decade, receiving repeated visits from prominent politicians, including the former president, Jiang Zemin.[9]

As Marxism–Leninism fades away, a new museological approach to the past is gradually emerging. A plethora of new museums have been created since the early 1990s to exhibit recently unearthed artefacts. Not only do these new museums subscribe to the new paradigm of the rehabilitation of antiquity, but they also sumptuously celebrate the beauty, refinement and technological achievements of ancient Chinese civilisation. This approach is manifested in exhibitions through an increased emphasis on the aesthetics of objects, as discussed above. The process of selection and reinterpretation of ancient relics has produced a vision of history purged of disturbing elements. Corruption, internal conflicts, famines and social discontent are evacuated from historical narratives, while emphasis is placed on the elements denoting a flourishing society: the splendours of the arts, the achievements of technology, the extension of the empire and the relative inferiority of ethnic minorities and foreign cultures. A study of the Palace Museum in Beijing reveals that displays sustain the image of an elegant, cultivated and scientifically advanced imperial court, while references to moral, political, economic and cultural decadence are carefully omitted (Hamlish 2000).

Another example further illustrates the political stakes of the reinterpretation of ancient history. In 1999, on the occasion of the 50th anniversary of the founding of the People's Republic, the State Administration of Cultural Heritage, in cooperation with the National Museum of Chinese History and the Museum of Chinese Revolution, organised an exhibition entitled *The treasures of a nation: China's cultural heritage 1949–99*. The declared aim of the exhibition was to show the cultural relics unearthed and collected since the founding of the New China. The catalogue

---

9   Shanghai Museum of Arts and Crafts. Visited in August 2004.

of the exhibition asserts that cultural relics 'are material evidence of how the Chinese nation has risen from humiliation to glory [...] They are the most precious legacy and spiritual wealth of our nation' (State Cultural Relics Bureau 1999, 7). A subtler, implicit objective of the exhibition was to assert the positive role played by the Communist Party in the protection of cultural heritage. The exhibition was meant to respond to allegations of governmental censure, repression, neglect and even destruction of cultural heritage and artistic production during the Cultural Revolution. At the same time, with its focus on the splendours of ancient art, the exhibition contributed to shifting attention away from the relatively scant production of art under Communist rule. Ultimately, the initiative was meant to improve and reshape the image of the government itself, both by asserting its legitimacy in representing China's past, and by providing visibility to the government's philanthropic endeavours.

The dual narratives of the past in Chinese museums – the progress-oriented narratives of Communist imprint, and the celebratory narratives rehabilitating ancient and 'traditional' China – are emblematically expressed in the galleries of the newly refurbished National Museum of China.

THE NATIONAL MUSEUM OF CHINA

The National Museum of China was officially inaugurated in Beijing in 1959 and was originally named the National Museum of Chinese History.[10] The Museum was one of the Shi Da Jianzhu, the 'Ten Great Buildings' created in 1959 to celebrate the tenth anniversary of the People's Republic of China. The National Museum of China is today not only one of the most prominent museums in China, but also the one that is most intimately linked to the rise and rule of the Communist Party.

Beginning in 2000, the Museum underwent several major transformations. In 2001, its permanent historical exhibitions were closed and dismantled with a view to the complete restructuring of the collections and their relocation to a new building. The process took almost a decade as the new National Museum of China – established in 2003 following the merging of the National Museum of Chinese History with the Museum of the Chinese Revolution[11] – reopened to the public in spring 2011.

The stated mission of the National Museum of China is 'to be leading within China and first-class internationally [...] protecting Chinese cultural heritage, displaying the time-honoured history of China, providing education on history and culture for the public – especially for the young people, and promoting cultural exchange with other countries and regions' (National Museum of China 2012d). The Museum offers a rich programme of permanent and temporary exhibitions, distributed across five floors. At the heart of the displays are the two main permanent exhibitions: *Ancient China* and *The Road of Rejuvenation*. The two exhibitions are complementary from a chronological point of view: the historical narrative in *The Road of Rejuvenation* starts right where *Ancient China* ends.

The permanent exhibition devoted to Ancient China includes over 2500 objects presented in chronological order. The exhibition aims to present China's entire history, from prehistory

---

10   The Museum had incorporated the Preparatory Office of the National Museum of History, an institution dating back to 1912.

11   The two institutions had previously merged in 1969 and then separated again in 1983.

FIG 7.2. THE NATIONAL MUSEUM OF CHINA, BEIJING.

(around two million years ago) to the fall of the Qing Dynasty in 1911: 'a comprehensive review of the political, economic, cultural and social development as well as China's foreign relations in different historical periods. The exhibition focuses on the continuous progress of Chinese civilisation and the historical course of building a multi-ethnic country.'[12]

Objects in the *Ancient China* galleries are presented using a perfect synthesis of Marxist–Leninist museology and decontextualising and aesthetising approaches. The concepts and terminology used in the galleries' panels reveal a Marxist–Leninist imprint: objects are categorised by material and function (eg food; music; modes of production; economy and daily life; ritual systems and nobility).[13] However, the labels for individual objects (mostly unearthed cultural relics) are succinct: they give the Chinese name and function of the objects, periodisation, and place and time of archaeological excavation. Relatively little or nothing is said about the objects' original contexts of production and use, or their social biographies. Display techniques invite an aesthetic appreciation of objects. Unobtrusive cases line the gallery walls, while the most visually stunning items occupy individual glass boxes in the centre of the exhibition space; in other instances, sets of valuable relics are exhibited in niche-like exhibition spaces encased in the wall and illuminated with boutique lighting.

Interesting changes in the classification and presentation of collections have occurred as a result of the Museum's refurbishment. Prior to its reopening in 2011, the National Museum of China had set up an *ad interim* exhibition called *The treasures of a nation: China's cultural heritage*

---

12   National Museum of China, introductory panels. Last visited in May 2012.
13   Museum panel titles, *Ancient China* galleries, National Museum of China. Last visited in May 2012.

1949–99, which included a selection of around 300 objects from the collections of the former National Museum of Chinese History and the National Museum of the Chinese Revolution. The objects featured in that special exhibition – presented in that context as 'selected treasures' – can now be seen in the permanent *Ancient China* galleries. However, in the current display they are no longer singled out as 'treasures' but have been incorporated in a broader historical depiction of Ancient China. Their significance as self-standing artistic and technological achievements has been effaced by their new role as tokens of the millennial Chinese culture and civilisation. In most instances, the uniqueness and visually arresting properties of the objects on display beg for richer information and access to curatorial research. Yet the *Ancient China* galleries are much less about exploring Chinese culture through the specific features of individual artefacts, than about tracing its trajectory of ascent.

The historical narrative in the other permanent exhibition at the Museum, *The Road of Rejuvenation*, presents the recent history of China beginning with the Opium War in 1840. The exhibition's emphasis is on the history of the Communist Party and its political achievements. The introductory panel sets the tone of the exhibition:

> The Chinese nation is a great nation whose people are industrious, courageous, intelligent and peace loving and have made indelible contributions to the progress of human civilization. For generations and generations the Chinese people have been pursuing a dream of national strength and prosperity. The Road of Rejuvenation is a permanent exhibition showcasing the explorations made by the Chinese people from all walks of life who, after being reduced to a semi-colonial, semi-feudal society since the Opium War of 1840, rose in resistance against humiliation and misery, and tried in every way possible to rejuvenate the nation. The exhibition also highlights the glorious history of China under the leadership of the Communist Party of China (CPC), in which all the ethnic groups joined forces to achieve national independence and liberation and strove to build a strong and prosperous country for the well-being of the people. The exhibition therefore clearly demonstrates the historical course of the Chinese people of choosing Marxism, the CPC, the socialist road and the reform and opening-up policy and China's firm determination in building socialism with Chinese characteristics through adherence to this great banner, this special road and this theoretical system. Today, the Chinese nation is standing firm in the east, facing a brilliant future of great rejuvenation. The long-cherished dream and aspiration of the Chinese people will surely come to reality.[14]

In terms of display techniques, the exhibition relies extensively on enlarged reproductions of photos (including a considerable number of graphic photos of war victims), maps and historical documents, interspersed with life-size dioramas (mostly made of bronze sculptures) reproducing historical events. This material largely outnumbers the historical artefacts on display. The latter include written documents, paintings (some of which are reproductions) and a miscellaneous set of mundane objects of which the 'museum quality' lies in their indirect association with historical events and persons. These paraphernalia include microscopes used by Sun Yat-Sen when he was a doctor, army generals' uniforms and badges, an alarm clock used by railway workers, a washbasin

---

[14] National Museum of China, *The Road of Rejuvenation* introductory panels. Last visited in May 2012. A slightly different version of this text has been published on the museum's website: http://www.chnmuseum.cn/english/tabid/520/Default.aspx?ExhibitionLanguageID=83 [10 July 2012].

FIG 7.3. YOUNG MEMBERS OF THE CHINESE MILITARY ADMIRE THE NATIONAL MUSEUM OF CHINA'S RECONSTRUCTED SECTION OF THE IMPERIAL PALACE FROM WHICH MAO DECLARED THE BIRTH OF THE PEOPLE'S REPUBLIC OF CHINA IN 1949.

used by a Red Army soldier and a piece of an iron chain from a bridge conquered by the Red Army during the Long March.

In contrast to the *Ancient China* gallery, replicas are not always labelled as such, and the visitor is left to guess the historical authenticity of the objects on display. Curators have used different lighting and background colours to create gallery sections and impart rhythm to the historical narrative. For instance, in the first section of the gallery devoted to the Qing Dynasty (AD 1644–1911), the lights are dim and the walls are covered with reproductions of historical photos in shades of grey. As the narrative moves into the 20th century and Republican China, the gallery space gradually becomes clearer; the gallery sections devoted to the rise of the Communist Party, and specifically to Mao's persona, are marked by deep pink and red walls and powerful lighting. In the last section, devoted to the open reforms and the liberalisation enacted by Deng Xiaoping, Jiang Zemin and Hu Jintao, the walls turn cream, the space is brightly lit and the floor takes on a deep red hue. The sensory experience is complemented by loud music in the style of a military march, its crescendo drawing visitors to the closing section of the gallery.

The historical narrative in *The Road of Rejuvenation* is dominated by Party ideology. Exhibition texts are more concerned with presenting political slogans – such as 'Building socialism in China is the inevitable outcome of the course of modern Chinese history'[15] – than with providing an

---

[15] National Museum of China, panels with text translated into English. Last visited in May 2012.

accurate and comprehensive historical account. While some photo captions (untranslated) are dated, virtually no historical dates appear in panel texts.

Historical periods are indicated through obscure references such as 'the third plenary session of the 11th CCP party committee', and rhetorical phrasing. For instance, Deng Xiaoping's 1978 reforms are described as:

> the CCP central collective leadership with comrade Deng Xiaoping as [sic] its core thoroughly reviewed the lessons from its experience in socialist construction, emancipated their minds, sought truth from facts, made the historic decision to shift the focus of the Party and country's work to economic development and to implement reform and opening up […] (ibid)

The historical account is plagued with shortcuts and strategic omissions. While some elements are emphasised – such as the historical role of Mao Zedong, his popularity and personal cult, and the atrocities committed by Japanese soldiers during the Second Sino-Japanese War (1937–45) – others are downplayed or omitted. For instance, the Great Leap Forward (1958–61), the policy that should have propelled China into modernity by increasing productivity but actually caused a famine that killed millions, is glossed over; the exhibition refers to increases in production and the construction of new roads, bridges and industries. The tragedy of the Cultural Revolution (1966–76) is reduced to one photo and the comment 'the project of constructing socialism suffered severe complications'. In the same vein, no reference is made to the popular protests of 1989 and the ensuing massacre on Tian An Men Square, nor to the ongoing unrest in Xinjiang, in Tibet and in other minority areas.

In many respects, the two permanent displays, *Ancient China* and *The Road of Rejuvenation*, are quite contrasting exhibitions. They capture some of the ambivalences inherent in the representation of the past in Chinese museums. *Ancient China* presents a wealth of cultural relics of high historical, scientific, technical and artistic value (and some replicas), whereas *The Road of Rejuvenation* is largely based on replicas of historical photos and documents. While China's ancient past is framed through an aesthetic gaze – reminiscent of Stephen Greenblatt's (1991) idea of the 'wonder' effect – China's recent history in *The Road of Rejuvenation* is presented in a storytelling style, as a (re)collection of facts, historical figures and images. While *Ancient China* focuses on the materiality, aesthetics, skills and cultural richness of Chinese civilisation, *The Road of Rejuvenation* is concerned with the singular trajectory of Communist China, its emergence from a 'dark', 'oppressive' and 'feudal' past, and its march towards the future.

A certain degree of ambivalence also emerges from the Museum's portfolio of temporary exhibitions, as Communist propaganda exhibitions, such as *Rising Sun in the East: Marxism in China and 90th Founding Anniversary of People's Publishing House* (September 2011) and *Exhibition on the Achievements of Chinese Women and Children in the Past Decade* (March 2012) alternate with blockbuster commercial events such as *Louis Vuitton Voyages* (May 2011) and *BVLGARI Retrospective Exhibition* (September 2011), generously sponsored by global corporations of the luxury sector. However, inconsistencies in display and narrative approaches are ultimately transcended by the superposition of narratives of nationalism and patriotism. The two galleries work in synergy in conveying the ideas of longevity, cultural unity, epic struggle and progression of the Chinese nation towards a bright future. These ideas are at the core of nationalist rhetoric in contemporary Chinese museums.

Nostalgia and Market Economy

The era of reforms and the opening up to a market economy have been marked by a progressive loss of faith in Communist ideology. Today, the Chinese people's attitude towards the revolutionary past has lost most of its patriotic ethos. Paradoxically, however, disillusionment, scorn and cynicism mingle with nostalgia (Jing 2006) for an idealised, indefinite ancient past (when Chinese civilisation was considered to be at its peak, a 'Golden Age' of scientific progress, cultural splendour and artistic refinement), as well as for a more recent past imbued with revolutionary ideals (see Lee and Yang 2007).

Nostalgia looms in museum representations of both ancient and revolutionary history. On the one hand, increasingly, museum exhibitions focus on the material culture of antiquity; bronzes, paintings, calligraphy, ceramics and textiles are presented as materialisations of such a Golden Age. On the other hand, exhibitions of revolutionary artefacts, now relieved of their ideological charge, take on nostalgic overtones. This is the case not only for artefacts (Beijing flea markets are brimming with Communist paraphernalia and gadgets bearing the effigy of Mao), but also for whole villages, as seen in Shaoshan, Mao's birth village (Anthony 2004), or Nanjie village (Chen 2004) in Henan, transformed into a utopian commune for nostalgic tourists' consumption. As James Flath (2002, 53) notes, 'museum and relic management in the post-Mao era reveals that although stateist narratives are still promoted in some contexts, that interpretation is now divided by subnarratives that promote a localized and increasingly commercialized interpretation of the past that has a problematic relationship with the nation'.

While such nostalgia for the past is fuelling the tourism industry, it would be inaccurate to dismiss its motivation as purely commercial. This nostalgic turn is also a facet of the ideological void left by disillusionment with Communist values; despite the tragic mistakes of the Maoist era, the period was infused with ideals, trust in progress, hope and high expectations for the future, which helped people make sense of difficulties and hardship. In today's remembrance of that era, most negative memories are voluntarily omitted, while the most positive are kept alive and enhanced through repetition. This dynamic, which one might compare to a process of 'invention of tradition' (Hobsbawm and Ranger 1983), is operating at not only the individual, but also the collective level. In both cases of nostalgia – for an ancient Golden Age of China and for the more recent revolutionary past – museums play a key role in expressing and fomenting nostalgic feelings. As Pan Lu (2012, 125) points out:

> The balance is subtly kept between the still orthodox continuity with a past narrative and the silent adaptation to a new, self-contradictory and parallel one. As a result, this type of narrative conceals much of the contested collective memory present and latently foments a radical or cynical attitude of the public towards a not yet fully discussed past.

The Shikumen Open House in Shanghai provides an interesting example of a 'nostalgic site'. The house is a detailed reconstruction of a typical high-class dwelling of 1930s Shanghai, called Shikumen. Most of the items of interior decoration are replicas; they can be freely touched by visitors and there are no labels or explanatory texts in the various rooms, except for a general introductory panel in the entrance hall. The decor is reminiscent of the exotic image of early 20th-century Shanghai, complete with reproduction posters of the time, depicting alluring girls in silk *qipao*. Shikumen is located in the heart of Xintiandi, a luxury shopping and tourist area reconstructed in Shanghai pre-war style. The complex is a commercial celebration of Shanghai's bygone era, where even an artificial lake 'evokes nostalgia about the local past when rivers crisscrossed taipingqiao area'.[16]

In Shanghai, a constellation of nostalgic sites has appeared over the last two decades. The reconstructed neighbourhood of Xintiandi – a project of urban redevelopment initiated in the late 1990s – is a large-scale celebration of 'old' Shanghai. Formerly a popular residential neighbourhood in the heart of the city, Xintiandi is today a tourist area boasting upmarket restaurants, cafés and boutiques. With its cobbled pedestrian streets and architectural forms recalling traditional pre-war houses, the area has become one of the symbols of the city. In a similar vein, a road in a historic Shanghai district, Duolun Lu – also known as 'Shanghai culture street' – has been transformed into a tourist area. The area is dotted with preserved ancient buildings, among which can be found the ancient residences of political leaders, writers and artists. The pedestrianised street with restored 'ancient-looking' buildings is now lined with restaurants, cafés and souvenir shops. Displays at the Shanghai History Museum, in the basement of the Oriental Pearl TV station building, echo the appeal of Xintiandi and Duolun Lu and largely draw on the 'old' Shanghai atmosphere through reconstructions of period roads and reproductions of period photographs. In Shanghai, a further nostalgic touch is added in the form of the former residences of famous people (Song Qingling, Sun Yat-Sen and Song Meiling, among others); the residences are mostly located in the former French concession and are today a popular tourist attraction. Visitors succumb to the charm of these villas, immersed in luxuriant gardens of magnolias and eucalyptus, the interiors of which, frozen in time, speak of the comfort, cultivation, taste and luxury of a bygone era.

A MUSEUM OF THE CULTURAL REVOLUTION?

Despite renewed interest in the past, one period of Chinese history remains largely inaccessible and is still considered taboo in museum representations: the Cultural Revolution (1966–76). In spite of strong criticism, public critique of this decade is still scant. In most museum texts, reference to this period, when unavoidable, is made in vague terms such as the 'dark era' or 'dark decade', and at most it is dismissed as 'a mistake'.

The mere idea of setting up a museum devoted to the Cultural Revolution seems daring. Yet the writer Ba Jin, himself a victim of persecution at the hands of the Red Guards, relished this project. As Ba explains, 'It is only by engraving in our memory the events of the "Cultural Revolution" that we will prevent history from repeating itself, that we will prevent another "Cultural Revolution" from recurring' (1986). Taking the example of museums devoted to the Holocaust, the philosophy behind this project is 'let history not be repeated'. Museum representation would here act as an educational tool: by providing a historical account of this tragic decade, visitors and the authorities would be forced to acknowledge the reality of historical events.

A small Museum of the Cultural Revolution inspired by the spirit of Ba Jin was opened in Shantou in Guangdong Province in 2005, under the patronage of local politicians and with the financial support of wealthy Hong Kongese benefactors. The initiative has not been well received by government authorities; the Museum's founders have been discouraged from releasing inter-

---

[16] Shikumen Open House, Shanghai. Visited in August 2004.

views about the Museum, and journalists have been prevented from covering it (Cody 2005; Coonan 2006). In addition to the museum in Guangdong, a Virtual Museum of the Cultural Revolution has been established online (http://www.cnd.org/cr/english) with material collected from readers and intellectuals, including interviews, witness statements and personal accounts, literary and artistic works, and bibliographies for interested readers.

As Vera Schwarcz (1994, 54) remarks, 'the Cultural Revolution museum envisioned by Ba Jin cannot be built until Chinese society is able to challenge and dislodge the party's monopoly on public remembrance'. This would require, in the first instance, the coalescence of a collective willingness to remember. For the time being, public debate on responsibilities during the Cultural Revolution is avoided, and the full restoration of social ties indeterminately postponed. Amnesia is the strategy chosen to deal with personal and collective ordeals. Future generations, having no direct memory of the events, will be in a better position to address these pages of Chinese history.

This chapter has discussed how museum narratives of the past have changed over the course of Chinese history as a result of changing ideologies (from Maoism to nationalism) and changing demands (from political indoctrination to a market economy). Yet these contrasting ideologies and discourses are not incompatible in contemporary Chinese museums, as demonstrated by the ambivalent narratives of the past presented in the recently revamped National Museum of China. If the representation of the past in Chinese museums emerges as changeable, inconsistent and fragmented, museum narratives of Chinese national identity appear more stable, though multilayered. This crucial topic will be discussed in the following chapters.

8

The Politics of Identity

The previous chapter examined how the national past has been interpreted and represented in Chinese museums. In most instances, the re-evocation of the past is instrumental to the unfolding of narratives centred on the present and future of the Chinese nation. As the scholars of China Yih-Jye Hwang and Florian Schneider (2011, 42) remark in their analysis of the People's Republic of China's 60th anniversary celebrations in 2009, 'the parade has moved the ideological legitimacy basis of the Party significantly away from its revolutionary heritage to a mixture of nationalism and the current administration's interpretation of Chinese modernity'. Notions of nationalism and modernity are key to the interpretation of current Party rhetoric and shed light on the narratives of the nation presented in contemporary Chinese museums. This chapter focuses on how the narratives of the ancient and recent past are used in museums to shape the image of the present-day Chinese nation. The expression of Chinese national identity is changing. Increasingly, narratives on cultural nationalism are replacing political indoctrination. Analysis suggests that two main narrative strands emerge from current museum representations of the Chinese nation.

A first set of narratives focuses on the Chinese nation as a civic project and extols aspects of Chinese culture, industry, science and technology. Museums as diverse as those representing silk, tea, tobacco, post and banks all convey a nationalistic message. In these museums, the development of a cultural tradition, an industry or a service sector are inscribed in the broader framework of the history of the Chinese nation, with special emphasis on the Communist Party and its achievements. A second cluster of narratives focuses on the multi-ethnic nature of the Chinese nation and the role of ethnic minorities in the making of China.

Although each museum has its own specific story to tell when taken individually, when juxtaposed they provide a plurality of versions of a similar 'master narrative' centred on the longevity, continuity, cultural richness and ingenuity of Chinese civilisation from its Yellow River origins, to its revolutionary glory, and its march to modernity. While drawing on different national facets, all narratives ultimately aim to convey notions of unity and pride in the Chinese nation. In so doing, they substantiate a crucially important connection between Chinese civilisation and the Chinese nation.

Exhibiting the Chinese Nation: Culture, Industry and Science

The museum depiction of the Chinese nation revolves around three major themes: Chinese culture and civilisation, productive forces (industries and public services) and scientific and technological achievements. Representations and narratives of Chinese culture and civilisation centre on the 'Huaxia' civilisation. The Huaxia civilisation is considered the ancestor of the Han and the depositary of the distinctive characters of 'Chineseness'. Huaxia would be, in other words, the

cultural substratum from which Chinese civilisation flourished. References to the Huaxia civilisation confer cultural grounding and historical depth to contemporary narratives of the Chinese
nation. A second set of narratives develop around the notion of the nation as a civic project.
Displays here aim to substantiate the link between the state and the Chinese nation. The nation
is institutionalised and understood as an efficient and modern apparatus of production. This
rhetoric of efficiency – echoing the grand social projects of the Maoist era – celebrates the state
and acknowledges the contribution of the various service and industrial sectors to the making
of a modern China. The last group of narratives projects the Chinese nation into the future by
extolling the country's scientific advancements and new technologies.

EXHIBITING CHINESE CULTURE AND CIVILISATION

The long, uninterrupted history of Chinese civilisation and the aesthetic refinement of its material culture constitute the axis of museum narratives of Chinese national culture. The historical
depth of Chinese civilisation is complemented by an emphasis on the aesthetic appeal of objects
exhibited – often cultural relics of high historical value – which suggests feelings of pride and
admiration. A parallel is tacitly established between the beauty and technical skills encapsulated
in objects and the taste and refinement of Chinese culture. In this way, the notion of Chinese
national identity is embedded in Chinese culture and civilisation. These dynamics have been
discussed with reference to the Ancient China galleries at the National Museum of China, but
they are also played out in a range of other museums representing aspects of Chinese culture.

Examples include the China National Silk Museum and the Tea Museum in Hangzhou,
Zhejiang Province. These museums focus on iconic features of Chinese culture – silk and tea –
their status here elevated to tokens of national culture in China. The main narratives in these two
national museums revolve around the development of the production and consumption of silk
and tea. These are portrayed as the trademarks of the Huaxia culture – the mythical civilisation
of the Central Plains thought to be the origin of Chinese civilisation – spreading out towards
the periphery, in a movement framed as a 'civilising process'.

The permanent exhibition at the China National Silk Museum focuses on the development of
textile activities, understood as a mark of civilisation, and draws a link between sericulture and
the Huaxia civilisation. This is done through museum texts' assertion that the use of textiles for
clothing purposes represents 'a milestone for human civilization. [...] not only a symbol of the
splendor of Chinese civilization, but also of its profound contributions to human civilization'.[1]
Expanding on the notion of textiles as a sign of civilisation, the display establishes parallels
between the Chinese silk culture and the textile traditions of other 'ancient' civilisations: Indian
cotton, Egyptian linen, Babylonian wool. Through the statement 'the Yellow River Valley was
the center of silk production' (Yu 2005, 4), the development of silk culture is depicted as a
distinguishing and defining feature of the Huaxia civilisation, which is thus elevated to the same
status as other ancient world civilisations. This point is also stressed in the texts of the Museum's
permanent gallery: 'the traditional clothing and accessories of the northern nomads and the
Han nationality created a historic nation of clothing and accessories, which became a symbol of
the culture of the Chinese nation'. This text draws together the concept of Chinese culture and

---

[1]   China National Silk Museum, Hangzhou, Zhejiang Province. Visited in May 2006.

civilisation (Huaxia) and the Chinese nation by establishing a direct link between silk culture, the Han majority and the Chinese nation.

Chinese culture and civilisation are similarly at the centre of narratives at the Tea Museum in Hangzhou. The permanent exhibition presents paintings, literary texts, poems, scientific dissertations and financial data related to tea production, distribution, preparation and appreciation. The materials on display, which include not only tea and tea-related implements but also poems, novels, calligraphy scrolls and paintings celebrating tea, aim to demonstrate the concept of 'tea culture' and place the consumption of tea into the larger framework of Chinese art, literature, history and customs. Tea culture is linked to the Chinese nation through references to its 'noble national sentiment' which 'infiltrated into the lofty life ideal of the Chinese nationality'.[2]

In the same vein as the Silk and Tea Museums, other museums are developing narratives that frame specific artistic forms as 'traditional', presenting them as 'the arts of the nation'. For instance, the Shanghai Arts and Crafts Museum – devoted to traditional works such as wood, ivory and jade carvings, textile embroidery, painted ceramics and paper works – and the Oriental Musical Instruments Museum of the Shanghai Conservatory of Music are undergoing a process of transition. The re-evaluation of national 'traditional' features is also evident in the general revival of interest for Chinese Traditional Medicine over the last two decades in China (Hsu 1999). This revival has been accompanied by the creation of new museums devoted to Chinese Traditional Medicine within universities in Beijing (in 1990) and Shanghai (relocated to Pudong in 2003), and the renewed popularity of the Traditional Medicine Museum in Hangzhou, Zhejiang Province. Having been neglected for decades, these small, thematically specific museums are today regaining relevance in the context of an ongoing revival of traditions, which are considered markers of cultural identity. At the same time, such revived traditions are often connected with nostalgia and the commodification of culture, as illustrated by the Shanghai culture street Duolun Lu and the Xintiandi area.

INDUSTRIAL AND SERVICE MUSEUMS

Narratives about the Chinese nation are not confined to 'traditional' culture, but also develop around other facets of the nation, such as industrial production and public services. In most instances, industrial museums are set up by state-owned enterprises, as discussed earlier. Within these museums, the development of specific industrial or service sectors is explicitly connected to the process of nation-building by narratives highlighting the contribution of the industry or service to the accomplishments of the Chinese nation.

Shanghai is one of the cities boasting the largest number of museums devoted to industrial sectors and services. Industrial museums in Shanghai reflect and enhance the image of the city as an industrial, commercial and financial hub. In 2002, the Shanghai Tourism Administrative Committee stated that 'these specialized museums, intended to introduce the industries to the public, are expected to become tourist attractions in the coming years' (*China Daily* 2002).

The Tobacco Museum is emblematic of these industrial museums. Opened in 2004, financed and managed by the powerful national tobacco lobby, this Museum portrays the tobacco industry as a pillar of the Chinese economic system and, intriguingly, as a symbol of national culture.

---

2 Tea Museum, Hangzhou, Zhejiang Province. Visited in April 2006.

Since 1949, the Communist government's monopoly of tobacco has provided this sector with an enormous protected domestic market; as Museum panels put it, 'after 1949, the tobacco industry acquired a new life'.[3] Today, tobacco production is a flourishing industry,[4] aiming to 'satisfy the needs of 300 million consumers'. The displays at the Tobacco Museum make a link between smoking and charismatic smokers, including prominent political and intellectual personalities such as Mao Zedong, Deng Xiaoping and the writer Lu Xun. Smoking is so intimately associated with politics and power that, until 1984, a Beijing factory produced high quality cigars exclusively for members of the government. Exhibitions at the Tobacco Museum strive to depict the tobacco industry as a goodwill benefactor. Visibility is given to the charitable activities carried out by the sector's industries: providing assistance to developing countries, contributions to medical research, poverty alleviation, education programmes and suchlike. The rationale behind such initiatives is synthesised in one of the Museum's panels: the 'tobacco industry can bring profits to both the country and the people and is congenial to national conditions'. By asserting that 'tobacco has integrated with Chinese traditional culture, leading to the birth of the rich and colorful tobacco culture', the exhibition frames the production and consumption of tobacco as 'cultural' activities. This discourse shifts emphasis away from health concerns linked to smoking and inscribes it in the framework of Chinese national identity.

The Shanghai Museum of Public Security provides an example of a museum devoted to a national service. The Museum portrays the history of the public security service, its social function and the moral values that inspire it. In the introductory panels, one can read:

> Shanghai public security organs, relying on the broad masses of the people, successfully waged arduous struggles against enemy agents, spies and all types of criminals eradicated every description of vile social evils left over from the old society and endured the smooth progress of the socialist revolution and construction.[5]

This statement sets the tone of the exhibition: an efficient police service is regarded as a condition upon which to build a safe society. A section of the exhibition is devoted to public security officers who lost their lives in service. Personal belongings are exhibited as symbols of authority: uniforms, whistles, white gloves and badges are part of the paraphernalia designed to move the visitor and elicit feelings of admiration. Police officers are elevated to the status of national heroes; exhibition texts use the term 'martyrs'. The display also includes pictures of formally attired policemen on a new bridge in Shanghai; another photograph shows the same policemen on a concrete square against a background of skyscrapers. These images convey ideas of modernity, social utility and efficiency. The exhibition omits any reference to widespread corruption and the mistreatment and abuse perpetrated by police, especially during the Cultural Revolution. By framing police officers as indispensable social actors, and by depicting them as model citizens (and, in some cases, national heroes), the Museum of Public Security unfolds a hagiography of authority: police forces implement the law and provide a safe and ordered society, thereby playing a pivotal role in the Communist social project.

3 The quotes in this paragraph refer to the Tobacco Museum, Shanghai. Last visited in May 2012.
4 Museum labels report that one-third of the world's tobacco is produced in China.
5 Shanghai Museum of Public Security. Last visited in July 2004.

The Bank Museum provides another example of how public services are used in narratives of nation-building. Created in 1998 by the Industrial and Commercial Bank of China (ICBC) – one of the largest corporate banks in the world, backed by the Chinese government – the Bank Museum illustrates the development of financial activities in China with a special focus on Shanghai. Strategically located in the Pudong area, the financial core of the city, the Museum's mission is 'to report the lagging, humiliation, and advancing the glorious bank history'.[6] Exhibitions illustrate the development of financial activities from the 'credit enterprise in Chinese late feudal society', to the rise of a bourgeois class, and the subsequent commercial and financial buoyancy of the 1920s and 1930s. The Chinese banking system's difficulties in the 1940s are linked to the rule of the Kuomintang, which 'deprived people of their wealth through the reform of money system in 1948'. The advent of the Communist Party is seen as a turning point, introducing the reforms that led to the modernisation and success of the Chinese banking system. Exhibitions at the Bank Museum include a section devoted to coins and paper money. The banknotes issued by the Communist government after 1949 are particularly interesting for their patriotic and propagandistic themes. In addition to the portrait of Mao Zedong, workers and peasants labouring for the nation are the main subjects represented. Banknotes depicting a woman driving a tractor allude to the centrality of agriculture and the peasant class, while acknowledging women's role in agriculture and highlighting the mechanisation of rural activities. Another common theme for banknote images is technology: boats, bridges and aeroplanes celebrate the country's technological achievements.

The Post Museum in Shanghai is another example of a service museum. The opening panels announce that the exhibitions show 'the historical path that the Shanghai Post Party Committee had taken to lead the direction of the post workers' revolution, the contribution to our early revolution leaders to the birth of the People's Republic of China'.[7] The narrative emerging from the Museum's texts echoes the Marxist–Leninist evolutionary theory: 'the system of post station, starting from the ancient slave society and prevailing through the feudal dynasties played a non-replaceable function in the course of history'. The postal service is framed 'as part of the social infrastructure and national communication service administration', while postage stamps 'showcase the profound Chinese culture background'. The modernisation of the postal system is presented as a token of the country's modernisation.

Other museums devoted to industrial or service sectors include the China Fire Museum in Beijing, the Beijing Car Museum, the Shanghai Museum of Glass (all opened in 2011), the China National Film Museum (opened in Beijing in 2007) and the China Dairy Museum (opened in Shanghai in 2001); this list is by no means exhaustive. Representations in these museums point to narratives of modernity understood as a civic project – a modernity translated into efficiency of services and expansion of the possibilities of production and consumption.

EXHIBITING THE FUTURE: MUSEUMS OF SCIENCE AND TECHNOLOGY

The narratives of modernity presented in industrial and service museums take on futuristic tones in museums of science and technology, where descriptions and images of possible futures for the Chinese nation are unfolded before visitors' eyes. In the museums considered up to this point,

6   All quotes in this paragraph refer to the Bank Museum, Shanghai. Last visited in August 2004.
7   All quotes in this paragraph refer to the Post Museum, Shanghai. Last visited in May 2006.

Fig 8.1. The majestic entrance to the Shanghai Science and Technology Museum.

representations of the Chinese nation revolve around its past, its cultural heritage and present achievements. However, narratives may also be framed by a different discourse, centred not on the past but on the future. Among the museum categories that best illustrate such future-oriented discourses are museums of science and technology.

In contemporary China, museums of science and technology have overshadowed their fore-runners, museums of natural history and natural sciences. As recently as 2006, at the Museum of Natural History in Shanghai, one could read 'this exhibition hall was first established in 1972. As we are limited by time, ability and financial capacity the exhibition might have many short comings. Therefore we will be very grateful to those who will give us good opinions.'

The new China Science and Technology Museum opened in Beijing in September 2009. Symbolically, the museum is located in the Olympic Park, not far from the Olympic Stadium, in an area visually and materially removed from the ancient character of the Chinese capital. The introductory panels describe the Museum as 'a large scale science popularization facility for the implementation of the national strategy of invigorating the country through science and educa-tion and strengthening the comprehensive national power of the country by relying on talented people as well as for the enhancement of the scientific literacy of the general public'. Consistent with such a nationalistic tone, one of the main permanent galleries, entitled *The Glory of China* and devoted to the main inventions and discoveries contributed by China to the world, opens with a large photo of Hu Jintao at the Museum, surrounded by children (including some in ethnic minority costumes), the children wear the red neckerchief symbolising membership of the Communist Party.

The Shanghai Science and Technology Museum (SSTM)[8] is another prominent museum in this category. Inaugurated in 2001, the Museum focuses on the themes of information technology, robotics and science, which are made accessible to the wider, non-specialist public; school groups are prime target audiences. Through interactive tools, simulations and the latest technological devices, displays explain basic scientific principles and allow the observation of natural science phenomena, such as the geological structure of the Earth or aspects of astrophysics. While exhibitions offer education in an entertaining and interactive way, they also serve to showcase the country's achievements in the domains of science and technology. For instance, the activities of Chinese scientists in the aerospace industry are emphasised, particularly in regard to space missions.

The Shanghai Children's Museum offers similar science-oriented content and narratives, but adapted to younger audiences. The Museum focuses on Chinese accomplishments in the domains of astronomy and space sciences. Aerospace expeditions are imbued with patriotic undertones through photo displays of prominent Chinese political figures officially congratulating astronauts. The Museum's permanent exhibition closes with a panel stating 'in order to meet the space time [sic], it is necessary to train a new generation with strong constitution, wide range of knowledge, to create more brilliant achievements. Our country places hopes on you!'[9] Similarly, the postal worker and the police officer, the scientist and the astronaut are portrayed as national heroes, as 'model citizens' that the younger generation are encouraged to admire and emulate.

The narrative tone is similar at the Shanghai Urban Planning Exhibition Center, a futuristic building on the main Shanghai square. The Exhibition Center opened in 1999 to enhance and celebrate the city's 'modern' character. Objects are relatively scant at the Exhibition Center; interactive screens and video projections portray the city of Shanghai's development, from the opening of the port to foreign trade in 1843, to the contemporary city's 'highly technological urban sites':[10] the Stadium, the Central Library, the Grand Theatre, the Shanghai Museum and the Science and Technology Museum. The exhibition also strives to improve the historic image of Shanghai. Since the early 1920s, the city had become famous as the Asian centre of gambling, dubious trade, criminality and forbidden pleasures. Today, the exhibition explains:

> The education in patriotism, collectivism, and socialism is becoming ever popular in Shanghai residents. A mass movement to promote socialist culture and ideology is going on through the city and many outstanding individuals and model workers have appeared. There is a notable improvement in social conduct and cultural life of Shanghai people.

Thus rehabilitated, the city of Shanghai can now claim a first-rank position among Chinese cities, as well as a grand future: 'By the year 2020, Shanghai will have become a world-class metropolis and an international center of economy, finance and trade […] The city will emerge as a regional

---

8   Shanghai Science and Technology Museum. Visited in September 2004.
9   Shanghai Children's Museum. Last visited in September 2004.
10 Unless stated otherwise, all quotes in this paragraph are related to the Shanghai Urban Planning Exhibition Center. Last visited in July 2004.

center of shipping, manufacturing, service and technology, and a sparkling pearl on the Western coast of the Pacific.' The point that the Shanghai Urban Planning Exhibition Center clearly puts across is that, now rid of old vices and reshaped by new technologies, Shanghai can legitimately aspire to represent China and the Chinese in the world – a role that Shanghai has already proved itself fit to play on the occasion of the World Expo 2010.

The museums discussed in this section, depicting the Chinese nation from cultural, industrial, scientific and technological perspectives, demonstrate that, once couched in national narratives, everyday and mundane objects – such as silk fabrics, tea implements, smoking pipes, police whistles and postage stamps – may be transformed into national tokens. While this chapter has focused on the 'civic' element of national narratives – through emphasis on the Han Chinese cultural heritage, the productive forces of the industry and service sectors, and science and technology – the next two chapters will be devoted to an analysis of the ethnic components of the Chinese nation and their representation in museums.

9

The Museum Representation of Ethnic Minorities

This chapter considers the relevance of ethnic minorities in discourses on Chinese national identity and explores the representation of Chinese ethnic groups in museums. The Chinese expression used to designate ethnic groups is *shaoshu minzu*, which literally means 'minority nationality' or 'national minority'. The term *shao* is a diminutive; it may refer to a small number and/or small size. *Minzu* also appears in the official denomination of China as a 'unified, multinational state', *duominzu guojia*, literally a 'country with many nationalities'. The term *minzu* is laden with political significance. As the historian of China Frank Dikötter (1996, 594) notes, 'The conflation of "race", descent and nation has been expressed throughout the twentieth century by the term *minzu*, signifying both a descent group and a cultural community.' Moreover, it should not be overlooked that the term 'ethnic minority' (*minzu*) defines a group by means of its relative, subaltern position to another group. Bearing these terminological nuances in mind, the expressions 'ethnic minorities', 'ethnic groups' and 'nationalities' are here used interchangeably for the sake of simplicity and to conform with their use in museum texts in China.

The Official Discourse About Ethnic Minorities

Ethnic groups occupy a central position in the representation of the Chinese nation. The opening ceremony of the 2008 Beijing Olympic Games, with its emphasis on the performances of the various ethnic groups, provided a powerful illustration of China's 'unity within diversity'.

The problematic integration of Chinese ethnic minorities in the national framework reveals the difficulties inherent in China's transition from the multicultural dimension of a millennial empire to the logic of a modern nation-state needing to cement its citizenship basis. As Prasenjit Duara (2002, xiv) has noted, 'it is China as a modern nation-state that undertook the most unprecedented measures to homogenize and standardize the population'. Indeed, China presents a unique history of internal colonisation, understood as a gradual process of cultural assimilation of the peoples inhabiting its peripheral regions. As a former empire, China is in essence multicultural, but this has not hindered the elaboration of a cohesive narrative of the Chinese nation and the formulation of ethnic policies aimed at containing, domesticating and integrating ethnic groups into the national mould.

Such policies date back to the early years of the People's Republic of China. In 1953, the Chinese government initiated a project to register the ethnic groups inhabiting the Chinese territory. To date, 56 nationalities have been officially recognised, the Han representing the vast majority of the population (over 90 per cent) (C Wang 2004, 6). The identification of ethnic groups was made following Stalin's definition of nationality, that is, a group that shares 'territory, language, economy and psychological nature' (Harrell 1995, 23). Once thus identified, ethnic groups were classified according to their stage of development (primitive, slave, feudal or capitalist). Five provinces – Guangxi, Xinjiang, Tibet, Inner Mongolia and Ningxia – enjoy the status of 'autonomous regions' in consideration of their substantial ethnic populations.

The cultural rights of ethnic groups are formally enshrined in the Chinese Constitution,[1] which also defines China as a 'unified, multinational state' (*duominzu guojia*), the nationalities of which 'consider themselves as descendants of common ancestors and members of the same big community' (Fei 1979, 3). This narrative maintains that 'from earliest antiquity China has been a united country made up of people of many different nationalities, who have worked together to develop its resources and create a civilization that is as rich as it is ancient' (Museums Department of the State Administrative Bureau of Museums and Archaeological Data 1980, 174). These formulations conflate two sets of contrasting arguments that inform Chinese discourse on ethnic minorities: on the one hand, the continuity and unity of the Chinese nation – epitomised by the common descent and the belonging to the same 'big family' – are emphasised, and on the other, ethnic diversity is only partially embraced. Official rhetoric[2] advocates the inclusion of ethnic minorities in the nation, while flattening their cultural difference. Ethnic minorities are presented as inferior to the Han majority. Dikötter (1996, 598) explains:

> 'national minorities' are represented as less evolved branches of people who need the moral and political guidance of the 'Han' in order to ascend on the scales of civilization. The representation of the 'Han' as a more highly evolved and better endowed nation-race has generally increased within popular culture, scientific circles and government publications in the Deng Xiaoping era.

It follows that the purpose of central government policies has been to 'free' ethnic minorities from their backward social structures through education programmes and development plans. This process has been described as 'internal colonialism' (Jonsson 2000, 74) – indicating the civilising mission that Chinese central authorities claim to perform towards minorities – and 'Chinese Orientalism', implying varying amounts of exoticisation (Gladney 1994) and essentialisation (Dahl and Stade 2000, 159) of ethnic groups.

Ethnic groups are identified by contrast to the Han majority (cf Jonsson 2000, 60). Indeed, 'like gender – nationality is a relational term whose identity derives from its inherence in a system of differences' (Parker quoted in Gladney 1994, 93). In the same vein, Hjorleifur Jonsson (2000, 62), referring to a case study of the Yao minority, maintains that 'the practices of difference

---

[1] In Article 4: 'All nationalities in the People's Republic of China are equal. The State protects the lawful rights and interests of the minority nationalities and upholds and develops a relationship of equality, unity and mutual assistance among all of China's nationalities. Discrimination against and oppression of any nationality are prohibited; any act which undermines the unity of the nationalities or instigates division is prohibited.

The State assists areas inhabited by minority nationalities in accelerating their economic and cultural development according to the characteristics and needs of the various minority nationalities.

Regional autonomy is practised in areas where people of minority nationalities live in concentrated communities; in these areas organs of self-government are established to exercise the power of autonomy. All national autonomous areas are integral parts of the People's Republic of China.

All nationalities have the freedom to use and develop their own spoken and written languages and to preserve or reform their own folkways and customs.'

[2] The expression 'official rhetoric' refers to the narratives on ethnic minorities emerging from museum texts, specialised publications and statements of public officials or scholars.

have been increasingly erased but their markers are sanctioned by the state's agents, in relation to national identity'. While the homogeneity of the Han majority is in itself disputable – 'Han' being an umbrella term including peoples of diverse languages, cultures and ethnicities (see Mullaney *et al* 2012) – Han culture and civilisation are invoked as a reference model. As Dru Gladney (1994, 93) notes, 'the homogenization of the majority [is made] at the expense of the exoticized minority'. This implies that the construction of the minority is instrumental to the construction of the image of the Han majority, and ultimately of the Chinese nation. As Jonsson (2000, 68) sums it up, 'the nation and the minority are mutually constitutive'.

Yet, it is important to point out that while the Communist government did not grant ethnic minorities the right to self-determination, neither did it pursue fully a policy of assimilation. Rather, the politics of cultural difference took a third approach, based on a temporary 'tolerance' and a selective celebration of ethnic minorities' cultural differences. In an effort to make sense of this move, some scholars have suggested that the ethnic policies of Communist China actually renewed the ideological basis of the empire. Magnus Fiskesjö (2006, 15, 28) holds that:

> [The] new China is also a new formulation of the imperial Chinese model, which resurrects the corollary idea of civilisation as a transformative force that requires a primitive, backward periphery as its object [...] Imperial tradition favoured the explicit recognition of 'ethnic minorities', formulated as 'barbarians' (that is, as a limit figure which simultaneously represents the threat which justifies imperial power, and serves as its favourite object of benevolent tutelage and civilising).

From this perspective then, the construction of the ethnic minority as 'backward' and peripheral is instrumental to the production of the Han as 'central' and 'modern'. In museum displays of ethnic minorities, it is possible to locate a tension between 'China the nation-state', and 'China the empire' – and by extension, a tension between the unity and the cultural diversity of the Chinese nation. The repeated clashes between members of ethnic minorities and the Han majority – such as the Uyghur anti-government riots in 2009 and 2012 (*The Guardian* 2012) are manifestations of such tension.

The opening of the Tibet Museum in Lhasa in October 1999 (to mark the 50th anniversary of the People's Republic of China and the 40th anniversary of Tibet's annexation to China), and of other museums in similarly politically unstable areas such as Xinjiang (where the Ili Kazak Autonomous Prefecture Museum was inaugurated in 2004) and Inner Mongolia (where the Museum of the Xinjiang-Uyghur Autonomous Region opened in 2004) (*China Heritage Newsletter* 2005b), indicates that ethnic minority museums in China are symbolically powerful sites of cultural appropriation. Ethnic museums also serve the purpose of making visible the political authority and the glorious narratives of the Chinese state where these most need to be enforced. As Harrell (1995, 7) points out, the implementation of the Chinese government's 'civilising project' entails that 'the civilizing center, in its formulation of its project, needs to develop formal knowledge of the other and of itself'. It is precisely in light of this need that one can fully appreciate the role of museums as privileged loci for the interpretation of ethnic minorities' cultures, and the dissemination of images and narratives aiming to objectify and standardise the ethnic 'Other'.

Narratives of Inclusion and Exclusion in Ethnic Minority Displays

In the postcolonial era, a self-reflective museology has emerged at an international level as a critique of hegemonic practices of cultural representation. These works have highlighted museums' potential to foster social inclusion and intercultural dialogue. Indeed, in the postcolonial period, ethnic groups and source communities have been increasingly involved in the representation and reinterpretation of their own cultural heritage (Golding 2009; Peers and Brown 2003; Simpson 1996).

Acting as both a 'differentiating machine' and a 'facilitator of cross-cultural exchange' (Bennett 2006a, 59), museums have the potential to transform cultural difference from a problem into a resource and from a barrier into a link, making cultures mutually intelligible. However, to this end the prior recognition of cultural difference is essential; the non-denial of difference is necessary in order to engage with it. This is not quite the case in Chinese museums.

Mieke Bal (1996, 3) notes that the act of display creates a subject/object dichotomy that 'enables the subject to make a statement about the object'. This observation is a valuable starting point for the analysis of museum representations of ethnic minorities in China. Here, the voices of ethnic groups are marginal, if not absent, from museum displays. The minority tale is not an emanation of the minority itself, nor is it the fruit of a collaborative project. Rather, it is the unilateral vision of a group of actors – Chinese public authorities – mediated by the museum.

Drawing from Benedict Anderson's seminal theory (1991), a parallel can be drawn between the public press and museums in China. Like the press, museums enable us to imagine the nation and its collectivity; for instance, they make it possible for a Han Chinese from Beijing, who has never visited southern Yunnan, to imagine the Dai ethnic group inhabiting this area, as well as their relationship with the other ethnic groups and with the Han majority. Through specific narratives and display techniques, museums contribute to the objectification of ethnic minorities' cultures and to their subordination to the Han Chinese majority. Through a purposeful threading of exhibits, texts and exhibitionary techniques, museums construct ethnic minorities as passive, inert objects that can be arbitrarily interpreted and 'narrated'.

Interestingly, in China, ethnic minority material is rarely displayed in museums of anthropology or ethnographic museums; museums of this kind are relatively scant in the country.[3] Rather, exhibits pertaining to ethnic minorities feature in a broad range of exhibitions which may be framed by historical, artistic, anthropological or scientific exhibition approaches.

Three main sites of display and modes of contextualisation of ethnic minority artefacts can be identified. Firstly, ethnic minority objects feature in displays of national or local history and culture; in such instances the artefacts are presented as 'attributes' of the Chinese nation. This is the case at the Shanghai Museum, which aims to showcase the most prominent cultural artefacts of Chinese culture and which displays ethnic costumes next to 'traditional' Chinese arts and antiquities such as Shang and Zhou bronzes, Buddhist sculpture, calligraphy, paintings, coins, jades and ceramics. Similarly, the Museum of the University of Sichuan in Chengdu, which focuses on the history and culture of the province, exhibits material culture of ethnic minorities next to archaeological finds, Qing furniture and items from the imperial collections.

---

[3]   Among the most prominent museums of anthropology in China are the Museum of the University of Xiamen and the Museum of the University of Yunnan.

Alternatively, ethnic minority material culture features in museums, ecomuseums and 'ethnic parks' (mostly at a provincial level) specifically aiming to showcase ethnic cultures framed as tourist attractions. This is the case for the Yunnan Nationalities Museum in Kunming and the Ethnic Minorities Park, an open-air museum in Beijing that provides an overview of Chinese ethnic groups, including reconstructions of traditional dwellings, dance performances and craft demonstrations.

Lastly, ethnic minority artefacts can be found in university museums, where they are presented as objects of study. Minzu Museum, Minzu University of China in Beijing and the corresponding museums in Sichuan (the Museum of the Southwest University for Nationalities, Chengdu) and Yunnan (the Museum of Anthropology of the Yunnan University and the Museum of the University of Ethnic Minorities, both in Kunming) illustrate this approach.

Regardless of the typology of museums in which ethnic minority objects are exhibited, visitors to these museums might be struck by the relative homogeneity of displays. In Beijing as in Shanghai, in Chengdu as in Kunming, in ethnic parks as in university museums, ethnic minorities are represented through arrays of colourful ethnic costumes, textiles, embroideries, cooking and smoking tools and musical instruments. The great attention paid to costumes and textiles in exhibitions can be better understood in light of the historical social significance of textiles in China. A historian of Chinese textiles, Valery Garrett (1994, xiii), explains that since the Zhou Dynasty (1046–256 BC), dress codes have expressed social status and position in China. The artistic and technical qualities of garments are presented as tokens of ethnic minorities' cultures: 'customs and conventions, art traditions, religious beliefs, ways of lives and the alike are all represented to some extent by the costumes and accoutrements of various minorities. [...] China's ethnic costumes are more than just a material system of culture. They have a spiritual resonance' (Beijing Institute of Clothing Technology n.d., Prologue). Ethnic minority artefacts are thus presented as indexes of traditions, skills and craftsmanship and, ultimately, of the ethnic group itself. The visitor is told that a certain ethnic group wears a certain kind of clothes, consumes a certain kind of food and is 'good at' a certain kind of music, dance or performance. Overall, it is emphasised that all Chinese ethnic groups are equal, actively contributing to the prosperity of the country and living in harmony, somewhere far away. By establishing cross-cutting associations among items of different ethnic groups, museum displays create a framework for comparison and hierarchisation. Forcing cultural variation into pre-established object categories equals forcing difference into ideological moulds, uniforming and ultimately domesticating it. In short, focusing exclusively on material culture, essentialising and folklorising ethnic groups, museum displays reduce cultural complexity to its minimum terms, reinforcing through reiteration the reductive association between objects and ethnic groups.

As mentioned earlier, official rhetoric about the ethnic composition of the Chinese nation revolves around the themes of inclusion and diversity; museum representations of ethnic minorities are pivotal loci to substantiate and disseminate such rhetoric. But how are such ideas and concepts actually translated into museum exhibitions? Through what kind of narratives and displays techniques? Analysis of ethnic minority displays points to a set of narratives and display techniques that reveal how museums approach ethnicity and cultural difference in contemporary China.

CO-OPTING THE ETHNIC OTHER

In line with official discourse that postulates the formal equality of all ethnic minorities, museum exhibitions assert ethnic minorities' status as Chinese citizens through a discourse centred on the notion of inclusion of ethnic groups in the Chinese nation. The theme of inclusion is pervasive in politically and visually prominent sites such as the Cultural Palace of Nationalities, in Beijing. The Palace is one of the *Shi Da Jianzhu*, the 'Ten Great Buildings' created in 1959 to celebrate the tenth anniversary of the People's Republic of China. The institution is a centre for the study, display and celebration of minority cultures; it aims to show how ethnic groups 'come together for cultural exchange' in a 'microcosm of the greater family of diverse peoples that make up China' (Li and Luo 2004, 40). A 1958 State Council circular entitled 'Artifacts and Books for the Exhibition at the Cultural Palace of Nationalities' (quoted in Hung 2012, 582) reveals the political objectives of this institution:

> The main purpose of the museum and the library – the two key components of the Palace – was to propagate the great victory of the Party's ethnic policies and the extraordinary results of its ethnicity projects in the last ten years [...] Through exhibited objects and books, we educate various nationalities in matters of patriotism and internationalism in order to consolidate the unification of the motherland, enhance the unity of nationalities, and strengthen socialist education.

The theme of ethnic minority inclusion in the national mould is similarly a prime concern at the Beijing Institute of Clothing Technology, where ethnic costumes are presented as 'not just part of our national culture, they are a pure form of folk art [...] these costumes are China's national treasures'. This presentation is situated within a broader discourse extolling China's ethnic and cultural diversity: 'China is a multi-ethnic country, and during its long history of social progression each ethnic people has developed its own unique cultural traditions' (Beijing Institute of Clothing Technology n.d., Prologue).

Until the late 2000s, when the Kadoorie Gallery of Chinese Minority Nationalities was revamped, the Shanghai Museum explicitly endorsed the themes of unity and diversity of the Chinese nation. The introductory panel to the gallery originally stated:

> Our splendid and glorious Chinese civilization is the result of the assimilation of various nationalities that have lived in China. Due to varying social conditions and means of livelihood, the different nationalities in China have developed quite diverse cultures. The unique features of each culture are best expressed through their decorative arts. The numerous different artifacts, often magnificently coloured, exhibit diverse skills and reflect the flavour of each culture's rich and varied lifestyle. The unusual and original arts and crafts of minority cultures have made great contribution to the culture and art of the Chinese nation.

Here, in tune with the Marxist–Leninist theory of evolution, the cultural diversity of ethnic minorities is causally linked to their different stage of development, of which material culture (and notably, decorative arts) is considered to be evidence. Consistently, panels even in the refurbished gallery state that 'metalwork reflects an ethnic group's level of scientific and technological skill'. Interestingly, the introductory text at the Shanghai Museum was subsequently rewritten in a much-diluted ideological and nationalistic tone following the renovation of the gallery.[4]

Historical inclusion is attained through the inscription of ethnic minorities into Chinese history. This strategy is pursued through the representation of harmonious relations between government officials and members of ethnic minorities. For instance, at the Yunnan Museum of Nationalities, the exhibition *Social Forms, Reform and Development of Yunnan Ethnic Minorities*, on display until 2006,[5] included propagandistic museum texts explaining how 'since 1949, under the leadership of the Communist Party of China all the nationalities of Yunnan Province have turned to be masters of their own destiny and stepped into Socialism together'. In the same exhibition, the visitor could see life-size sculptures depicting officials from the People's Liberation Army (the military body of the Communist Party) being warmly greeted by members of ethnic minorities during the Long March.[6]

Similarly, at the Museum of the University of Ethnic Minorities in Kunming, a large wall painting depicts members of the People's Liberation Army being welcomed by an exultant crowd in a village in southern Yunnan. By materialising the positive role of ethnic minorities in the revolutionary cause and in the making of the Chinese nation, these fictional scenes aim to strengthen the civic bond between ethnic minorities and the Chinese government. At the same time, by providing a visual representation of harmonious inter-ethnic relations – where no reference is made to hierarchies among groups, discrimination, tensions or conflicts – they also ease the imagination, in Anderson's sense (1991), of the multicultural Chinese nation.

Similar narratives of integration appear in a catalogue of the National Museum of Chinese History, where ethnic groups are described as 'inhabiting the peripheral areas of the Central Plains, with which they gradually merged and mingled' (National Museum of Chinese History 2002, 57). Within the same line of text and with reference to the role of ethnic minorities during the Tang Dynasty (AD 618–906), the museum catalogue reports that 'the minorities assimilated

---

[4] During my last visit, in May 2012, the introductory panel read: 'China has had a long and established history as well as a multi-ethnic culture. As a result of the ecological environments, their ways of living, and the differences in customs, each ethnic group has its own unique culture. The arts and crafts that are produced reflect each ethnic group's history and identity. These works were not only made from a multitude of materials but were also crafted using a variety of techniques. In addition to their aesthetic functions, they also served pragmatic use as well. The works produced by China's ethnic minorities contribute an exotic flavour to the whole of Chinese art.'

Another version of this text, similar to the original but diluted in its Marxist–Leninist and nationalistic content, still features in the visitor leaflets available at the entrance of the Museum's gallery. This version reads: 'China is a large country consisting of 56 ethnic groups of people. Various ethnical [sic] civilizations and cultures have assimilated each other and bring forward the splendid Chinese culture. Costumes of these ethnic peoples, as symbols of their cultures, vary greatly in material, design, color, style and associated ornaments with their different ways of life, modes of production, religious faiths, aesthetic standards and geographic environments. Beautiful textiles with woven, printed or embroidered designs and distinctive artifacts such as metal ware, lacquer ware, pottery, masks and carved and knitted works are the reflection of people's wisdom in art creation, skills of craftmanship and deep love for life.' (Shanghai Museum leaflet, collected in May 2012.)

[5] Yunnan Nationalities Museum, exhibition *Social Forms, Reform and Development of Yunnan Ethnic Minorities*, visited in May 2006. For a comprehensive discussion of the original exhibition see Wu (2011, 221ff).

[6] The expression 'Long March' refers to the series of battles initiated in 1934 between supporters of the Communist Party and the Chinese Nationalist Party (Kuomintang) which led to the establishment of the Communist Party as the main political force under the leadership of a young Mao Zedong.

Fig 9.1. Mural depicting Chinese nationalities at the Minzu Museum, Minzu University of China, Beijing.

the advanced economy and culture of the Han' (ibid, 116). Consistently, the Ancient China permanent gallery of the National Museum of China (successor to the National Museum of Chinese History) emphasises the topic of the harmonious coexistence of ethnic groups. The gallery strives to convey the idea (reiterated in several museum panels) that China has always been a multinational country and that all ethnicities have contributed, equally and peacefully, to the making of China.

The rhetoric of inclusion is not, however, confined to the past. It also appears in the present through the theme of civic inclusion expressed by the notion of 'nationalities unity' (*minzu tuanjie*). This is epitomised by the metaphor of the 'Chinese big family', whereby ethnic minorities allegedly 'consider themselves as descendants of common ancestors and members of the same big community' (Fei 1979, 3). The opening panels at the Minzu Museum, Minzu University of China in Beijing eloquently illustrate this idea: 'China is a unified multi-ethnic country. Its fifty-six nationalities and their forebears are of one great cultural tradition, and they have formed a diligent, intelligent and peace-loving Chinese nation.'[7]

One of the most visually powerful ways in which museum displays communicate notions of the unity and equality of all ethnic minorities is by juxtaposing similar items of ethnic minority material culture in such a way that invites comparison, while at the same time containing the potential for variation. For example, at Yunnan University's Anthropology Museum, the Yunnan Nationalities Museum, the Minzu Museum, Minzu University of China in Beijing, the Sichuan University Museum and the Museum of the Southwest University for Nationalities in Chengdu,

7   Museum panels, Minzu Museum, Minzu University of China, Beijing.

visitors are consistently presented with arrays of mannequins dressed in ethnic minority costumes, juxtapositions of musical instruments, or of cooking vessels. Establishing material and aesthetic analogies across items of ethnic minority material culture is implicitly meant to reinforce the rhetoric of national unity and feelings of 'belonging' to the Chinese nation.

Narratives of inclusion of ethnic minorities feed on the metaphor of the 'Chinese big family', which is central to Chinese nationalist rhetoric. Such a metaphor is often translated in museum displays through the medium of wall paintings and murals. Large wall paintings featuring different ethnic groups can be seen in the Minzu Museum, Minzu University of China in Beijing, the Yunnan Nationalities Museum, the Museum of the University of Ethnic Minorities in Kunming, or the Mengle Museum in Jinghong, located in Xishuanbanna in southern Yunnan. These paintings usually depict members (mostly female) of ethnic groups immersed in lush natural environments in the context of creation myths, or happily tending to everyday activities such as agriculture, embroidery or paper-making.

These depictions are reminiscent of the notion of assemblage elaborated by Tony Bennett. Bennett (2008, 7) suggests that museums operate as 'sites of assemblage, bringing together varied objects, practices and persons'. Museums can do this because of their 'capacity, through the studied manipulation of the relations between people and things in a custom-built environment, to produce new entities that can be mobilized – both within the museum and outside it – in social and civic programmes of varied kinds' (Bennett 2005, 525). Wall paintings enable the depiction of friendly and harmonious relationships among ethnic groups, and between ethnic groups and the Han majority.

MINORITIES AND HIERARCHY

As a corollary to the theme of inclusion, one can identify in Chinese museums the theme of subordination of ethnic minorities to the Han majority (see also Gladney 2004). Despite the emphasis of ethnic minorities' equal status within official discourse, not all groups are represented in museum exhibitions, nor are they equally represented. Some ethnic minorities, for instance the Naxi, Dai and Miao, appear widely.[8] The Miao in particular, are the iconic ethnic minority: their spectacular silver headdresses and body ornaments have become a trademark of displays

---

8   Members of the Naxi ethnic group mostly inhabit the area of Lijiang in northern Yunnan. A matrilinear society, the Naxi developed an independent pictographic script, mainly used for religious texts. Naxi women are known for their elaborate clothing, including a sheepskin cape embroidered with seven stars, which often features in museum displays. The Dai ethnic group is predominantly located in the southern areas of Yunnan. The influence of Thai culture – to which the Dai culture is closely related – is present in Dai language, architecture, food, clothing and religion (most Dai people are Theravada Buddhists). Since the late 1990s, Xishuanbanna, the area of Yunnan inhabited by the Dai, has become a major tourist attraction for wealthy coastal Chinese. The Miao is an ethnic group that mainly inhabits the mountainous province of Guizhou in southern China. The Miao are immediately recognisable by their extraordinarily rich costumes, including complex embroideries and elaborate silver headdresses and personal adornments. In contrast to the Naxi, Dai and Miao, the Hui ethnic group is less visually prominent – members of the Hui are hardly distinguishable from the Han majority – and much less 'exotic'. In recent years, members of the Hui ethnic group have been involved in violent clashes with Han Chinese due to social discrimination and demands for autonomous rule in Hui areas. For an overview of Chinese ethnic minority cultures, see Mackerras (2003).

of ethnic minorities in Chinese museums. Conversely, others, such as the Hui, are relatively under-represented in museum displays. The reasons for such different treatment revolve around notions of cultural and geographical distance, spectacular costumes and plain exoticism. Susan Blum (2001, 142–3) explains that 'the Hui, like the Tibetan, are salient because they are a source of uncertainty and discomfort, but they are scarcely typical', while 'for accessible and positively-valued typicality, one must look to the more 'docile' nationalities, such as the home-grown Naxi, Yi, or Bai'.

References to the alleged cultural and technological inferiority of ethnic minorities vis-à-vis the Han majority are a recurrent element in museum representations. This is mostly the by-product of the evolutionist theories of social development embraced by the Communist Party. Museum texts and displays hint at the subaltern status of minorities through references to the 'traditional' modes of production 'still' in use among minorities. At the Yunnan Nationalities Museum, one can read that 'science and technology are an indication of human civilisation and progress [...] to our amazement, even until today when science and technology are well developed, some traditional techniques [...] still exist among the people of Yunnan'. In the same vein, traditional manual techniques of oil-pressing and paper-making are openly defined as 'comparatively primitive ones'. Consistently, the modes of transport and lifestyles of minorities are often described as 'a treasure house of the evolution of farming' and tagged as 'an integral page of the history of science and technology of the Chinese nation'.[9] These texts reveal a Marxist–Leninist vision of society, and at the same time contribute to normalising unequal social relations. The unequal status of ethnic minorities in relation to each other and their collective subordination to the Han majority emerge from a system of related narratives which, taken together, are meant to reveal the degree of 'backwardness' of each ethnic group. Such narratives revolve around the disruption of temporalities, specific gender construction and the treatment of ethnic minorities as immature and childlike citizens.

The Minority as an Ancient Entity

The representation of ethnic minorities in China is informed by a concern for the 'vanishing', 'traditional', 'authentic' and allegedly 'unspoilt' ethnic 'Other'. As Louisa Schein (1997, 72) has pointed out, 'the suppressions of the Cultural Revolution [...] combined with the perceived emptiness of imported culture from abroad seem to have left a void at the core of Chinese ethno-nationalism, leading individual and state culture producers to turn to minority cultures as reservoirs of still-extant authenticity'.

Defined in museum texts as 'living fossils' (see also Harrell 1995, 16), ethnic minorities are depicted as ancient, almost ageless entities, the history of which has its roots in an undetermined, remote past. Statements such as 'they live here since remote antiquity' (Yunnan Provincial Museum 2001, 4), 'looking at them, you will learn [...] all the things since time immemorial' (Anthropology Museum of Yunnan University, introductory panel) and expressions such as 'in the early days', 'in the past', 'over thousands of years' (Yunnan Nationalities Museum) locate contemporary communities in the historical realm, condemning them to atemporal immobility.

---

[9]   All quotes in this section originate from the text panels of the Yunnan Nationalities Museum. Last visited in April 2008.

This approach is in line with Lewis Henry Morgan's theory of social evolution (1985 [1877]), according to which ethnic minorities can be located at an early phase of development along an evolutionary path leading from primitive to slave, feudal and capitalist societal forms. This construct is particularly intriguing when considering that ethnic minorities are actually denied a historicity of their own: their non-Han, pre-Communist past is dismissed or omitted in displays and thus, in the long term, erased from collective consciousness. For instance, the development of independent scriptural systems among ethnic groups is downplayed and presented as ancillary to Han Chinese culture in the permanent exhibition *Memories of Mankind: Exhibition of Ancient Documents of the Yunnan Ethnic Groups* at the Yunnan Nationalities Museum. Here, museum panels explain that the ancient scriptural systems of the Yao, Zhuang, Bai and Sui ethnic groups of Yunnan were derived from Chinese characters ('by adding or cutting strokes from a Chinese character') as a result of the 'strong influence' of Han Chinese nationality. Moreover, the visitor is reminded of the benevolent, salvaging role of government authorities, as museum texts emphasise that 'the Chinese Communist Party and government have paid a lot of attention to the ancient documents of ethnic peoples since the People's Republic of China was founded in 1949'.

Historical references to events prior to the creation of the People's Republic are dismissed through the use of expressions such as 'dark era' and 'feudal system of oppression'. The existence and recollection of ethnic minorities' pasts are accepted to the extent and on the condition that they support the ethnic minorities' assertions of antiquity, and the longevity and continuity of the Chinese nation. Yet, the same recognition is denied by its main conceptual implication: that ethnic minorities have historically enjoyed varying degrees of cultural independence from the Han Chinese.

The denial of ethnic minorities' historicity is coupled with a corresponding denial of modernity. The consistent representation of minorities as ancient, static entities means that indexes of change and hybridisation are largely overlooked in favour of a crystallised, essentialised image. In texts devoted to ethnic minority cultures, one learns that ethnic minorities enjoy 'ways of life and customs that have changed little for decades or even a century' (C Wang 2004, 4). Museums displays of ethnic minorities usually include a section devoted to 'traditional techniques of production'. Within such displays, the material culture of ethnic minorities is presented as though it is frozen in time: the visitor is led to believe that ethnic groups make daily use of manual mortars and handmade wooden fish-traps, rely on oxen and slash-and-burn farming methods and dwell in bamboo, wooden or clay shelters. What is omitted from the picture are present-day conditions of poverty, illiteracy and discrimination. Ethnic minorities can at best emulate the modernity of the Han; modernity is hardly ever ascribed directly to them. In a striking installation at the Museum of the Southwest University for Nationalities, Chengdu, Sichuan, 56 ethnic groups are represented by small-scale plastic figurines; all nationalities except the Han majority are depicted in their traditional ethnic costumes, while the Han figurine is dressed in blue, workman-style overalls.

As James Clifford (1988, 161) has noted, 'what's different about peoples seen to be moving out of "tradition" into "the modern world" remains tied to inherited structures that either resist or yield to the new but cannot produce it'. While ethnic minority cultures are repeatedly described as 'ancient' and 'traditional', assumptions of the modernity and superiority of Han culture are implicit in museum texts, such as at the Yunnan Nationalities Museum: 'in the past, some ethnic groups in Yunnan Province, paid a lot of attention to learning advanced Chinese Han culture'. In these instances, the representation of ethnic minorities as backward and locked in a 'traditional' world is meant to provide a contrast to the modernity of the Han majority. As Louisa Schein (1997, 90) notes with reference to China, 'in the official regime of representation, that which was excluded from state-defined modernity (i.e., local tradition) was not "disappeared," but rather rendered hyper-visible in order to highlight, by contrast, the civilized character of the state'. In this sense, museum displays help to instantiate the argument that the peripheral, backward minority is instrumental to the construction of the modern Han political and cultural core. More precisely, the narrative constructions about ethnic minorities' 'backwardness' and 'antiquity' have the effect of disrupting temporalities on two levels: firstly, they establish an 'internal temporality' for each ethnic group (through the attribution of a more or less 'backward' position) and, secondly, they transform the 'backwardness' of ethnic minorities into a backdrop for the expression of the modernity of the Han-centred state.

Furthermore, the idea that ethnic minorities are simply 'lagging behind' the Han bears the important conceptual implication of constructing the cultural difference of the ethnic minority as temporary, transient and bound to disappear over time, as the ethnic minority 'evolves' along the path of development to eventually reach the level of the Han. This discourse enables the transposition of cultural difference on a temporal rather than substantial level. In a move not too dissimilar from the one described by Johannes Fabian in *Time and the Other* (1983) – whereby anthropological accounts transpose the object of study to a different temporal level by spatialising time (there is the past, here is the present) – the Chinese government is constructing the 'Otherness' of ethnic minorities as a temporary category. The ethnic minority lives far away, in a there that is past, whereas the Han live in a here that is present and modern.

GENDER CONSTRUCTION: THE MINORITY AS FEMALE

Narratives of the subordination of ethnic minorities to the Han majority also develop around ethnic minorities' gender, and more precisely the construction of ethnic groups as female. Almost invariably, pictorial museum representations of ethnic minorities portray young, attractive women with subdued smiles, wearing colourful clothes (see also Gladney 1994; Harrell 1995). The iconic female minority is embodied by the Dai. For instance, the exhibition on minorities' lifestyles and production methods at the Yunnan Nationalities Museum includes a diorama of a forest environment featuring bare-breasted Dai women. The caption reads, 'a miniature of topographical conditions of Yunnan Province'. The feminisation of minorities is often accompanied, as in this case, by varying degrees of eroticisation; as Dru Gladney (1994, 103) argues, in China, minority women are considered attractive and 'easily accessible'. This kind of representation aims to crystallise a close association between a set of features considered female prerogatives – submission, docility, exoticism, simple-mindedness, inarticulateness, 'closeness to nature' – and the 'character' of ethnic groups, thus contributing to the construction of the ethnic minority as female, as opposed to the Han male (cf Gladney 1994).

REPRESENTING ETHNIC MINORITIES AS CHILDREN

Narratives of subordination also adopt the metaphor of life stages to construct the ethnic minority as a child, with a corollary of condescending and paternalistic approaches (see also Schein 1997, 75). Panels at the Yunnan Nationalities Museum describe members of ethnic groups in these terms: 'brave, intelligent and unsophisticated people [...] working together with diligence and intelligence'. The strategy of infantilisation has intriguing Confucian undertones. By portraying the ethnic minority as a child, the Han assign themselves the role of the knowledgeable, wise, guiding adult. The relationship thus established between the ethnic group and the Han is not simply one of generational disparity, but rather is of the typically Confucian 'father–child', 'master–student' or 'emperor–subject' kind. This brings into play the Confucian moral imperatives of respect for the elderly and for the ritual, which confers moral and philosophical legitimacy to the Han's claims to superiority. Thus, the life stage metaphor is a discursive device that not only enables the transposition of the ethnic group in a different temporal framework, but also facilitates its subordination to the Han.

The image of childhood is complemented by other attributes. Naivety is one of these, as demonstrated by this catalogue text: 'though the living utensils of Yunnan ethnic groups are made primitively, they are the symbol of human developing [sic]: though they are simple, they are full of natural beauty' (Yunnan Provincial Museum 2001, 11). Purity is another attribute commonly associated with minorities. As Susan Blum (2001, 169) notes from her fieldwork experience, 'Han views of ethnicity are visible here: ethnic groups must have a kind of purity of practice, purity of descent, and cultural content. Without these features, the groups may be accused of being jia (false) or kong (empty).'

Closeness to nature is a theme associated with animist beliefs and shamanism, but may also be linked to (and stem from) ideas of naivety and purity. Minorities are often described as having a special relationship with the natural world. It is no accident that minorities are often presented in natural settings. Alternatively, enlarged photos of natural settings are juxtaposed with exhibits to provide contextualisation and to reinforce ideas of ethnic minorities' distance, remoteness, inaccessibility and mystery.

OBJECTIFICATION AND ESSENTIALISATION

Exhibitions of ethnic minorities in China privilege objects rather than intangible cultural aspects of living communities. This is not entirely surprising. The relevance of material culture in contemporary China can be understood as a result of the long-term influence of historical materialism – the search for evidence of theoretical constructions in concrete things – on scientific thought. In that theoretical and ideological framework, material culture is regarded as 'scientific evidence'. It follows that museum catalogues define the 'material forms of nationality culture […] [as] tangible carriers of nationality culture' (Yunnan Provincial Museum 2001, 4). One of the implications of this approach is that material culture comes to stand for ethnic groups in museums, rather than simply representing them. By privileging material culture and by stressing the associations between objects and ethnic groups, museum exhibitions essentialise and 'freeze' images and identities. This is also the result of specific display layouts. For instance, the dress styles of the various ethnic groups are almost invariably presented through an array of identical, featureless, plastic mannequins – a vision that, in an uncanny way, succeeds in conveying equality, but also anonymity. (Given the prominence of this mode of display in ethnic minority exhibitions, the implications of mannequins, miniatures and dioramas will be discussed in the next chapter.)

In Yunnan – a Chinese province with one of the highest ethnic populations – descriptions of ethnic minorities in museum texts and panels often refer to an aggregate subjectivity identified by the (capitalised) expression 'Yunnan Ethnic Groups'. Thus, artefacts become a metonym not only of the specific ethnic group who produced or used them, but of all ethnic minorities,

FIG 9.2. MANNEQUINS REPRESENTING ETHNIC MINORITY GROUPS AT THE SHANGHAI MUSEUM.

grouped into an organic, undifferentiated 'Other'. Consistent with the effacing of the individual in an aggregate entity, the question of objects' authorship is disregarded in displays. In this sense, both display techniques and discursive practices concur in reinforcing the idea of ethnic groups as seamless and homogeneous. The process of assimilation of ethnic minorities rests here on the flattening of cultural specificity and variation, and the erasure of individual agency. Notably, displays overlook cultural elements dismissed by the Han Chinese majority as 'superstitious' practices and 'remnants of primitive societies'. These may include specific marriage customs (such as the 'walking marriage' practised among the Mosuo ethnic group in northern Yunnan), funerary rites (such as the celestial burial practised by some Tibetan communities) or shamanic practices. Museum exhibitions shun engagement with the changing political, hierarchical, ritual, religious and social meanings of the objects on display. The cultural practices that suit the official discourse and image of ethnic minorities are acceptable (such as the often-cited 'water-splashing festival' of the Dai group, transformed into entertainment for tourists: see Cable 2008; Komlosy 2004), while other cultural features are excluded from museums' selective representations. Gradually distancing themselves from 'undesirable' and 'backward' cultural features is the condition for ethnic groups' inclusion within the 'Chinese family'.

The taxonomic system that informs the representation of ethnic minority material culture – revolving around a standardised set of narratives and object categories: costumes and textiles, musical instruments, everyday tools, ritual objects and masks – reveals the realms in which cultural difference is allowed to be 'safely' expressed without threatening the centrality of the Han's cultural system, while at the same time instantiating the 'Chineseness' that all ethnic minorities are supposed to share.

FOLKLORISATION

Based on the assumption that 'most of China's ethnic minorities are good singers and dancers' (C Wang 2004, 69), traditional songs and ritual dances of ethnic groups have become exotic and entertaining performances for Chinese urban audiences. Today, the folklorisation of minority cultures sustains a flourishing tourist industry in minorities' areas (see Henderson *et al* 2009; Hillman 2003; Yang *et al* 2008). However, these performances rarely find their way into a museum. As mentioned previously, museum exhibitions mainly focus on ethnic minority material culture, with an emphasis on the utilitarian dimension of objects. The fulfilment of utilitarian purposes is, for example, one of the criteria that inform acquisition policies at the Anthropology Museum of Yunnan University (Li 2008, *pers comm*).[10] Exhibitions of 'ethnic minority art' usually refer more specifically to 'folk art' – such as paper-cutting, wood-carving and embroidery – which is understood as a minor, popular form of art (as opposed to the high arts of calligraphy, painting and poetry practised by the Han Chinese). For example, the gallery devoted to ethnic minorities at the Shanghai Museum – the Kadoorie Gallery of Chinese Minority Nationalities – includes ethnic costumes, weaving and embroideries, bamboo items, wood carvings and ritual masks, but does not include item categories such as paintings or sculpture, which one might expect to find in an art exhibition.

This chapter has discussed the narratives and modes of display of ethnic minorities in Chinese museums. The next chapter will develop a more focused analysis of the techniques used in exhibitions to display ethnic minority cultures. The aim is to move beyond museum texts and narratives to decrypt the subtle messages conveyed by the use of specific display techniques.

---

[10]   Ms Li, curator at the Museum, explains that acquisition policies request that the object be in current use in the society that produced it.

10

Techniques and Sites of Display
of Ethnic Minorities

The use of mannequins, miniatures, small-size figurines and dioramas is sufficiently wide-spread within ethnic minority displays in China to justify a critical reflection on their use and implications as display techniques. At the Museum of the Southwest University for Nationalities in Chengdu, the capital of the Sichuan Province in south-western China, the visitor can see the 56 Chinese ethnic groups represented by small-scale plastic figurines positioned side-by-side to form a materialised picture of the Chinese nation. This depiction is consistent with China's self-definition as a 'multinational state'. The display technique adopted by the museum in Chengdu is not an isolated case; it can be found in a number of other Chinese museums exhibiting ethnic minority material culture.

The concept of the miniature (Lévi-Strauss 1962; Stewart 1984) is useful in exploring the agency of Chinese museums in shaping the image of ethnic minorities, as it reveals how specific museological practices and display techniques – such as mannequins, miniatures, dioramas, figurines and maps – enable the containment of ethnic minority cultural difference. In particular, following on from Tony Bennett's theory of museums as sites for the development of 'civic seeing', mannequins, figurines and miniatures in displays of Chinese ethnic minorities can be understood as devices aimed at imparting a 'civic lesson' (Bennett 2006b) on the 'unity within diversity' of the Chinese nation. This analytical perspective suggests that the development of a 'civic seeing' in museums may be pursued not only through particular display arrangements, but also through specific museum objects and display techniques. The term 'miniature' is here used with the extended meaning developed by Claude Lévi-Strauss. For Lévi-Strauss (1962, 23), miniatures are not so much defined by their reduced scale as by the loss of some features of the original: details, volume, smell, colour, etc. In this sense, museum mannequins, figurines, models, dioramas, maps and other reproductions can all be considered miniatures to the extent that they have lost several of the dimensions of complexity of the originals – in this case, individuals and communities.

Miniatures occupy a significant place in the Chinese cultural system and have been deployed in a range of diverse contexts, modalities and significations. Miniatures were, for instance, included in funerary sets in Ancient China (Clunas 1997a, 27). During the Ming Dynasty (AD 1368–1644), miniature gardens were fashionable among scholars (see Clunas 1996, 91; Stein 1990); also, at this time, miniatures that reproduced natural features, such as miniature rock carvings and miniature curio cabinets, featured in the paraphernalia of the literati. China also developed a significant tradition of reduced-scale landscape architecture (Stanley 2002, 272), of which the Forbidden City may be the most spectacular example.

FIG 10.1. MINIATURE FIGURINES OF ETHNIC GROUPS AT THE MUSEUM OF THE SOUTHWEST UNIVERSITY FOR NATIONALITIES IN CHENGDU, SICHUAN PROVINCE.

The use of miniatures, figurines and life-size mannequins in museums has become relatively common, and is by no means unique to China. Mannequins, miniatures and reduced-scale reproductions were, for instance, used in 19th-century European museums, notably in zoological, ethnographic and archaeological displays, as tools enabling the pristine display of natural and cultural human habitats (see Haraway 1984). Albeit globally widespread, the use of miniatures, mannequins and small-scale reproductions to depict ethnic minority cultures invites reflection in the case of China particularly, since here the narratives of equal and harmonious inter-ethnic relations unfolded in museum displays by means of such representational devices are in sharp contrast to the reality of inter-ethnic friction regularly reported in newspaper chronicles, such as the riots that broke out in summer 2009 in the Xinjiang Uyghur Autonomous Region between the Uyghur ethnic minority and the Han Chinese majority.

Mannequins as Substitutes for Ethnic Minorities

At the Yunnan Nationalities Museum, the glass wall cases in the gallery devoted to ethnic minority costumes contain identical mannequins, offering an overview of the Yunnan ethnic groups' costumes. Very similar displays are found at the Anthropology Museum of Yunnan University, the Museum of the Southwest University for Nationalities in Chengdu, the Sichuan University Museum, the Shanghai Museum, the Minzu Museum, Minzu University of China and the Museum of the Institute of Clothing Technology in Beijing, among others. Despite the differences that exist between these institutions, ethnic minorities in all of these museums are presented with an emphasis on their costumes.[1]

The use of mannequins in such museum displays casts light not so much on the position of the subject represented (ethnic minorities) as on the position of the author of such representations (the museum and, by extension, the Chinese state). In general terms, these interpretations of the human body can be understood as museums' claims to be able not only to reproduce variation and diversity in ethnic outfits' styles and materials, but also to reduce the complexity of ethnic minorities' physical, cultural and historical features. As Deborah Root (1996, 114) notes about the use of mannequins in museums, 'what is being displayed is the ability to construct the real'. Thus, the ability of the museum, through the acts of curators, to present the detail of the elaborate embroideries and unique fabrics of ethnic minority costumes is instrumental in conveying the idea that museum displays are 'authentic' in that they closely reflect real-life conditions.

This kind of representation is not without contradiction; while some of the objects on display – textiles, garments and body ornaments – are presented as 'authentic', their material support – the plastic mannequin – denies any claim to authenticity. The mannequin, like the model, the miniature, the diorama, the map and other reproductions, does not make any attempt to be taken for 'real', its function being, by definition, auxiliary. The mannequin, with its standardised features and static body postures, resists variation, uniqueness and individuality by imposing

---

[1] These museums vary in status, availability of funds, audience and visibility, among other considerations. For example, displays at the Anthropology Museum of Yunnan University have been largely funded by the Ford Foundation, while the other museums mentioned are public institutions. The Museum of the Southwest University for Nationalities in Chengdu is open only to researchers and only by appointment, whereas the Shanghai Museum draws thousands of visitors daily.

an element of artificiality and anonymity that disrupts the person–object correspondence: the mannequin depersonalises the object in order to enable the generalisation of the representation. When transposed in museum displays of ethnic minorities, such disruption means that what is retained and communicated by mannequins is a superficial and reductive notion of cultural difference limited to diverse dress codes, headdresses and physical appearance. Conversely, the fact that the mannequins are identical suggests that, beyond the superficial aspect of differing body adornments, all ethnic groups are essentially similar in that they are all 'Chinese' – as is painstakingly reiterated in museum labels and panels, and through the visual juxtaposition of the mannequins. Tellingly, museum displays do not provide information on the social biography of the objects on display – who made them, when, how, who used them, how they entered the museum collections and so on – as this would anchor the object to real-life situations and specific individuals. On the contrary, it is the object's capacity to become representative of a group that is emphasised in museum displays. The mannequin is key to enabling such abstraction.

MINIATURES AS A METONYM OF THE ETHNIC GROUP

The relationship between the figurines and the ethnic groups they represent can be said to be metonymic insofar as, within the museum setting, the figurines become substitutes for the ethnic group. The metonymic relationship between the ethnic group and the figurine can be explained as a 'strategy of "reduction" used to bring some higher or more complex realms of being (down) to the terms of a lower or less complex realm of being' (Burke 1969, 506). In the case of Chinese ethnic minorities, such a strategy of reduction also reflects the relative position of ethnic minorities within Chinese society, as the small stature of ethnic minority figurines can be seen as reflective of Chinese ethnic minorities' subordinate status vis-à-vis the Han Chinese majority.[2] One is here reminded of the (mostly positive) words of Lévi-Strauss (1962, 23) on the effects of scale reduction: 'being smaller, the object as a whole seems less formidable. By being quantitatively diminished, it seems to us qualitatively simplified.' The subordinate status of ethnic groups is revealed in the use within museum panels (for instance, at the Minzu Museum, Minzu University of China) of adjectives such as 'diligent', 'peace-loving' and 'colourful' (the use of similar terms has also been noted by Gladney 1994, 103), and expressions such as 'brave, intelligent and unsophisticated people [...] working together with diligence and intelligence'.[3]

Miniatures, however, are not deprived of agency in Alfred Gell's terms (1998). As Lévi-Strauss (1966, 24) aptly notes, '[Miniatures] are not just projections or passive homologues of the object: they constitute a real experiment with it.' For instance, at the Museum of the Southwest University for Nationalities in Chengdu, Sichuan Province, the visitor can find the 56 Chinese ethnic groups represented by small-scale plastic figurines positioned side-by-side to form a physical picture of the Chinese nation. Within this display, the agency of the figurines operates on at least two levels. Firstly, through their static postures and facial expressions, the figurines convey a specific body-type and attitude – in short, they embody an idealised image of the ethnic group. Secondly, their reduced scale hinders the possibility of an equal relationship between the viewer and the exhibit. This is further reinforced by the spatial position of the miniatures in relation

---

[2]   For a broader discussion of the political significance of museum representations of ethnic minorities in China see also Varutti (2011a; 2011b; 2010b; 2010d; 2008a).
[3]   Yunnan Nationalities Museum, text in English and Chinese.

to the viewer. In the display at the Museum of the Southwest University for Nationalities, the viewer, empowered by a panoptical gaze, looks down at the miniatures, visually encompassing them from a position of comfort and control. If, as mentioned above, the intention is for the mannequin to contribute to the 'homogeneity through anonymity' of the ethnic group, the miniature figurine contributes to instantiating its subaltern status.

However, this is not to imply that the use of small-scale figurines in museum displays reflects hostility towards the ethnic groups represented; quite the contrary. Due to the figurines' dimensions and features, the viewer is invited to approach them as fragile, valuable, pretty things. In her discussion of miniatures, Susan Stewart (1984, 111) introduces a useful distinction between the 'dwarf' and the 'midget' to describe the more or less benevolent gaze that is bestowed on the small-scale object. Following on from Stewart, the miniatures of ethnic minorities that one sees in Chinese museums tend to present human figures as 'midget' rather than as 'dwarf' – that is, as positive, charming entities, non-threatening yet not entirely familiar.

Nostalgia may also play a role in the popularity of miniatures within and outside Chinese museums. The standardisation and commodification of cultural goods and practices brought about by the turn towards a market economy and socio-political changes since the early 1990s have drastically altered the lifestyle of Chinese families in the space of only one generation. The idealised image of 'exotic' communities living in a distant, undefined place and time, 'peacefully' and 'in harmony with nature' appeals to the nostalgic desire for an ideal world 'unspoilt' and 'uncorrupted' by modernisation (see also Wang *et al* 2001, 81). Such nostalgic feelings are nevertheless not immune to commercial exploitation. Museum souvenir shops, ethnic minority parks (such as the Ethnic Minorities Park in Beijing) and ethnic villages (such as the ethnic minorities village on the outskirts of Kunming, Yunnan Province) are filled with ethnic minority costumes and paraphernalia available for sale. Also, the widespread practice (at these sites) of having one's photo taken in ethnic garments is quite telling of the degree to which ethnic identity can be appropriated and, literally, worn and divested. Here, 'being ethnic' is a game, it is a safe estrangement, a close encounter with the Other within the non-threatening realm of the *mise en scène*.

Dioramas and the Power of Contextualisation

Due to their realistic appearance, the detailed reproductions of real-life scenes and *tableaux vivants* encapsulated by the term dioramas were particularly popular in museums of the Maoist era (1949–76). At that time, museum displays were informed by principles of historical materialism and by the imperative to provide historical and scientific evidence in support of Marxist–Leninist theories of socio-economic development. Despite critiques of the use of this medium in museums (see Haraway 1984), dioramas remain a museological tool, notably featuring prominently in displays of ethnic minorities in China. At the Tea Museum in Hangzhou, for example, the interior of a Tibetan house has been recreated to provide contextualisation for the practice of tea-making among members of ethnic groups. This enables the visitor, if not physically to walk into the house and occupy the seats as an imaginary host (due to restricted access), then at least to inspect and visually appropriate a private space. Similarly, at the Museum of the University of Ethnic Minorities in Kunming, the capital of Yunnan, typical ethnic dwellings have been reconstructed for visitors' appraisal. At the Yunnan Nationalities Museum in Kunming, curators have reconstructed the sacred spaces of ethnic minorities; for instance, the visitor is presented with a ritual altar of the Bai group, complete with wooden and rock sculptures of deities and embroidered banners, set against the backdrop of a painted panel featuring a view of the snow-capped mountains and the three pagodas of Dali, the main centre of the Bai ethnic area. In a gallery of the Yunnan Nationalities Museum (currently undergoing refurbishment), there could previously be found a life-size bronze sculpture of Red Army soldiers being greeted by female members of ethnic minorities – a propaganda image illustrating the socialist discourse on the contribution of ethnic minorities to the revolutionary cause. The historical accuracy of the scene might be questionable, but its hyperrealism approximates a historical document.

The peculiarity and potency of dioramas as tools of representation is partially due to their ability to be comprehended not only visually but also through feelings of proprioception – that is, through the perception of the relative position and movements in space of one's body. Through such perceptions, the diorama enables the viewer to position him- or herself vis-à-vis the object. A relationship – of solidarity, authority, distance or opposition – is thus established not only between the viewer and the exhibit, but also, by implication, between the viewer and the ethnic groups represented.

By aiming to represent a real-life community within the walls of a museum, dioramas produce a spatial, temporal and cultural displacement. In so doing, they act as powerful evocative tools capable of bridging the gap between reality and the abstract narrative of the museum exhibition. In this sense, the diorama is a good illustration of the miniature in Lévi-Strauss' terms (1966, 22), given its capacity to conjure up both real-life subject matter and the image of an idealised, magical world. So for instance, at the Tea Museum in Hangzhou, the visitor is able to enter a Tibetan dwelling and experience the depth of a tropical forest in the air-conditioned comfort of the exhibition room. Because the diorama is ultimately fictitious, its efficacy in providing object contextualisation can only be achieved on the basis of a tacit understanding between museum curators and visitors of the fictional nature of the scene represented. This tacit understanding also entails a degree of trust and of the 'suspension of disbelief' on the part of the viewer. As mentioned, this may be in part the result of a culturally specific Chinese understanding of miniature representations. Yet the suspension of disbelief also entails a recognition of museums' legitimacy and authority in authoring such representations. By recreating real-life communities in the space of the exhibition room, dioramas assert museums' capacity to manufacture images and validate narratives. But they do so, once again (as for the miniature and the mannequin) within safe boundaries, as the object of observation – ethnic minorities in this case – is confined to the passive, speechless and motionless setting of the inanimate world.

VISUALISING THE CHINESE NATION

Having considered some of the conceptual implications of the use of mannequins, miniatures and dioramas in displays of ethnic minorities in Chinese museums, this chapter will now examine the effects of their juxtaposition in museum displays. Displays at the Museum of the Southwest University for Nationalities in Chengdu include a large wall map of China with ethnic minority figurines fixed to it. The map achieves in this case two complementary objectives. Firstly, the positioning of ethnic minority figurines on the map contributes to the fixing of their identities by anchoring each group to their territory. This method of representation reinforces the stereotype of ethnic groups as discrete communities that can be unproblematically linked to a specific geographic area, ruling out migration, cohabitation, intermarriage, exchanges among groups, hybrid cultural forms and blurred cultural and ethnic boundaries. Cultural homogeneity across the territory is artificially constructed at the expense of a reality where, even over a small distance, from one valley or one village to another, cultural features can vary significantly. China's efforts at defining ethnic groups and mapping them over the territory have been the guiding principle of Chinese official rhetoric on ethnic minorities since well before the 1953 ethnic minorities census,[4] and the subsequent institution of autonomous regions, prefectures and counties in areas densely populated by ethnic groups (cf Duara 2002; Harrell 1995). Secondly, on a broader level, the map enables the panoptic visualisation of the ethnic dimension of the Chinese nation – in accordance with Shelly Errington's (1998, 196) argument that 'maps emblematize and naturalize the boundaries of the nation-state'. This point also chimes with Ann Anagnost's (1997, 162) comment on miniature landscapes to the effect that 'they speak the totality of the nation in time and space'. In particular, maps also carry the advantage of representing and including contested areas of China, such as Taiwan, Tibet and Xinjiang, while visualising the extent of Han presence across the Chinese territory.

Similarly, displays at the Minzu Museum, Minzu University of China in Beijing present an overview of the 55 Chinese ethnic minorities through an array of life-size plastic mannequins dressed in the ethnic costumes of each group. The juxtaposition of mannequins emphasises the cumulative and classificatory dimensions of the display. Consistently, the Museum panels inform the visitor that the Chinese nation is composed of 56 nationalities, of which 22 ethnic groups constitute the northern nationalities, and 34 the southern. Not only does this concern with classification express a need for the ordering and hierarchisation of ethnic groups (cf Blum 2001; Gladney 1994), but also and once again it aims to create homogeneity (Mullaney 2010). By reducing ethnic communities to the minimum common denominator of a costume worn by a mannequin, such displays render ethnic groups quantifiable and allow for such statements as '[the Chinese visitor can] touch history, understand the present situation, appreciate the charm and glamour of the traditional culture of the Chinese nation […] and strengthen our national solidarity'.[5] Even more direct and visually powerful is the display at the Museum of the South-west University for Nationalities in Chengdu, mentioned above, featuring 56 small-size figurines positioned side-by-side in three rows against a backdrop of the Chinese national emblem. This layout has a considerable visualising potency; the whole Chinese nation is here encompassed in a single glance. Unusually for exhibitions of this kind, the Han Chinese are also represented; yet in contrast to the others, the Han figurine is male and is wearing blue work overalls instead of an ethnic costume. This layout aims to display China's ethnic groups as a collective, a single constituency unified by its belonging to the Chinese nation.

Interestingly, with the exception of the miniature figurines at the Museum of the South-west University for Nationalities, collective displays of ethnic groups do not include the Han majority. Their absence contributes to the construction of the Han's modernity; Han Chinese do not feature in ethnic displays since Han do not wear costumes, practise 'superstitious' rites or engage in peculiar marriage practices. The absence of the Han majority is thus meaningful in a Derridean sense (Derrida 1982); the Han's non-representation reinforces their distance and difference from ethnic groups.

---

4   See Mullaney (2010) for a history of China's ethnic classification project.
5   Minzu Museum, Minzu University of China, Beijing. 'Preface' panel; text in Chinese and English.

Susan Stewart (1984, 132) has argued that through the miniaturised world of the freak show, 'we derive an image of the normal; to know an age's typical freaks is, in fact, to know its points of standardization'. Paraphrasing Stewart, one could argue that by looking at displays of ethnic minorities, one derives an image not only of the ethnic Other, but also of the extent of its conformity to an idea of 'Chineseness' embodied by the Han majority. This is particularly signifi-cant given the fact that most visitors of museums displaying ethnic minorities are Han Chinese (the Yunnan Nationalities Museum and the Nationalities Village in Kunming are some of the main destinations for Han Chinese tourists, and large tour buses of hundreds of tourists can be seen unloading at these spots every day). The alterity of the ethnic minority is instrumental in the definition of the viewer's own identity. Displays of ethnic minorities' 'exotic' lifestyles may reas-sure the viewer of his or her own cultural, moral and technological superiority and 'modernity'. Dru Gladney (1994, 98) argues that:

> the objectified portrayal of minorities as exoticized, and even eroticized, is essential to the construction of the Han Chinese majority, the very formulation of the Chinese 'nation' itself [...] the representation of the Han as 'normal' and 'un-exotic' is critical for understanding the construction of present-day Chinese identity.

As a result, the representation of ethnic minorities' exoticism in museums ultimately contributes to the definition of the Han majority's identity (see also Jonsson 2000; Fiskesjö 2006).

'Civic seeing' in Chinese Ethnic Minority Museums

The scholar Tony Bennett (2006b, 121) has noted that historically:

> the functioning of museums as civic institutions has operated through specific regimes of vision which, informing both the manner in which things are arranged to be seen and the broader visual environment conditioning practices of looking, give rise to particular forms of 'civic seeing' in which the civic lessons embodied in those arrangements are to be seen, understood, and performed by the museum's visitors.

Bennett's assertion rests on an analysis of museums and displays in Europe and the United States during the 19th and 20th centuries. However, his predicate can plausibly be extended to China; museum displays featuring all 56 officially recognised nationalities can be understood as a device aimed at instilling the constitutional principle of the 'unity within diversity' of the Chinese nation.

In his analysis, Bennett notes that the model of the 19th-century evolutionary museum differs from the Enlightenment museum in the unprecedented significance attributed to ideas of progress and evolution of the species. The evolutionary museum was mainly concerned with presenting to viewers not the wonder of natural objects in themselves, but rather the relationships between them in order to communicate notions of progress and evolution. Bennett (2006b, 128) notes that 'far from looking into things, the visitor's eye had to be directed to look along the relations between them'. Likewise, Chinese audiences are not invited to view the ethnic minority figurines as museum objects – displays make no claims about their artistic, historical, cultural or scientific relevance – rather they are taught to look at the connections that bind them; that is, their common Chinese identity. In addition, audiences are invited to regard the relationships as harmonious. The body postures, facial expressions and attitudes of the figurines in the Museum of the Southwest University for Nationalities in Chengdu are telling: the figurines mostly depict scenes of dancing and happiness, but crucially they are not facing each other, there is no interaction between them and they are all facing the viewer. Their aligned, front-facing position reveals not only the staged, theatrical nature of the scene – a characteristic feature of miniature representations (Stewart 1984, 54) – but also betrays the agency of museum curators who arranged the figurines, and beyond that, the agency of the Chinese government and its nationalist principles which inspired the installation.

Yet, for such agency to be effective, maps, miniatures and mannequins representing ethnic minorities need to be exposed to public view. As in Bennett's 'civic seeing', and in contrast to Renaissance cabinets of curiosities where aristocrats could comfortably admire the exotic Other in the privacy of their dwellings (Abt 2006), here it is the public view – the shared, collective experience of observing the exhibit – that makes the display consequential. While there are sound arguments for regarding (Chinese) museums as sites for the organisation and control of an audience's view in ways reminiscent of Foucault's panopticon (cf Bennett 1995), the extension of this argument to Chinese museums displaying ethnic minorities calls for some specification. Miniatures in ethnic minority museums – be they mannequins, models, dioramas or maps – act upon viewers in ways that transcend the mere regulation of sight: they not only organise vision, but also establish specific relationships between the viewer and the object on display, and transversely among the objects on display (ie among ethnic groups). Ultimately, paraphrasing Marilyn Strathern (1993), what is miniaturised in the figurines is not only the features of ethnic groups, but also the set of social relations in which these are embedded, inter-ethnic and minority–majority relationships.

Analysis of ethnic minority museum displays in Chinese museums shows that miniatures are used in an effort to anchor identities to ideal types, to regulate social and intercultural relations and to promote understandings of the Chinese nation as 'united and diverse'. In this sense, miniatures, mannequins and figurines in Chinese museums can be understood as tools for the dissemination of 'civic lessons' (Bennett 2006b).

The museum visitor is invited to see ethnic groups in terms of harmonious relations, docile character, laboriousness, dancing and musical skills and folklore traditions. Conversely, concealed from view are the effects of modernisation, hybridisation and change, as well as inter-ethnic conflictual and hierarchical relations. As a result, the ethnic minority is on display yet absent, visually available yet physically inaccessible. As a replacement for the 'real' ethnic minority, the miniature is ultimately an index of its absence. As Susan Stewart (1984, 134) puts it, 'the possession of the metonymic object is a kind of dispossession in that the presence of the object all the more radically speaks to its status as a mere substitution and to its subsequent distance from the self'. Here, the miniature acts as a form of magic and 'like other forms of magic, it guarantees the presence of an absent other through either contagion or representation' (Stewart 1984, 126). While the debate is open on whether the object on display is 'authentic', its effects are real.

Understood as the expression of the unfulfilled desire to turn human beings into manipulable, docile objects, the miniature becomes the materialisation of the gap between ideology and reality. In this perspective, the miniature is an index of the incompleteness of the Chinese political body, and of the idealised objectives of Chinese cultural and nationalistic policies.

Yet, there is more to museum miniatures than their use as propaganda tools. The miniatures featured in displays of Chinese ethnic minorities are not merely vehicles for state narratives of the nation. By virtue of their materiality, they are also agents in producing meanings, relations, emotions and world views far more complex and nuanced than government-inspired master narratives. In the insightful book *Fieldwork Connections* (Bamo *et al* 2007), Bamo Ayi discusses the issues encountered when collecting and displaying ethnic minority artefacts of the Nuosu ethnic group from Sichuan Province. The issues discussed include, among others, how to define 'hand-made', 'traditional', 'authentic', or 'representative' objects; how to set a fair acquisition price for objects that most often either do not have a market (because they are heirloom possessions) or circulate in a market of collectors at highly inflated prices; how to appropriately present ethnic minority artefacts to non-Chinese audiences in ways that make ethnic cultures intelligible while also retaining their cultural complexity. These issues reveal the contested, negotiated character of ethnic identities and cultural representation in China (see Harrell 2001), as well as the multiplicity of perspectives, approaches, concerns, assumptions and sensitivities that shape museum representations which are generally concealed in the context of public museum displays in China.

ETHNIC MINORITIES AND ECOMUSEUMS

Since the late 1990s, a new category of museums devoted to ethnic minorities has appeared in China: ecomuseums. Peter Davis (2011, 85) explains that an ecomuseum is 'a community-led heritage or museum project that supports sustainable development'. The defining features of ecomuseums are:

> The adoption of a territory that may be defined, for example, by landscape, dialect, a specific industry, or musical tradition.

> The identification of specific heritage resources within that territory, and the celebration of these 'cultural touchstones' using in-situ conservation and interpretation.

> The conservation and interpretation of individual sites within the territory is carried out via liaison and co-operation with other organizations.

> The empowerment of local communities – the ecomuseum is established and managed by local people. Local people decide what aspects of their 'place' are important to them.

The concept of the ecomuseum was pioneered by the French museologists Georges Henri Rivière and Hugues de Varine in the 1970s. In China, this concept was introduced in 1986 through a special issue of *China's Museums*, the journal of the Chinese Museum Institute, which included translated articles on ecomuseums in other areas of the world (Su 2008, 34). However, it was only in 1997 that the first ecomuseum in China was established in the Suoga Miao village in Western Guizhou Province (S Pan 2012, 48). Other ecomuseums in the same province devoted to the Buyi, Dong and Miao ethnic groups were set up in cooperation with Norwegian museum professionals (Zhang 2008, 7). In 2001, two more ecomuseums were established: one in Inner Mongolia, the other in Guangxi Province. In 2008, there were 16 ecomuseums in China and several others are planned (Su 2008, 38). The introduction of ecomuseums in ethnic minority areas is linked to the Chinese government's recognition of 'the failure of previous attempts to open up rural areas and minority for tourism and economic benefit' (Davis 2011, 237). In recent years, the Chinese government has become increasingly active in establishing ecomuseums in ethnic minority areas. The creation of ecomuseums in remote areas inhabited by ethnic minorities is made possible by the mobilisation of funds from central government and occasionally from international sources; Norway, for example, contributed to the creation of several ecomuseums in the late 1990s (see Davis *et al* 2006).

In the late 2000s, the Minzu Museum, Minzu University of China in Beijing became involved in managing government funds for the creation of ecomuseums in Guizhou Province – notably the Gong-mi-a Village Museum in Leishan county and the Xiao-huang Village Dong Chorus Museum in Congjiang county – devoted to the Kaili Miao and Dong ethnic groups (S Pan 2012). A different initiative, emanating from Yunnan University and funded by the Ford Foundation, led to the creation in the early 2000s of six 'Ethnic Cultural and Ecological Villages' and museums in Yunnan Province. In the words of project leader Professor Yin Shaoting (2003, 47), 'cultural and ecological villages are not the same as ethnic villages, folk custom villages, tourism villages, or holiday and recreation villages. Rather, they aim at a pattern of sustainable community development that incorporates high cultural standards and ecological quality.' The projects were variously successful, although in several instances the museums failed to integrate with the daily lives of villagers. In spring 2008, I visited the ecological village of Nanjian, central Yunnan, considered to be the most successful of the project. The local museum was opened for me and closed again after my departure, while locals did not enter or use it, preferring to use the area in front of the museum as a meeting and recreational venue. This example raises a number of questions around the conditions for success of ecomuseums in China. As the museologist Su Donghai (2006, 6) has noted, 'In China, it is not that difficult to found an ecomuseum but it is very hard to sustain it. The government and academics can be major forces in establishing an ecomuseum, but the community residents are the only ones who can sustain it.'

An important role of ecomuseums is that they benefit local communities. 'Benefits may be intangible, such as greater self-awareness or pride in place, tangible (the rescue of a fragment of local heritage, for example), or economic [...] These features indicate the strong connection between ecomuseums and specific geographical localities, with the latter two points demanding that ecomuseums embrace local empowerment and heed local voices' (Davis *et al* 2010, 81). It is worth considering the impact of an externally driven project on the cultural and social structures of a community that has previously been relatively secluded. It may be difficult to reconcile urban planning development projects aimed at creating new homes and buildings in economically deprived ethnic areas (a huge emerging phenomenon in China) with concerns over the preservation of a village's original cultural features. Moreover, training local museum staff can be challenging in areas where resources (human and financial) are scarce. It is also hard to evaluate the actual participation of local villagers in the setting-up of these museums, and consequently their degree of commitment once the museum has been completed and the academics, professionals, funding bodies and central authorities have left. In addition, there is a real risk of presenting ethnic minority cultures as 'exotic goods' for tourist consumption (see also Davis 2011, 246), as is often the case with 'ethnic parks', such as the Nationalities Park in Beijing and the Yunnan Ethnic Village. Ecomuseum projects in China – as in many other countries – are caught between social development and cultural preservation (see White 1997). They are strategically located at the crossroads of economic development and community empowerment, revitalisation of local 'traditional' cultures and tourist exploitation.

Concluding Notes on Museum Representations of Ethnic Minorities

This section has endeavoured to disentangle the various strands of arguments, assumptions, narratives and display techniques that contribute to shaping the image of ethnic minorities in Chinese museums. The rich intangible heritage of Chinese ethnic minorities does not find full expression in museum displays, which privilege a limited range of objects. By focusing on a set of fixed object categories – textiles and costumes, musical instruments, ritual objects, everyday implements – and by displaying side-by-side the material culture of each ethnic group, displays of ethnic minorities in Chinese museums contain cultural variation within a pre-established matrix in order to produce a sense of seriality and homogeneity which makes ethnic minority cultures comparable (hence scalable) and ultimately suitable for integration within the national frame-work. In other words, through the manipulation of their material culture, ethnic minorities' cultural diversity is being 'standardised' in order to produce similarity and, consequently, a sense of national unity. This is achieved by overlooking substantial cultural differences and maintaining only marginal, irrelevant difference which, through folklorisation, upholds the superficial image of a culturally varied and rich nation.

Extolling ethnic minorities' folklore, and in the same breath describing them as culturally and technologically in need of modernisation, museum representations succeed in precluding the expression of substantial cultural difference. Conversely, the expressions of cultural difference that do find their way into museums consistently focus on ethnic minorities' materiality. These kinds of displays are non-threatening since they do not call into question the links between ethnic minority cultures and Han Chinese culture – as would, for instance, a comprehensive representation of the historical trajectories of ethnic groups, of ethnic scriptural and language systems, or religious cosmologies. The cultural differences of ethnic minorities are thus embraced only to the extent that they do not threaten the unity and 'harmony' of the Chinese nation. To this effect, it could be said that museums contribute to the production of an array of similar forms of difference. As a result, the representation of ethnic minorities in Chinese museums does not involve a process of construction or translation of cultural difference, but a containment of alterity. Such a strategy entails not so much the assimilation or integration of difference, but more its internalisation via standardisation. While assimilation implicitly requires the prior recognition of some form of difference (the process of othering is also, in a way, constitutive of the Other), in the Chinese case we are confronted with a process of 'neutralisation' of difference. China defines itself as a 'container' of nationalities, but crucially these are constructed as differing not in their cultural substance but in their degree of 'Han-ness' (see Blum 2001; Harrell 1995; Schein 2000).

What these strategies reveal is an anxiety about real difference, as this is associated with fears of separatism and disaggregation. As the scholars Yang, Wall and Smith (2008, 752) point out in their analysis of the development of ethnic tourism in China, 'the expression of an ethnic sense of identity can be seen as a threat to the unity of a nation'. Conversely, expressions of difference revolving around dress codes, musical traditions and folklore are not perceived as menacing. There are two reasons for this: firstly, there is no direct corresponding Han figure whose centrality might be displaced (Han do not wear 'colourful costumes' or practise 'superstitious rituals'); and secondly, there is no threat because ethnic minorities' cultural expressions are constructed as subaltern and as subordinate to Han civilisation.

Yet, because threats of separation (regularly highlighted by, among other examples, the Tibetan question) are real, and because the harmony and unity of the 'Chinese family' are far from real, the Chinese government needs to enforce its idealistic harmonious vision. The result is that the recognition and representation of cultural diversity is partial and conditional. By celebrating some cultural features and dismissing others, museum representations of minority cultures become a means to define them and, ultimately, to domesticate them. In this way, the nation factually contains the potential of ethnic minorities for cultural diversity, while 'authenticating' their identity as Chinese citizens.

In broader terms, the representation of ethnic minorities in contemporary China lies at the intersection of at least four connected dynamics of change affecting the ideological, political, socio-economic and cultural spheres. As with representations of the national past, the image of Chinese ethnic minorities is entangled with the country's ideological transition from Communist ideology, informed by Marxist–Leninist theories, to cultural nationalism. Ethnic minorities are portrayed as 'backward' but are also celebrated as members of the Chinese family, embodying the 'colourful' richness of the Chinese nation.

In parallel to its politicisation, ethnic minority tangible and intangible heritage has also become an economic resource, leading to the development of a flourishing tourism industry. Over the last decade, a significant number of cultural sites, ethnic minority villages, ecomuseums and theme parks have been created all over the Chinese territory – notably in provinces highly populated by ethnic minorities, such as Yunnan, Inner Mongolia and Guizhou. These initiatives often involve the folklorisation, commercialisation and exploitation of ethnic minority cultures, raising questions about the authenticity of displays and staged performances, cultural ownership and rights of representation (Yang *et al* 2008; Liu *et al* 2005).

The representation of ethnic minorities is also couched in complex dynamics of socio-cultural change. The employment of ethnic minorities as a tourism-enhancing asset creates a tension between cultural exoticism and modernity (Yang *et al* 2008). Ethnic groups are negotiating their right to development and to cultural expression (Davis 2005), but the terms of their modernisation are often dictated by central government policies (Shih 2002; Walsh and Swain 2004). Ethnic groups stage and exhibit their 'exotic', 'traditional' and 'colourful' cultural features for the benefit of the tourism industry and China's global image (for example, at the opening ceremony of the 2008 Olympic Games in Beijing). In parallel, the Chinese government is showing growing concern for cultural preservation, having successfully inscribed items of Chinese ethnic minority cultures on the UNESCO Intangible Cultural Heritage list (the Uyghur Muqam of Xinjiang and the Mongolian Urtiin Duu Traditional Folk Long Songs feature on the list) and China has established legal regulations under UNESCO's aegis to specifically protect ethnic minority cultures.[6] All of these developments have occurred against a backdrop of cultural transformation; the boundaries among ethnic groups and between ethnic and Han identities are increasingly fluid and blurred. As ethnic cultures possess a growing appeal among wealthy Han urbanites, phenomena of emulation and hybridisation contribute to challenging formal definitions of identity.

This chapter has developed a critical analysis of the techniques most frequently used in exhibitions when displaying ethnic minorities. Complementing the previous chapter on ethnic minority narratives in museums, this section rounds off discussion about the representation of

---

[6] For further details on the measures taken by China to protect its intangible heritage, see the document 'National Implementation – Periodic report' [online], available from: http://www.unesco.org/culture/ich/index.php?lg=en&pg=00311&cp=CN [22 May 2013].

the Chinese nation's ethnic components. This chapter also concludes analysis of the main facets of museums in China – their development, actors, collections and narratives of the national past and of national identity. These elements will be revisited in a critical light in the concluding remarks.

Conclusions: The New Museums of China

Throughout Chinese history, the meanings and values attributed to cultural heritage have reflected the stability and the transformations, the weaknesses and the virtues deployed in the exercising of authority. Since the 19th century, Chinese museums have provided not only a framework for the viewing, appreciation and interpretation of cultural heritage, but also a setting for the representation of contrasting narratives of the past and present of the Chinese nation.

In China, perhaps more than anywhere else, museums have played a crucial role in rooting political authority, instilling a sense of unity, creating a common identity and developing images of the national self. Post-1949, museums became key institutions in the process of nation-building, of which the Communist Party was the sole architect. Museums' contents, forms, objectives and priorities were (re)designed to fulfil the requirements of the new ideology. Providing 'political education' was the primary function of museums.

At the outset of the new millennium, against the backdrop of what Kirk Denton (2005, 565) has called the 'ideology of market reform', China's socio-economic evolution is transforming the profile of the country, impacting on virtually every aspect of social life: social relations, living standards, working life, education, leisure activities, mobility, health and the environment, to mention just a few. In such a volatile, complex context, it is perhaps not so strange that the Chinese government is again turning its attention to museums. In times of uncertainty, with a need for political legitimation, museums are tools through which to foster cohesion and national belonging; to paraphrase Benedict Anderson (1991), museums uphold the image of a 'Chinese imagined community'.

Analysis of the representations of the Chinese nation under the dual perspectives of temporality (in the ancient and recent past) and identity (the nation in its cultural, productive and multi-ethnic dimensions) suggests an ideological shift in the sources of political legitimation. The Chinese government is gradually abandoning the Marxist–Leninist paradigm in favour of cultural nationalism. Pride in belonging to the Chinese nation is instilled through the emphasis of China's extraordinarily long history and glorious civilisation, and through the promise of future technological advancement, generalised wealth and harmonious social relations. These concepts are conveyed in museums on at least three distinct, but connected, levels. Firstly, museum objects are presented as indexes (in Alfred Gell's sense) of the antiquity, glory, refinement and achievements of the Chinese civilisation (Gell 1998). Secondly, museum narratives apply these attributes to the nation through discourses on the longevity, continuity and unity of the Chinese nation. On a third and subtler level, such narratives uphold the legitimacy of the Communist Party as keeper of Chinese cultural, historical, political and moral heritage.

Museum representations of the past and of identity are still very much under government control. While the Chinese government is not relinquishing its authoritative role vis-à-vis politically crucial questions (such as the representation of the Chinese nation), it is reducing and focusing its control. The government is not a passive subject, but the orchestrator of the ongoing process of change in museums. Although the Chinese government will most probably continue to play a key role in the development of museums in China, it seems uncertain whether it will continue to be in full control in the longer term, and doubtful that it will continue as the sole legitimate narrator of Chinese history and identity.

The Communist Party's grip on museums may not have changed substantially since 1949, but there are indications that the scope of its influence has diminished. What has changed is the discourse that is put forward in museums: no longer centred on Communist ideology, it now focuses on cultural nationalism.

While analysis of displays has elicited official narratives of the past and of national identity, it has also cast light on the transformations that museums in China are undergoing. It is not only what one can see through museums that is changing, but also the very medium through which one is looking. The need for sources of legitimation has triggered a broader transformation, reshaping the building blocks of the museum institution: new actors (corporations, entrepreneurs, art collectors) are entering the museum scene; narratives of national pride have replaced political indoctrination; political education has receded to the most politicised exhibitions, while most museums choose to attract their audiences through displays emphasising the aesthetics of objects and futuristic museum architecture.

While wealthy art-lovers open private museums and galleries, and successful businessmen reinvent themselves as art patrons (thereby increasing visibility for both their business ventures and the beneficiary museum), a new generation of museum professionals is scaling the museum hierarchy. Most have no direct experience of the Maoist period, nor of the tragedy of the Cultural Revolution (1966–76); their references, increasingly, are museums and curatorial practices in the West. Museum visitors, long considered as recipients of propaganda messages, are now framed as 'customers' and have become the target of museums' marketing activities. Increasingly young, cultivated, wealthy and demanding, Chinese museum audiences expect to be entertained, surprised and able to satisfy their 'cultural thirst' in museum bookshops and souvenir outlets. Foreign actors are also gradually entering the museum scene, including foreign museums (through collaborations, loans and exchange programmes for museum staff), foreign investors (as sponsors of prestigious exhibitions), donors and collectors.

Approaches to the object have also evolved. From a purely didactic evaluation, the object is now also (and increasingly) appreciated aesthetically. This shift involves – to varying extents – the disconnection of the object from its historical, social and political background. The 'aesthetisation' process is also the result of an increasing awareness of the rarity of cultural relics, in turn linked to the wider movement for the protection and conservation of cultural heritage.

The content of museums is also changing, with the definition of 'museum object' being stretched to include unusual items: from the trousers worn by a soldier during the Long March, to Mao's personal pipe. Museum categories are expanding and becoming blurred: art and history as museum genres are slowly merging (the best example being the Shanghai Museum and the new National Museum of China), as are science and technology (intertwined in 'industrial' museums). As a result, museums are gradually opening up to unusual topics: industry is the most prominent (industrial museums are a relatively recent but important phenomenon, especially in Shanghai), but also service activities such as public security, banking, the postal service and urban development, to name but a few.

Even more noticeable is the way in which museum architecture is changing. As discussed earlier (notably in Chapter 4), a bold architectural style can significantly enhance the visibility of a museum in the urban context and help to draw audiences. Soviet-style architectural forms, in vogue from the 1950s to the 1980s, have been gradually abandoned. New sources of architectural inspiration are being found in Chinese traditional architecture, which is being reinterpreted to produce innovative forms and designs. One of the earliest and most prominent examples of this remains the Shanghai Museum, but other institutions – such as the Capital Museum in Beijing and the Sanxingdui Museum in Sichuan – have shown that innovative architecture can be one of a museum's most effective advertising tools.

As a result of such changes, Chinese museums are gradually moving away from the monolithic dimension of political indoctrination, and new museum paradigms are emerging after decades of stern adherence to Communist ideology. The old model of monofunctional museums operating under the strict control of central government is steadily giving way to a more composite and dynamic museum scene.

Considered globally, these changes point to processes of diversification and specialisation. Museum typologies, functions, content, actors and architectural forms are diversifying. Mirroring the growing complexity of Chinese society, museums in China are today increasingly called upon to perform tasks as diverse as enhancing the image of a city or of the country as a whole, acting as a platform for nation-building, tackling identity issues, supporting the local or national economy, promoting tourism and encouraging investment. The latest generation of Chinese museums is also increasingly specialised and market-oriented, as suggested by a novel attention to profit and an approach to visitors which increasingly views them as customers.

Beyond their specificities, contemporary museums in China share a crucial feature: they all seem driven by an ideal of modernity. Indeed, within the most recent museums in China, one even senses an 'anxiety to be modern' – modernity being perceived as both a condition and evidence of success. Historically in China, the advent of modernity in the museum realm has been linked to the end of the imperial system and the events following the 1911 Revolution (Li and Luo 2004, 2). At the end of the 19th century, museums were considered emblems of colonial power and tokens of China's technological and scientific backwardness. The reformist movement of 4 May 1919, however, led to a reappropriation of the notion of modernity, which was to be reformulated in Chinese terms. In the museum domain, this was marked by the opening of the Forbidden City to public view, and its transformation into a public museum. The opening of the Palace Museum in 1925 substantiated the public appropriation of imperial accoutrements, the desacralisation of the emperor's persona and the delegitimation of his rule. China and its museums could thus be said to have entered 'modernity'.

In the current context of significant changes in Chinese society and in Chinese museums, notions of modernity resurface in discourses and practices. Modernity appears to function as an intellectual tool that helps to integrate innovation and make sense of change. Indeed, the quest for modernity emerges as an overarching theme in the history of Chinese museums. The whole movement of re-evaluation of Chinese cultural heritage can be interpreted as a process of 'modernisation'. The transformation of museum features discussed in this book – the new national narratives, display techniques, actors and architecture of museums, among other aspects – can be understood as an attempt to grasp, define and express modernity in Chinese terms. But what, then, does modernity mean for museums in China today?

The observations of Chinese museums conducted during this study suggest that one of the elements that has come to indicate modernity in museums most strongly is an emphasis on the aesthetics of objects. Over the last decade, I have observed an increasing number of museum exhibitions adopting an aestheticising approach. In these instances, objects – most notably ancient cultural relics – are presented through display techniques that singularise them and emphasise their formal properties, while museum texts provide minimal historical and cultural contextualisation. The Shanghai Museum is a case in point. Generally considered the paradigmatic 'modern' Chinese museum, the Shanghai Museum successfully blends sophisticated displays of visually arresting masterpieces of ancient Chinese art with stunning architecture. This Museum has been conceptualised as an art object – a work of art meant to contain other works of art.

However, as discussed, aesthetics refer not so much to the formal properties of objects as to their mode of display. It is the way in which visitors are invited to look at museum objects that is aesthetic and aestheticising, and it is this, I contend, that is associated with modernity in Chinese museums. Barbara Saunders corroborates this point when she writes, 'the ritual of aesthetic contemplation […] [is] the foundational myth of modernism' (2001, 24).

Part of the reason why aesthetic display approaches have been adopted so widely in museums is the potential of aesthetics to allow for a disengagement from the historical, cultural and social contexts in which objects are embedded. While objects' multiple and changing meanings, associations and values make them historically and culturally salient, these elements are often omitted in displays within contemporary Chinese museums. As suggested, the emphasis on aesthetics presents objects as atemporal; this exhibitionary mode is apt when unfolding the narrative of a similarly atemporal and abstract concept: the Chinese nation. The glorious Chinese past can thus be actualised and cultural difference transcended through their transfiguration into the 'universal' value of Beauty. Moreover, the emphasis placed on aesthetics enables museums to elude potentially contentious issues such as the ownership and interpretation of objects. Recast in this light, aesthetics represent a device through which Chinese museums can negotiate their political and ideological role, and shift attention away from historical discrepancies and the ideological content of their narratives and representations.

In addition, the essentialisation and objectification implied in aesthetic display approaches enable the commercialisation of museum objects, or better, of their simulacra. Aestheticising displays can be understood as a facet of the ongoing transformation of Chinese museums and society at large. Chinese museums are facing a vast array of challenges, not least a growing domestic appetite for cultural consumption and the scrutiny of increasingly informed, cosmopolitan and consumption-oriented audiences. 'Aesthetisation' is one of the strategies that museums deploy to meet such challenges. Visitors are invited to buy objects in the museum shop as simulacra of Beauty, the Past, or the Ethnic Other. The exhibition catalogue, the merchandise and gadgets in the museum shop metaphorically play the role of everyday colonial trophies. Cultural consumption (in China as elsewhere) is increasingly a crucial factor in the definition of museums' priorities and policies.

What will the museum of the future offer to its visitors? Given the increasingly similar challenges that museums are facing globally, will museums in China develop in ways similar to their foreign counterparts? In what respects would they continue to be uniquely Chinese? Although the answers to these questions are outside the scope of this book, it is certain that Chinese museums will continue to change and develop in ways that reflect the changing culture and society of China itself.

Over the course of a century, museums in China have evolved from colonial imports to shrines for imperial treasures, from ideological classrooms to key assets in the economies of tourism and international prestige. As I write, new museums are being conceptualised in China.

In the process, new displays are being set up and new narratives, new images and new meanings are being woven around museum objects.

For centuries, the stories of the objects on display in Chinese museums – the material witnesses of Chinese civilisation – have been listened to, silenced, questioned or ignored. And those objects no doubt still have many more stories to tell. The appearance, content and narratives of Chinese museums will most likely keep changing in the future. Nonetheless, insofar as museum objects will continue to speak to our imagination, memories and emotions, Chinese museums will continue to provide a unique tool to map and explore the itinerary of Chinese culture and society.

Appendix
Museums in China Visited by the Author

BEIJING
Arthur Sackler Museum of Art and Archaeology
Beijing Art Museum
Capital Museum
China Millennium Monument
China Science and Technology Museum
Ethnic Minorities Park
Guanfu Museum of Classic Arts
Military Museum
Minzu Museum, Minzu University of China
Museum of the Institute of Clothing Technology
National Art Museum of China
Natural History Museum
National Museum of China (formerly the China Museum of National History)
Palace Museum (Forbidden City)
Poly Art Museum
Revolutionary Museum

SHANGHAI
Bank Museum
Chanying District Revolutionary Relics Show Room
Former residence of Sun Yat-Sen
Jewish Refugees Memorial Hall
Liu Hai Su Art Gallery
Lu Xun Museum
Museum of Natural History
Museum of Oriental Musical Instruments
Post Museum
Shanghai Art Museum
Shanghai Children's Museum
Shanghai History Museum
Shanghai Museum
Shanghai Museum of Arts and Crafts
Shanghai Museum of Glass
Shanghai Museum of Public Security
Shanghai Science and Technology Museum

Shanghai Urban Planning Exhibition Center
Shikumen Open House, Xintiandi
Site of the First Congress of the Communist Party of China
Song Qingling Residence
Tobacco Museum

JIANGSU PROVINCE
Nanjing Museum
Suzhou Museum
Zisha Ceramics Museum, Dingshan

ZHEJIANG PROVINCE
China National Silk Museum, Hangzhou
Tea Museum, Hangzhou
Traditional Medicine Museum, Hangzhou
Zhejiang Provincial Museum, Hangzhou

SICHUAN PROVINCE
Museum of the Southwest University for Nationalities, Chengdu
Sanxingdui Museum, Guanghan
Sichuan University Museum, Chengdu

YUNNAN PROVINCE
Anthropology Museum, Yunnan University, Kunming
Dongba Museum, Lijiang
Mengle Museum, Jinghong
Museum of the University of Ethnic Minorities, Kunming
Nanjian Ecomuseum
Yunnan Nationalities Museum, Kunming
Yunnan Provincial Museum, Kunming

TAIWAN
National Palace Museum, Taipei

Bibliography and References

Abt, J, 2006 The Origins of the Public Museum, in *A Companion to Museum Studies* (ed S McDonald), Blackwell, Oxford

Academic Exchanges on Conservation of China, 2003 *Relevant Information on Cultural Relics Protection in China* [online], available from: http://www.chinacov.com/EN/displaynews. asp?id=97 [3 September 2012]

Alpers, S, 1991 The Museum as a Way of Seeing, in *Exhibiting Cultures: The Poetics and Politics of Museum Display* (eds I Karp and S D Lavine), Smithsonian Institution Press, Washington DC

Alsop, J, 1982 *The Rare Art Traditions*, Thames and Hudson, London

Ames, M, 1986 *Museums, the Public and Anthropology*, University of British Columbia Press, Vancouver

— 1992 *Cannibal Tours and Glass Boxes: The Anthropology of Museums*, University of British Columbia Press, Vancouver

An, L, 1991 Museums and Museology in China, paper presented at the Reinwardt Academie, Amsterdam, November

— 1999 An Historical Approach to Museums' Roles in China, lecture given at the Reinwardt Academie, Amsterdam, 29 September

Anagnost, A, 1994 The Politicized Body, in *Body, Subject, and Power in China* (eds A Zito and T Barlow), University of Chicago Press, Chicago

— 1997 *National Past-Times: Narrative, Representation, and Power in Modern China*, Duke University Press, Durham NC

Anderson, B, 1991 *Imagined Communities: Reflections on the Origin and Spread of Nationalism*, Verso, London

Andrews, J F, 1994 *Painters and Politics in the People's Republic of China, 1949–1979*, University of California Press, Berkeley

Anthony, T, 2004 What hath capitalism wrought? In Chairman Mao's hometown, a much-changed China, *Associated Press* [online], 4 March, available from: http://www.highbeam. com/doc/1P1–91959242.html [19 September 2012]

Appadurai, A (ed), 1986 *The Social Life of Things: Commodities in Cultural Perspective*, Cambridge University Press, Cambridge

Ba, J, 1986 *A Museum of the 'Cultural Revolution'* [online], available from: http://museums.cnd. org/CR/english/articles/bajin.htm [3 September 2012]

Bal, M, 1996 *Double Exposures: The Subject of Cultural Analysis*, Routledge, London

Bamo, A, Harrell, S, Ma, L, and Bamo, Q, 2007 *Fieldwork Connections: The Fabric of Ethnographic Collaboration in China and America*, University of Washington Press, Seattle

Baniotopoulou, E, 2001 Art for whose sake? Modern art museums and their role in transforming societies: The case of the Guggenheim Bilbao, *Journal of Conservation and Museum Studies* 7, 1–15

Barboza, D, 2010 Rival Museums Retrace Route of China's Imperial Treasures, *The New York Times* [online], 6 July, available from: http://www.nytimes.com/2010/07/07/arts/design/07treasures.html [3 August 2012]

Barmé, G, 2010 Shanghai: Harmonising History, *China Heritage Quarterly* 22 [online], June, available from: http://www.chinaheritagequarterly.org/editorial.php?issue=022 [22 May 2012]

Barnard, A, and Spencer, J, 1996 *Encyclopaedia of Cultural and Social Anthropology*, Routledge, London

Barringer, T, and Flynn, T, 1998 *Colonialism and the Object: Empire, Material Culture and the Museum*, Routledge, London

Becker, H, 1982 *Art Worlds*, University of California Press, Berkeley

Becker, J, 2001 Guardian of the Past, *South China Morning Post*, 3 January

Beijing Administrative Bureau of Cultural Relics, 2004 *Imperial Treasures from China*, Beijing Administrative Bureau of Cultural Relics, Beijing

Beijing Daily, 2003 *Five Changes of Cultural Relics Protection* [online], 7 October, available from: http://www.chinacov.com/EN/classify.asp?id=95&cate=24&page=1 [19 September 2012]

Beijing Institute of Clothing Technology, n.d. *Kingdom of Clothes: China's exquisite ethnic costumes and accoutrements*, Beijing Institute of Clothing Technology, Beijing

Bennett, T, 1995 *The Birth of the Museum: History, Theory, Politics*, Routledge, London

— 2005 Civic Laboratories, *Cultural Studies* 19 (5), 521–47

— 2006a Exhibition, Difference and the Logic of Culture, in *Museum Frictions: Public Cultures/ Global Transformations* (eds I Karp, C Kratz, L Szwaja, and T Ybarra-Frausto), Duke University Press, Durham NC

— 2006b Civic Seeing: Museums and the Organization of Vision, in *Critical Trajectories: Culture, Society, Intellectuals* (ed T Bennett), Blackwell, Oxford

— 2008 Anthropological assemblages: producing culture as a surface of government, *CRESC Working Paper Series* 52 [online], available from: http://www.cresc.ac.uk/publications/anthropological-assemblages-producing-culture-as-a-surface-of-government [3 September 2012]

Blum, S, 2001 *Portraits of 'Primitives': Ordering Human Kinds in the Chinese Nation*, Rowman & Littlefield, Oxford

Bobin, F, 2003 La Chine exige la restitution de ses antiquités, *Le Monde*, 29 March

Bourdieu, P, 1984 *Distinction: A Social Critique of the Judgement of Taste*, Routledge, London

Bourdieu, P, and Darbel, A, 1966 *L'amour de l'art, les musées et leur public*, Editions de Minuit, Paris

Brautigam, D, 2009 *The Dragon's Gift: The Real Story of China in Africa*, Oxford University Press, Oxford

Brindley, E, 2010 *Individualism in Early China: Human Agency and the Self in Thought and Politics*, University of Hawai'i Press, Honolulu

Burke, K, 1969 *A Grammar of Motives*, University of California Press, Berkeley

Cable, M, 2008 Will the Real Dai Please Stand Up: Conflicting Displays of Identity in Ethnic Tourism, *Journal of Heritage Tourism* 3 (4), 267–76

Capital Museum, n.d. *Introduction to Capital Museum* [online], available from: http://www.capitalmuseum.org.cn/en/ [3 September 2012]

Capon, E, 1977 *Art and Archaeology in China*, Westerham Press, London

Chang, K-C, 1983 *Art, Myth and Ritual: The Path to Political Authority in Ancient China*, Harvard University Press, Cambridge MA

Chang, W-C, 1999 Esquisse d'une histoire du concept chinois de patrimoine, *Publics et musées* 15, 81–117

Chen, A, 2004 Commune Inc milks Mao dream, *South China Morning Post*, 18 July

Chevrier, Y, 1990 Des réformes à la révolution (1895–1913), in *La Chine au XXe siècle* (eds M-C Bergère, L Bianco, and J Domes), Fayard, Paris

China Daily, 2000a Museum System to Be Restructured, *China Daily*, 13 October

— 2000b Museums Urged to Show China's Advanced Culture, *China Daily*, 12 October

— 2002 Shanghai to Build 10 Industrial Museums, *China Daily*, 7 August

— 2003 Tobacco Museum Shanghai, *China Daily*, 9 January

— 2004 Experts Muse over Museums, *China Daily*, 22 July

— 2011 Palace Museum covers up 4 more mishaps, *China Daily*, 6 August

China Heritage Newsletter, 2005a *Private Museums Threatened by Downtown Development* [online], March, available from: http://www.chinaheritagequarterly.org/articles.php?searchterm=001_privatemuseums.inc&issue=001 [19 May 2012]

— 2005b *A Tale of Two Cities: New Museums for Yining and Urumqi* [online], September, available from: http://www.chinaheritagequarterly.org/features.php?searchterm=003_twomuseums.inc&issue=003 [19 July 2012]

Chinese Government Official Web Portal, 2013 *Law of the People's Republic of China on Protection of Cultural Relics* [online], available from: http://english.gov.cn/laws/2005–10/09/content_75322.htm [22 April 2013]

Claypool, L, 2005 Zhang Jian and China's first museum, *Journal of Asian Studies* 64 (3), 567–604

Clifford, J, 1988 *The Predicament of Culture*, Harvard University Press, Cambridge MA

— 1997 *Routes: Travel and Translation in the Late Twentieth Century*, Harvard University Press, Cambridge MA

Clunas, C, 1987 *Chinese Export Art and Design*, Victoria and Albert Museum, London

— 1991 *Superfluous Things: Material Culture and Social Status in Early Modern China*, University of Illinois Press, Chicago

— 1996 *Fruitful Sites: Garden Culture in Ming Dynasty China*, Reaktion Books, London

— 1997a *Art in China*, Oxford University Press, Oxford

— 1997b Oriental antiquities/Far Eastern Art, in *Formations of Colonial Modernity in East Asia* (ed T E Barlow), Duke University Press, Durham NC

— 1998 China in Britain: The Imperial Collections, in *Colonialism and the Object: Empire, Material Culture and the Museum* (eds T Barringer and T Flynn), Routledge, London

Cody, E, 2005 Chinese Museum Looks Back in Candor, *The Washington Post* [online], 3 June, available from: http://www.washingtonpost.com/wp-dyn/content/article/2005/06/02/AR2005060201916.html [12 April 2012]

Cohen, M L, 1991 Being Chinese: The Peripheralization of Traditional Identity, *Daedalus* 120 (2), 113–34

Coombes, A, 2001 The Object of Translation, in *The Empire of Things: Regimes of Value and Material Culture* (ed F Myers), James Currey, Oxford

Coonan, C, 2006 China's first Cultural Revolution museum exposes Mao's war on 'bourgeois culture', *The Independent* [online], 21 February, available from: http://www.independent.co.uk/news/world/asia/chinas-first-cultural-revolution-museum-exposes-maos-war-on-bourgeois-culture-467265.html [12 April 2012]

Crane, S, 2000 *Museums and Memory*, Stanford University Press, Stanford

Croll, E, 2006 *China's New Consumers: Social Development and Domestic Demand*, Routledge, London

Cuno, J B, 2008 *Who Owns Antiquity?: Museums and the Battle over Our Ancient Heritage*, Princeton University Press, Princeton NJ

Dahl, G B, and Stade, R, 2000 Anthropology, Museums and Contemporary Cultural Processes: An Introduction, *Ethnos* 65 (2), 157–71

Davis, P, 2011 *Ecomuseums: A Sense of Place*, Continuum, London

Davis, P, Huang, H-Y, and Liu, W-C, 2010 Heritage, local communities and the safeguarding of 'Spirit of Place' in Taiwan, *Museum and Society* 8 (2), 80–9

Davis, P, Maggi, M, Su, D, and Zhang, J (eds), 2006 *Communication and Exploration: Papers of the International Ecomuseum Forum, Guihzou, China* [online], available from: http://www.trentinocultura.net/doc/soggetti/ecomusei/Atti_Convegno_eng.pdf [18 July 2012]

Davis, S, 2005 *Song and Silence: Ethnic Revival on China's Southwest Borders*, Columbia University Press, New York

De Bary, T, Chan, W, and Watson, B, 1960 *Sources of Chinese Tradition*, Columbia University Press, New York

Denton, K, 2005 Museums, Memorial Sites and Exhibitionary Culture in the People's Republic of China, *China Quarterly* 183, 565–86

— 2007 Heroic Resistance and Victims of Atrocity: Negotiating the Memory of Japanese Imperialism in Chinese Museums, *Japan Focus* [online], available from: http://japanfocus.org/-kirk_a_-denton/2547 [20 September 2012]

Derrida, J, 1982 *Margins of Philosophy*, University of Chicago Press, Chicago

Descola, P, 2007 Passages de témoins, *Le Débat: Le Moment du Quai Branly* 147, 136–53

Dewar, S, 1999 An Interview with Xiaoneng Yang, *Orientations* 30 (7), 62–4

— 2000 The Poly Art Museum, Beijing, *Orientations* 31 (1), 77–8

Dikötter, F, 1996 Culture, 'Race' and Nation: The Formation of National Identity in Twentieth Century China, *Journal of International Affairs* 49 (2), 590–605

Dirlik, A, and Meisner, M (eds), 1989 *Marxism and the Chinese Experience*, M E Sharpe, Armonk NY

Ditchev, I, 2001 Les métamorphoses de l'identité bulgare: musée et imaginaire national, *Ethnologie française* 31 (2), 329–36

Duara, P, 1988 Superscribing Symbols: The Myth of Guandi, Chinese God of War, *Journal of Asian Studies* 47 (4), 778–95

— 1993 De-constructing the Chinese Nation, *The Australian Journal of Chinese Affairs* 30, 1–26

— 2002 Foreword: Sovereignty and Citizenship in a Decentered China, in *China Off Center: Mapping the Margins of the Middle Kingdom* (eds S D Blum and L M Jensen), University of Hawai'i Press, Honolulu

Duke, M, 1989 Reinventing China, *Issues and Studies* 25 (8), 29–53

Duncan, C, 1995 *Civilizing Rituals: Inside Public Art Museums*, Routledge, London

Duncan, C, and Wallach, A, 2004 The Universal Survey Museum, in *Museum Studies: An Anthology of Contexts* (ed B Messias Carbonell), Blackwell, Oxford

Dunedin Public Art Gallery, 1999 *Chinese Splendour: 5000 years of art from the Shanghai Museum*, Dunedin Public Art Gallery, Auckland, NZ

Errington, S, 1998 *The Death of Authentic Primitive Art and Other Tales of Progress*, University of California Press, Berkeley

Fabian, J, 1983 *Time and the Other: How Anthropology Makes its Object*, Columbia University Press, New York

Fei, X, 1979 Modernisation and national minorities in China, *Occasional Papers of the Centre for East Asian Studies* 6, McGill University, Montreal

Fei, Y, and Fei, H, 1936 *Bowuguanxue Gailun* [Introduction to Museology], Shanghai Zhonghua, Shanghai

Feng, C, 1991 China's museums reveal a dynamic past as well as future, *Museum News* 70 (6), 16–19

— 1993 Chinese museums, windows and looking glasses of China's reality, paper presented at the Reinwardt Academie, Amsterdam, December

Ferguson, E, 1981 Interpreting a civilisation, *Museum News* 59 (6), 50–2

Fernsebner, S R, 2006 Objects, Spectacle, and a Nation on Display, *Late Imperial China* 27 (2), 99–124

Feuchtwang, S, 2011 Exhibition and Awe: Regimes of Visibility in the Presentation of an Emperor, *Journal of Material Culture* 16 (1), 64–79

Fiskesjö, M, 2006 Rescuing the empire: Chinese nation-building in the twentieth century, *European Journal of East Asian Studies* 5 (1), 15–44

— 2007 The trouble with world culture, *Anthropology Today* 23 (5), 6–11

— 2010 Politics of cultural heritage, in *Reclaiming Chinese Society: The new social activism* (eds C K Lee and Y-T Hsing), Routledge, London

Flath, J A, 2002 Managing Historical Capital in Shandong: Museum, Monument, and Memory in Provincial China, *The Public Historian* 24 (2), 41–59

Fowler, D D, 1987 Uses of the Past: Archaeology in the Service of the State, *American Antiquity* 52 (2), 229–48

Friedman, E, 1994 Reconstructing China's National Identity: A Southern Alternative to Mao-Era Anti-Imperialist Nationalism, *Journal of Asian Studies* 53 (1), 67–91

Fu, Z, 1957 *Introduction to Museology*, Shanghai Commercial Press, Shanghai [in Chinese]

Gabus, J, 1975 *L'objet témoin: les références d'une civilisation par l'objet*, Éditions Ides et Calendes, Neuchâtel

Galikowski, M, 1998 *Art and Politics in China 1949–1984*, Chinese University Press, Hong Kong

Gao, S, 1999 *Chinese Cultural Laws, Regulations and Institutions*, Culture and Art Publishing House, Beijing

Garrett, V, 1994 *Chinese Clothing: An Illustrated Guide*, Oxford University Press, Oxford

Gell, A, 1998 *Art and Agency: An Anthropological Theory*, Clarendon Press, Oxford

Giebelhausen, M, 2003 *The architecture of the museum: Symbolic structures, urban contexts*, Manchester University Press, Manchester

Gladney, D, 1994 Representing Nationality in China: Refiguring Majority/Minority Identities, *Journal of Asian Studies* 53 (1), 92–123

— 2004 *Dislocating China: Reflections on Muslims, Minorities and Other Subaltern Subjects*, Hurst & Company, London

Golding, V, 2009 *Learning at the Museum Frontiers: Identity, Race and Power*, Ashgate, Farnham

GOV.cn, 2008 *China opens more museums to public free of charge* [online], 28 March, available from: http://english.gov.cn/2008–03/28/content_931589.htm [2 July 2012]

Grasseni, C, 2007 *Skilled Visions: Between Apprenticeship and Standards*, Berghahn, New York

Greater London Authority, 2006 *London will benefit from strong economic and cultural ties with*

China, says Mayor [online], 26 January, available from: http://www.london.gov.uk/media/press_releases_mayoral/london-will-benefit-strong-economic-and-cultural-ties-china-says-mayor [3 September 2012]

Greenblatt, S, 1991 Resonance and Wonder, in *Exhibiting Cultures: The Poetics and Politics of Museum Display* (eds I Karp and S D Lavine), Smithsonian Institution Press, Washington DC

Gries, P, and Rosen, S (eds), 2004 *State and Society in 21st-Century China*, Routledge, London

Groys, B, 1994 The Struggle against the Museum; or The Display of Art in Totalitarian Space, in *Museum Culture: Histories, Discourses, Spectacles* (eds D J Sherman and I Rogoff), University of Minnesota Press, Minneapolis

The Guardian, 2012 *China riots leave 12 people dead* [online], 28 February, available from: http://www.guardian.co.uk/world/2012/feb/28/china-riots-dead [25 April 2013]

Guo, C, 2008 The Qing Palace: From a Forbidden City to a Public Heritage, *Museum International* 60 (1–2), 78–88

Guo, Q, 2004 Personal communication (interview with the author), 24 March, Shanghai

Guo, Y, 2004 Cultural Nationalism in Contemporary China: The Search for National Identity Under Reform, Curzon Press, London

Hamlish, T, 2000 Re-membering the Chinese Imperial Collections, in *Museums and Memory* (ed S Crane), Stanford University Press, Stanford

Handler, R, 1984 On sociocultural discontinuity: nationalism and objectification in Québec, *Cultural Anthropology* 25 (1), 55–71

Hansen, M H, and Svarverud, R (eds), 2010 *iChina: The Rise of the Individual in Modern Chinese Society*, Nordic Institute of Asian Studies Press, Copenhagen

Haraway, D, 1984 Teddy Bear Patriarchy: Taxidermy in the Garden of Eden, New York City, 1908–1936, *Social Text* 11 (1), 20–64

Harrell, S, 1995 *Cultural Encounters on China's Ethnic Frontiers*, University of Washington Press, Seattle

— 2001 *Ways of Being Ethnic in Southwest China*, University of Washington Press, Seattle

He, S, 2000 The mainland's environment and the protection of China's cultural heritage: a Chinese Cultural Heritage Lawyer's Perspective, *Art, Antiquity and Law* 5 (1), 19–35

Henare, A, 2005 *Museums, anthropology and imperial exchange*, Cambridge University Press, Cambridge

Henderson, J, Teck, G K, Ng, D, and Si-Rong, T, 2009 Tourism in Ethnic Communities: Two Miao Villages in China, *International Journal of Heritage Studies* 15 (6), 529–39

Hillman, B, 2003 Paradise Under Construction: Minorities, Myths and Modernity in Northwest Yunnan, *Asian Ethnicity* 4 (2), 175–88

Hobsbawm, E, and Ranger, T (eds), 1983 *The Invention of Tradition*, Cambridge University Press, Cambridge

Hodge, B, and Louie, K, 1998 *The politics of Chinese language and culture*, Routledge, London

Holden Platt, K, 2012 Chinese Museums Open to the World, *The New York Times* [online], 8 June, available from: http://www.nytimes.com/2012/06/09/arts/09iht-rartholden09.html?pagewanted=all&_r=0 [6 July 2012]

Holm, D, 1991 *Art and Ideology in Revolutionary China*, Clarendon Press, Oxford

Hooper-Greenhill, E, 1992 *Museums and the Shaping of Knowledge*, Routledge, London

— 2000 *Museums and the Interpretation of Visual Culture*, Routledge, London

Hsu, E, 1999 *The Transmission of Chinese Medicine*, Cambridge University Press, Cambridge

Humanities Research, 2001 Prominent Australians share their thoughts on museums of the future, *Humanities Research* 8 (1), available from: http://www.anu.edu.au/hrc/publications/hr/issue1_2001/article08.htm [20 September 2012]

Hung, C-T, 2005 The Red Line: Creating a Museum of the Chinese Revolution, *China Quarterly* 184, 914–33

— 2007 Oil Paintings and Politics: Weaving a Heroic Tale of the Chinese Communist Revolution, *Comparative Studies in Society and History* 49 (4), 783–814

— 2012 The Cultural Palace of Nationalities: Ethnicities Under One Roof?, *Journal of Contemporary History* 47 (3), 572–93

Hwang, Y-J, and Schneider, F, 2011 Performance, Meaning, and Ideology in the Making of Legitimacy: The Celebrations of the People's Republic of China's Sixty-Year Anniversary, *The China Review* 11 (1), 27–56

Jewsiewicki, B, 2007 La mémoire est-elle soluble dans l'esthétique?, *Le Débat: Le Moment du Quai Branly* 147, 174–7

Jing, W, 2006 Nostalgia as Content: Creativity Cultural Industries and Popular Sentiment, *International Journal of Cultural Studies* 9 (3), 359–68

Jisheng, L, 1987 Museum Training in China, *Museum International* 39 (4), 291–5

Johnson, I, 2011 At China's New Museum, History Toes Party Line, *The New York Times* [online], 3 April, available from: http://www.nytimes.com/2011/04/04/world/asia/04museum.html?pagewanted=all [12 July 2012]

Jonsson, H, 2000 Yao Minority Identity and the Location of Difference in the South China Borderlands, *Ethnos* 65 (1), 56–82

Kahn, D M, 1998 Domesticating a foreign import: museums in Asia, *Curator* 41 (4), 226–8

Kang, Y, 1905 *Yidali Youji* [Travels Around Italy], Ouzhou Shiyi Guo Youji, Shanghai

Kaplan, F E S, 1994 *Museums and the Making of 'Ourselves': The Role of Objects in National Identity*, Leicester University Press, London

Karp, I, Mullen Kreamer, C, and Lavine, S D, 1992 *Museums and communities: the politics of public culture*, Smithsonian Institution Press, Washington DC

Keane, W, 2001 Money is no object, in *The Empire of Things: Regimes of Value and Material Culture* (ed F Myers), James Currey, Oxford

King, A, 1991 Kuan-hsi and network building: a sociological interpretation, *Daedalus* 120, 63–84

Kleinman, A, Yan, Y, Jun, J, Lee, S, and Zhang, E, 2011 *Deep China: The Moral Life of the Person*, University of California Press, Berkeley

Komlosy, A, 2004 Procession and water splashing: expressions of locality and nationality during Dai New Year in Xishuangbanna, *Journal of the Royal Anthropological Institute* 10 (2), 351–73

Kopytoff, I, 1986 The cultural biography of things, in *The social life of things: Commodities in cultural perspective* (ed A Appadurai), Cambridge University Press, Cambridge

Kraus, R C, 2004 When Legitimacy Resides in Beautiful Objects, in *State and Society in 21st-Century China* (eds P Gries and S Rosen), Routledge, London

— 2009 The Repatriation of Plundered Chinese Art, *The China Quarterly* 199, 837–42

Lee, C-K, and Yang, G, 2007 *Re-Envisioning the Chinese Revolution: The Politics and Poetics of Collective Memories in Reform China*, Stanford University Press, Stanford

Legget, J, 1995 Pacific treasure trail, *Museums Journal* 95 (2), 29

Lengyel, A, 1991 Museums could be one of the vehicles for China's modernisation, paper presented at the Reinwardt Academie, Amsterdam, November

Lévi-Strauss, C, 1962 *La Pensée Sauvage*, Plon, Paris

— 1966 *The Savage Mind*, Oxford University Press, Oxford

Li, L, 2004 *China's Cultural Relics*, Cultural China Series, China Intercontinental Press, Beijing

Li, R, 2008 Personal communication (interview with the author), 22 March, Kunming

Li, X, 2004 Personal communication (interview with the author), 5 February, Beijing

— 2007 *20th Shiji zhongguo xueshu dadian: Kaoguxue, bowuguanxue* [Chinese academic canon in the 20th Century: Archaeology, museology], Fujian Jiaoyu Press, Fuzhou [in Chinese]

Li, X, and Jiang, L, 2003 Archaeological discoveries and studies on Ancient Chinese civilisation, *Social Sciences in China* 24 (1), 187

Li, X, and Luo, Z, 2004 *China's Museums*, Cultural China Series, China Intercontinental Press, Beijing

Lin, M, and Galikowski, M, 1999 *The Search for Modernity: Chinese Intellectuals and Cultural Discourse in the Post-Mao Era*, St Martin's Press, New York

Liu, K, 2000 Popular culture and the culture of the masses, in *Postmodernism and China* (eds A Dirlik and X Zhang), Duke University Press, Durham NC

Liu, P, Liu, A, and Wall, G, 2005 Eco-museum Conception and Chinese Application: A Case Study in Miao Villages, Suoga, Guizhou Province, *Resources and Environment in the Yangtze Basin* 14, 254–7

Lowenthal, D, 1985 *The Past is a Foreign Country*, Cambridge University Press, Cambridge

Lu, J, 1994 Museums and museology in China, paper presented at the *Annual Meeting of the ICOFOM*, 11–20 September, Beijing

Lu, J, 2004a Personal communication (interview with the author), 24 September, Shanghai

— 2004b Personal communication (interview with the author), 3 October, Shanghai

— 2006 Personal communication (interview with the author), 16 April, Shanghai

— 2012 Personal communication (interview with the author), 11 May, Shanghai

Ma, W, 2003 Significance and management of private-owned museums, *Social Sciences in China* 24 (1), 98–106

Ma, Z, 1994 Museums in China and its cultural policy, paper presented at the *Annual Meeting of the ICOFOM*, 11–20 September, Beijing

Macdonald, S, and Basu, P, 2007 *Exhibition Experiments*, Blackwell, Malden MA

Mackerras, C, 2003 *China's Ethnic Minorities and Globalisation*, RoutledgeCurzon, London

MacLeod, S, Hourston Hanks, L, and Hale, J, 2012 *Museum Making: Narratives, Architecture, Exhibitions*, Routledge, London

Mao, T, 1940 On New Democracy, *Selected Works of Mao Tse-Tung* [online], available from: http://www.marxists.org/reference/archive/mao/selected-works/volume-2/mswv2_26.htm [1 July 2013]

— 1967 Talks at the Yenan Forum on Literature and Art (May 1942), in *Selected Works Vol III*, Foreign Languages Press, Beijing

Maure, M, 1995 The Exhibition as Theatre: On the Staging of Museum Objects, *Nordisk Museologi* 2, 155–68

McKillop, B, 1995 Seoul searches for a new image, *Museums Journal* 95 (2), 27

Metropolitan Museum of Art, 1980 *Treasures from the Bronze Age of China: An exhibition from the People's Republic of China*, The Metropolitan Museum of Art, New York

Michaelson, C, 2007 Personal communication (interview with the author), 11 October, British Museum, London

Miller, D, 1987 *Material Culture and Mass Consumption*, Blackwell, Oxford

Min, Z, 1989 The administration of China's archaeological heritage, in *Archaeological Heritage Management in the Modern World* (ed H F Cleere), One World Archaeology, London

Mitter, R, 2000 Behind the Scenes at the Museum: Nationalism, History and Memory in the Beijing War of Resistance Museum, 1987–1997, *The China Quarterly* 161, 279–93

Morgan, L H, 1985 (1877) *Ancient Society*, University of Arizona Press, Tucson

Mullaney, T, 2010 *Coming to Terms with the Nation: Ethnic Classification in Modern China*, University of California Press, Berkeley

Mullaney, T S, Leibold, J, Gros, S, and Vanden Bussche, E, 2012 *Critical Han Studies: The History, Representation, and Identity of China's Majority*, University of California Press, Berkeley

Murowchick, R E, 2013 Despoiled of the garments of her civilization: Problems and progress in archaeological heritage management in China, in *A Companion to Chinese Archaeology* (ed A P Underhill), Wiley-Blackwell, Oxford

Museums Department of the State Administrative Bureau of Museums and Archaeological Data, 1980 Museums in China today, *Museum* 32 (4), 170–83

Myers, F, 2001 *The Empire of Things: Regimes of Value and Material Culture*, James Currey, Oxford

National Museum of China, n.d.a *Ancient China* [online], available from: http://en.chnmuseum.cn/tabid/520/Default.aspx?ExhibitionLanguageID=84 [24 May 2012]

— n.d.b *National Museum Collection Highlights of Chinese Modern Masterpieces* [online], available from: http://en.chnmuseum.cn/tabid/520/Default.aspx?ExhibitionLanguageID=85 [24 May 2012]

— 2012a *The Yellow River – Exhibition of Nakamura Sadao's Oil Paintings* [online], available from: http://en.chnmuseum.cn/tabid/520/Default.aspx?ExhibitionLanguageID=235 [24 May 2012]

— 2012b *African Cultures in Focus* [online], available from: http://en.chnmuseum.cn/tabid/522/Default.aspx?ExhibitionLanguageID=238 [24 May 2012]

— 2012c *Exhibition of Selected African Sculptures in the Collection of the National Museum of China* [online], available from: http://en.chnmuseum.cn/tabid/522/Default.aspx?ExhibitionLanguageID=232 [24 May 2012]

— 2012d *Introduction* [online], available from: http://en.chnmuseum.cn/tabid/497/Default.aspx [6 July 2012]

National Museum of Chinese History, 2002 *Exhibition of Chinese History* [exhibition catalogue], Morning Glory Publishers, Beijing

National People's Congress of the People's Republic of China, 2004 *Constitution of the People's Republic of China* [English version] [online], available from: http://www.npc.gov.cn/englishnpc/Constitution/node_2825.htm [9 July 2012]

Nerison-Low, R, 2001 Art Treasures and Social Transitions, *The Journal of the International Institute* 8 (3) [online], available from: http://quod.lib.umich.edu/j/jii/4750978 0008 307/--art-treasures-and-social-transitions?rgn=main;view=fulltext [3 September 2012]

Ni, X, 2001 *The Memorial Hall of the First National Congress of the Communist Party of China*, People's Publishing Society, Shanghai

Nora, P, and Kritzman, L D, 1996 *Realms of Memory: Rethinking the French Past*, Columbia University Press, New York

Ong, A, 1997 Chinese Modernities: Narratives of Nation and of Capitalism, in *Ungrounded Empires: The Cultural Politics of Modern Chinese Transnationalism* (eds A Ong and D Nonini), Routledge, London

Ong, A, and Nonini, D, 1997 Introduction: Chinese Transnationalism as an Alternative Modernity, in *Ungrounded Empires: The Cultural Politics of Modern Chinese Transnationalism* (eds A Ong and D Nonini), Routledge, London

Pagani, C, 1998 Chinese material culture and British perceptions of China in the mid-nineteenth century, in *Colonialism and the Object: Empire, Material Culture and the Museum* (eds T Barringer and T Flynn), Routledge, London

Pan, L, 2012 The Invisible Turn to the Future: Commemorative Culture in Contemporary Shanghai, *Culture Unbound: Journal of Current Cultural Research* 4, 121–46

Pan, S, 2012 The Social Benefits of Heritage and Chinese Ethnic Minorities, *Museum International* 63 (1–2), 43–54

Pearce, S, 1994 *Interpreting objects and collections*, Routledge, London

Peers, L, and Brown, A, 2003 *Museums and Source Communities: A Routledge Reader*, Routledge, London

People's Daily, 2002 *China to Have 3,000 Museums by 2015* [online], 20 December, available from: http://english.peopledaily.com.cn/200212/20/eng20021220_108815.shtml [28 May 2013]

— 2006 *China needs more, better museums* [online], 30 October, available from: http://english.peopledaily.com.cn/200610/30/eng20061030_316303.html [28 May 2013]

— 2007 *China's national museum closes for 3-year overhaul* [online], 31 January, available from: http://english.peopledaily.com.cn/200701/31/eng20070131_346278.html [28 May 2013]

Perin, C, 1992 The communicative circle, in *Museums and communities: the politics of public culture* (eds I Karp, C Mullen Kreamer, and S D Lavine), Smithsonian Institution Press, Washington DC

Perlez, J, 2012 China Extends Reach Into International Art, *The New York Times* [online], 23 April, available from: http://www.nytimes.com/2012/04/24/arts/design/china-focuses-on-museums-and-more-international-art-shows.html [5 July 2012]

Pohl, K-H, 2008 Identity and Hybridity: Chinese Culture and Aesthetics in the Age of Globalization, *Intercultural Aesthetics*, 87–103

Poly Art Museum, n.d. Undated museum leaflet collected by the author on the Museum's premises, February 2004

Preziosi, D, 2010 Myths of Nationality, in *National Museums: New Studies from Around the World* (eds S J Knell, P Aronsson, and A Bugge Amundsen), Routledge, New York

Price, S, 2007 *Paris Primitive: Jacques Chirac's Museum on the Quai Branly*, University of Chicago Press, Chicago

Pye, L, 1996 How China's nationalism was Shanghaied, in *Chinese Nationalism* (ed J Unger), M E Sharpe, Armonk NY

Qian, Z, 2004a Personal communication (interview with the author), 4 August, Shanghai

— 2004b Personal communication (interview with the author), 15 September, Shanghai

Qiu, M, 2000 On development of culture and comprehensive national power, *Shanghai Academy of Social Sciences Papers* 8, 314–26

Ren, Z, Hu, Z, Li, Y, Xue, C, Zhang, D, and Zhou, G, 1994 The collections of the Shanxi Provincial Museum, *Orientations* 25 (12), 26–42

Root, D, 1996 *Cannibal Culture: Art, Appropriation and the Commodification of Difference*, Westview Press, Oxford

Ruan, J, 1994 Features and values of cultural relics, paper presented at the *Annual Meeting of the ICOFOM*, 11–20 September, Beijing

Sandberg, M B, 2002 *Living Pictures, Missing Persons: Mannequins, Museums, and Modernity*, Princeton University Press, Princeton NJ

Sandell, R, 2002 *Museums, Society, Inequality*, Routledge, London

Sandell, R, and Nightingale, E, 2012 *Museums, Equality and Social Justice*, Routledge, London

Sanxingdui Museum, 1998 *The Sanxingdui Museum* [CD-ROM]

Saunders, B, 2001 The photological apparatus and the desiring machine, in *Academic Anthropology and the Museum: Back to the Future* (ed M Bouquet), Berghahn, Oxford

Schein, L, 1997 Gender and Internal Orientalism, *Modern China* 23 (1), 69–98

— 2000 *Minority rules: the Miao and the feminine in China's cultural politics*, Duke University Press, London

Schwarcz, V, 1991 No solace from Lethe: History, memory and cultural identity in twentieth century China, *Daedalus* 120 (2), 85–111

— 1994 Strangers No More: Personal Memory in the Interstices of Public Commemorations, in *Memory, History, and Opposition under State Socialism* (ed R Watson), School of American Research Press, Santa Fe NM

Shanghai History Museum website, 2004 English homepage [online], available from: http://www.historymuseum.sh.cn/en.php [29 October 2012]

Shanghai Museum, 1997 *Pan of Zi Zhong Jiang* [brochure], Shanghai Museum, Shanghai

— 2003 A series of activities of the exhibition, competition and forum on the *Chunhua ge tie* – To promote Chinese culture and national spirits [exhibition leaflet]

— n.d. *The Shanghai Museum* [brochure]

Shanks, M, and Tilley, C, 1987 *Re-constructing archaeology*, Cambridge University Press, Cambridge

Shelton, A, 1990 Post-modernist museography, in *Objects of Knowledge* (ed S Pearce), The Athlone Press, London

Shen, Q, 1994 Cultural relic and material, paper presented at the *Annual Meeting of the ICOFOM*, 11–20 September, Beijing

Shih, C, 2002 *Negotiating Ethnicity in China: Citizenship as a Response to the State*, Routledge, London

Simpson, M, 1996 *Making Representations: Museums in the Post-Colonial Era*, Routledge, London

Song, X, 2004a Personal communication (interview with the author), 2 February, Beijing

— 2004b Personal communication (interview with the author), 6 November, Beijing

— 2006 Personal communication (interview with the author), 26 May, Beijing

— 2008 The Development of Private Museums in China, *Museum International* 60 (1–2), 40–8

— 2012 Personal communication (interview with the author), 1 June, Beijing

Stafford, C, 2003 Langage et apprentissage des nombres en Chine et à Taiwan, *Terrain* 40, 65–80

Stanley, N, 2002 Chinese Theme Parks and National Identity, in *Theme Park Landscapes: Antecedents and Variations* (eds T Young and R Riley), Dumbarton Oaks, Washington DC

State Cultural Relics Bureau, 1999 *The treasures of a nation: China's cultural heritage 1949–99*, Morning Glory Publishers, Beijing

Stein, R A, 1990 *The World in Miniature: Container Gardens and Dwellings in Far Eastern Religious Thought*, Stanford University Press, Stanford

Stewart, S, 1984 *On Longing: Narratives of the Miniature, the Gigantic, the Souvenir, the Collection*, Johns Hopkins University Press, Baltimore

Stransky, Z, 1992 Museums in post-Communist countries, in *Museums and Europe 1992* (ed S Pearce), The Athlone Press, London

Stråth, B, 2005 Methodological and Substantive Remarks on Myth, Memory and History in the Construction of a European Community, *German Law Journal* 6 (2), 255–71

Strathern, M, 1988 *The Gender of the Gift*, University of California Press, Berkeley

— 1993 One-legged gender, *Visual Anthropology Review* 9, 42–51

Su, D, 1989 Museology in China, in *The Fourth Regional Assembly of ICOM in Asia and the Pacific: proceeding* [sic], *1–7 March 1989*, ICOM, Beijing

— 1994 Philosophy of Chinese Museums, paper presented at the *Annual Meeting of the ICOFOM*, 11–20 September, Beijing

— 1995 Museums and Museum Philosophy in China, *Nordisk Museologi* 2, 61–80

— 2004 Personal communication (interview with the author), 12 February, Beijing

— 2006 The establishment and sustainable development of ecomuseums in China, in *Communication and Exploration: Papers of the International Ecomuseum Forum, Guihzou, China* (eds P Davis, M Maggi, D Su, and J Zhang), Chinese Society of Museums, Guiyang, available from: http://www.trentinocultura.net/doc/soggetti/ecomusei/Atti_Convegno_eng.pdf [5 September 2012]

— 2008 The Concept of the Ecomuseum and its Practice in China, *Museum International* 60 (1–2), 29–39

Suresh, T, 2002 Rediscovering nationalism in contemporary China, *China Report* 38 (1), 11–24

Szántó, A, 2011 China's new Age of Enlightenment, *The Art Newspaper* [online], 4 April, available from: http://www.theartnewspaper.com/articles/Chinas-new-Age-of-Enlightenment/23495 [1 May 2012]

Thorp, R, 1988 *Son of Heaven, Imperial Arts of China*, Son of Heaven Press, Seattle

Tilley, C, Keane, W, Kuechler, S, Rowlands, M, and Spyer, P (eds), 2006 *Handbook of Material Culture*, Sage, London

Tong, E, 1995 Thirty years of Chinese archaeology (1949–1979), in *Nationalism, Politics and the Practice of Archaeology* (eds P Kohl and C Fawcett), Cambridge University Press, Cambridge

Tu, W-M, 1993 Introduction: cultural perspectives, *Daedalus* 122 (2), vii–xxiii

Tythacott, L, 2011 *The Lives of Chinese Objects: Buddhism, Imperialism and Display*, Berghahn, Oxford

UNESCO, 1970 *Convention on the Means of Prohibiting and Preventing the Illicit Import, Export and Transfer of Ownership of Cultural Property 1970* [online], available from: http://portal.unesco.org/en/ev.php-URL_ID=13039&URL_DO=DO_TOPIC&URL_SECTION=201.html [8 January 2013]

— 1972 *Convention on the Protection of World Cultural and Natural Heritage* [online], available from: http://www.unesco.org.uk/convention_on_the_protection_of_world_cultural_and_natural_heritage_(1972) [29 October 2012]

Unger, J, 1996 *Chinese Nationalism*, M E Sharpe, Armonk NY

UNIDROIT, 1995 *Convention on Stolen or Illegally Exported Cultural Objects* [online], available from: http://www.unidroit.org/english/conventions/1995culturalproperty/main.htm [22 April 2013]

Varutti, M, 2008a A Chinese puzzle: the representation of Chinese Ethnic Minorities in the

Museums of Kunming, Yunnan Province of China, *The International Journal of the Inclusive Museum* 1 (3), 35–42

— 2008b Representing and 'consuming' the Chinese Other at the British Museum, in *National Museums in a Global World* (eds A Bugge Amundsen and A Nyblom), Linköping University Electronic Press, Linköping, available from: http://www.ep.liu.se/ecp/031/ [3 September 2012]

— 2008c Thinking through the 'Other': comparing representations of cultural alterity at the British Museum and the Shanghai Museum, in *Comparing: National Museums, Territories, Nation-Building and Change* (eds P Aronsson and A Nyblom), Linköping University Electronic Press, Linköping, available from: http://www.ep.liu.se/ecp/030/ [26 September 2012]

— 2010a Using Different Pasts in a Similar Way: Museum Representations of National History in Norway and China, in *Culture Unbound: Journal of Current Cultural Research* 2 (40), 745–68

— 2010b Indexes of Exclusion, in *Narratives of Community: Museums and Ethnicity* (ed O Guntarik), MuseumsEtc, Edinburgh

— 2010c The Aesthetics and Narratives of National Museums in China, in *National Museums: New Studies from Around the World* (eds S J Knell, P Aronsson, and A Bugge Amundsen), Routledge, London

— 2010d The Politics of Imagining and Forgetting in Chinese Ethnic Minorities Museums, in *Outlines: Critical Practice Studies* 12 (2), 69–82

— 2011a Standardising difference: the materiality of ethnic minorities in the museums of the People's Republic of China, in *The Thing About Museums Objects and Experience, Representation and Contestation* (eds S Dudley, A Barnes, and J Walklate), Routledge, London

— 2011b Miniatures of the nation: ethnic minority figurines, mannequins and dioramas in Chinese museums, *Museum and Society* 9 (1), 1–16

Vergo, P, 1989 *The New Museology*, Reaktion Books, London

Vickers, E, 2007 Museums and nationalism in contemporary China, *Compare* 37 (3), 365–82

Vickery, J, 2007 Organising art: constructing aesthetic value, in *Museums in the Material World* (ed S Knell), Taylor and Francis, London

Virtual Museum of the 'Cultural Revolution', n.d. *Preface: About the Virtual Museum of the Cultural Revolution* [online], available from: http://www.cnd.org/cr/english/about.htm [August 2012]

Von Falkenhausen, L, 1995 The Regionalist Paradigm in Chinese Archaeology, in *Nationalism, Politics and the Practice of Archaeology* (eds P Kohl and C Fawcett), Cambridge University Press, Cambridge

Walsh, E, and Swain, M, 2004 Creating Modernity by Touring Paradise: Domestic Ethnic Tourism in Yunnan, China, *Tourism Recreation Research* 29 (2), 59–68

Wang, C, 2004 *Ethnic groups in China*, China Intercontinental Press, Beijing

Wang, H, 2001 *Zhongguo bowuguan xue jichu* [The basis of Chinese Museology], Guji Editing House, Shanghai

— 2004 Personal communication (interview with the author), 6 February, Beijing

Wang, J, 1996 *High Culture Fever: Politics, Aesthetics, and Ideology in Deng's China*, University of California Press, Berkeley

Wang, Z, Tan, C, Cheung, S, and Yan, H, 2001 *Tourism, anthropology and China: in memory of Professor Wang Zhusheng*, White Lotus Press, Bangkok

Watson, R, 1992 The Renegotiation of Chinese Cultural Identity in the Post-Mao Era, in *Popular*

Protest and Political Culture in Modern China: Learning from 1989 (eds J Wasserstrom and E Perry), Westview, Boulder

— 1994 Introduction, in *Memory, History, and Opposition under State Socialism*, School of American Research Press, Santa Fe NM

— 1995 Palaces, Museums, and Squares: Chinese National Spaces, *Museum Anthropology* 19 (2), 7–19

— 1998 Tales of two Chinese history museums: Taipei and Hong Kong, *Curator* 41 (3), 167–77

Wechsler, H, 1985 *Offerings of Jade and Silk: Ritual and Symbol in the Legitimation of the T'ang Dynasty*, Yale University Press, New Haven CT

Weiner, A, 1992 *Inalienable Possessions: The Paradox of Keeping While Giving*, University of California Press, Berkeley

— 1994 Cultural difference and the density of objects, *American Ethnologist* 21 (2), 391–403

White, S, 1997 Fame and sacrifice: The gendered construction of Naxi identities, *Modern China* 23 (3), 298–327

Williams, C A S, 1976 *Outlines of Chinese Symbolism and Art Motives*, Dover Publications, New York

Wu, H, 2011 Museum and Change: Regional Museums in the People's Republic of China, unpublished PhD Thesis, University of Bergen, available from: https://bora.uib.no/handle/1956/5181 [16 April 2013]

Wu, Y D, 1991 The construction of Chinese and non-Chinese identities, *Daedalus* 120 (2), 159–79

Xiao, X, 2000 *Sanxingdui Museum in China*, Sanxingdui Museum, Chengdu

— 2002 *Museums: treasure houses of history*, Culture of China series, Foreign Language Press, Beijing

Xinhua News Agency, 2004 *Private Museums Elbowed out in Shanghai* [online], 7 January, available from: http://china.org.cn/english/travel/84090.htm [5 September 2012]

Yang, L, Wall, G, and Smith, S, 2008 Ethnic Tourism Development: Chinese Government Perspectives, *Annals of Tourism Research* 35 (3), 751–71

Yang, M M, 1994 *Gifts, Favors, and Banquets: The Art of Social Relationships in China*, Cornell University Press, Ithaca

Yen, Y, 2005 *Calligraphy and Power in Contemporary Chinese Society*, Routledge, London

Yin, S, 2003 A Work Report on the Project for Construction of Ethnic Cultural and Ecological Villages in Yunnan, *Chinese Sociology and Anthropology* 35 (3), 37–50

Yu, M, 2005 *China National Silk Museum*, Hangzhou Donglian Advertising and Printing Co, Hangzhou

Yuan, K, 1992 The development of museology in China, in *Museums and Europe 1992* (ed S Pearce), The Athlone Press, London

Yuan, Y, 2011 Unpleasant nights at the museum, *People's Daily Online* [online], 21 September, available from: http://english.people.com.cn/102780/7601245.html [2 May 2012]

Yunnan Provincial Museum, 2001 *Selected cultural relics of the nationalities collected by Yunnan Provincial Museum*, Yunnan Provincial Museum Press, Kunming

Zemon Davis, N, and Starn, R, 1989 Introduction, *Representations Special Issue: Memory and Counter-Memory* 26, 1–6

Zhang, L, 2003 *La naissance du concept de patrimoine en Chine: XIX–XXe siècles*, Recherches, Paris

Zhang, W, 2008 Editorial, *Museum International* 60 (1–2), 5–11

Zheng, L, 2007 Auto query? Ask Shanghai museum, *China Daily*, 19 January

Zheng, Q, 1985 *Bowuguan cangpin baoguan* [Preservation of museum collections], Zijincheng Press, Beijing [in Chinese]

Index

aesthetics   6, 22, 27, 28, 41, 62, 67–75, 84,
   86, 104, 105, 111, 112, 114, 117, 122, 135, 137,
   160, 161, 162
   of restored objects   13, 15
   aesthetic appreciation   17, 38–9, 40, 49, 64,
      65, 66
African Cultures in Focus exhibition (National
   Museum of China, 2012)   84
Alpers, Svetlana   60
Alsop, Joseph   9, 15
Ames, Michael   60, 70
An, Laishun   29, 35, 36, 41
Anagnost, Ann   99, 151
Ancient China   9, 20, 26, 63, 68, 69, 70, 81,
   87, 90, 107, 112, 113, 114, 115, 116, 117, 122,
   136, 145
   inscriptions in Ancient China   13, 19
Anderson, Benedict   132, 135, 159
Anti-Spiritual Pollution Campaign (1982)   24
Anyang archaeological site, Henan   87, 92, 94
art and agency (anthropological theory)   60,
   79, 88
Art Antiquity and Law journal   31
art object   11, 15–16, 17, 40, 71, 79, 81, 86, 162
artwork   12, 15, 81
art world   43
Asia House, London   83
Asian Cultural Association Museum   26
assemblage   59, 137
auction houses   33, 34, 53
authenticity (*see also* 'replicas')   6, 12, 13, 39,
   60, 72, 108, 116, 138, 147, 153–4, 157

Ba, Jin (writer)   119
Bai ethnic group   138, 139, 149, 150
bamboo   11, 139, 143

Bamo, Ayi   154
Barmé, Geremie   85
Becker, Howard   43
Bennett, Tony   4, 89, 137, 145, 152, 153
Bo, Stråth   103
'bone energy'   11
Bourdieu, Pierre   54, 81
'Brilliance Period' (late Shang Dynasty)   19
British Library, London   83
Bronze Age   17, 82
bronze vessels (*see also jiu ding, taotieh*)   6, 11,
   12, 15, 16, 17–20, 41, 49, 54, 63, 68, 69, 70,
   81, 82, 83, 86, 88, 92, 94, 108, 109, 111, 112,
   115, 118, 132, 150
Bulgari Retrospective exhibition (National
   Museum of China, 2011)   84, 119
Buyi ethnic group   154

Cai, Yuanpei (Minister of Education)   27
calligraphy (*see also* inscriptions)   11, 12, 15, 16,
   23, 40, 56, 62, 64, 68, 81, 83, 86, 88, 95,
   118, 123, 132, 143
Capon, Edmund   11
Castiglione, Giuseppe   86
Chang, Kwang-Chih   13, 19
Chang, Wan-Chen   11, 19
ceramics (*see also* porcelain)   12, 16, 54, 63, 68,
   69, 88, 112, 118, 132
Chen, Boda   22
China-Africa relations   84–5
China Confucius International Tourism   52
China Design Now exhibition (Victoria &
   Albert Museum, 2008)   83, 88
China Foundation for the Development of
   Social Culture   50, 85
China International Culture Association   84

China's Lost Cultural Relics Recovery
  Program 50, 85
China in London celebrations, 2005–06 83
China Poly Group 50, 85
China: The Three Emperors, 1622–1795
  exhibition (London, 2005) 83, 88
China-UK relations 83, 87–8
Chinese art 6, 79, 84, 86, 87, 88, 111, 132,
  135, 162
  general principles 11
  'fine arts' 12, 70
Chinese characters 13, 139
  auspicious 13
  simplification 11
Chinese civilisation 23, 41, 63, 67, 68, 74, 81,
  90, 99, 104, 112, 117, 118, 121, 122, 159, 163
  origins of (*see also* Mandate of Heaven) 7,
    82, 91–5, 100
  and inscriptions 13
  Shu civilisation 63, 69, 87, 92–3, 94, 95
Chinese Constitution 31, 130, 152
Chinese Museum Association 28
Chinese National Committee of ICOM 32
Chinese Orientalism 130
Chinese Society of Agricultural Museums 30
Chinese Society of Museums 30, 32
Chinese Society of Natural Museums 30
Chongqing (Sichuan Province) 20
Chunhua Ge Tie (ancient calligraphic texts) 86
Ci, Jiwei (historian) 96
'civic seeing' 145, 152, 153
'civilising mission' 4, 78, 122, 130
Cixi (Qing Empress) 26
Clifford, James 139
Clunas, Craig 20, 77, 79, 87, 91, 92, 94
collections
  collecting practices and traditions 6, 10,
    15–17
  elite collections 15
  imperial collections 6, 15, 20, 24, 28, 82,
    63, 104, 105, 132
  scholarly collections 15
  private collections 16–17, 48
collectors 12, 15, 16, 17, 23, 34, 48, 53, 54,
  87, 154, 160
colonialism 4, 70, 78, 86, 99, 130
Communism
  Communist cultural policies 22, 23, 31–2,
    33, 34, 44, 48, 87, 157

Communist ideology 2, 7, 22, 28, 29, 31,
  36, 56, 66, 75, 89, 97, 118, 160, 161
Communist Party 2, 13, 15, 21, 22, 28, 36,
  39, 55, 56, 62, 60, 74, 75, 79, 84, 89,
  92, 96, 97–100, 104, 106, 109, 113, 111,
  121, 125, 135, 138, 139, 159, 160
Confucius 25, 52, 90, 99
  Temple of 25
Confucianism 9, 21, 26–7, 78, 79, 80, 97, 99
cross-straight relations 21
cultural diplomacy 21, 81, 82, 85
Cultural Palace of Nationalities 29, 32, 134
cultural relics (*see also* museum objects)
  2002 Law on the Protection of Cultural
    Relics 10, 31–2, 33
  and authenticity 12–13
  export of 32
  cultural relics diplomacy 82
Cultural Revolution (1966–76) 23, 29, 32, 48,
  56, 82, 96, 109, 113, 119, 120, 124, 138
culture fever (*wenhua re*) 68, 100

Dai ethnic group 132, 137, 140, 142
Dali, Yunnan 150
Davis, Peter 154
De Bary, Theodore 107
Deng, Xiaoping 2, 15, 24, 49, 60, 66, 97, 98,
  116, 117, 124, 130
Denton, Kirk 74, 89, 159
Dikötter, Frank 78, 99, 129, 130
diorama 39, 61, 62, 115, 140, 141, 145, 149,
  150, 153
discursive regime 89
Dong ethnic group 154, 155
Dong, Xiwen (painter) 24
Duara, Prasenjit 77, 80, 96, 129
Duncan, Carol 53, 71
Duolun, Lu (historic road in Shanghai) 119,
  123

ecomuseum 133, 154–5
Engels, Friedrich 105
Erligang (neolithic culture) 90
Erlitou (neolithic culture) 90
ethnic minorities 7, 78, 94, 112, 121, 127–58
ethnic parks 133, 155
exhibitions
  exhibition design 47, 59, 64, 69, 114–15,
    116–17, 145–58

travelling exhibitions   6, 17, 81–5
Exhibition on the Achievements of Chinese Women and Children in the Past Decade (National Museum of China, 2012)   117
European cabinets of curiosity   17, 26, 153
evolutionary theory   35, 104, 105, 108, 111, 125, 139

Fabian, Johannes   140
Fan, Jiachuan   48
Fei, Hongnian   35
Fei, Yu   35
Feng, Yuan   51
Feuchtwang, Stephen   97
figurines (as display technique)   139, 145–54
Fiskesjö, Magnus   51, 131
Flath, James   30, 43, 44, 111, 118
folk art   39, 48, 134, 143
Forbidden Palace *or* Forbidden City (*see also* Imperial Palace, Palace Museum)   1, 13, 25, 28, 34, 44, 145, 161
Foucault, Michel   4, 89, 153
'four modernisations'   30
Friedman, Edward   22
Fu, Zhenlun (Chinese museologist)   36

Galikowski, Maria   22
Garrett, Valery   133
Gell, Alfred   60, 79, 81, 88, 148, 159
Gilded Dragons: Buried Treasures from China's Golden Age exhibition (British Museum, 1999)   88
Gladney, Dru   78, 131, 140, 152
Great Leap Forward (1958)   23, 29, 117
Greenblatt, Stephen   60, 64, 117
Groys, Boris   105
Guandong Province   98
Guangxi Province   32
Guangxu (Qing Emperor)   26

Hamlish, Tamara   5, 20, 52, 89, 90, 104
Han majority-minority relations   130–43
He, Ping   49
He, Shuzhong   31
Heude, Pierre (French missionary)   26
historical materialism (*see also* Marxism-Leninism)   10, 29, 36, 70, 80, 104, 105, 108, 109, 111, 141
Hotung, Joseph   54

Huizong (1101–25), Emperor of the Song Dynasty   15
Hu, Jintao   2, 84, 98, 116, 127
Huaxia   91, 121, 122, 123
Hui ethnic group   137
Humudu (neolithic culture)   107
Hung, Chang-tai   22, 73, 103
Hwang, Yih-Jye   121

illicit trade   32, 70, 81, 87
imitation   6, 12
Imperial China   9, 11, 50
Imperial Palace (*see also* Forbidden Palace)   1, 25, 26, 27, 28, 116
Imperial Treasures from China exhibition (China Millennium Monument, 2004)   68
inalienable possessions   81–2
inscriptions (*see also* calligraphy)   13, 15
    as museum objects   15
    on bronze vessels   19
Inner Mongolia Province   32, 130, 131, 157
interaction spheres, theory of (*see also* Chinese civilisation – origins of)   92
internal colonialism   129, 130
International Committee of Museums (ICOM)   30, 32, 36, 41, 42
Issei, Temple of   9

Jade   12, 60, 81, 88, 123
Jiang, Zemin   15, 24, 98, 100, 116
Jewish culture   90
Jin, Shangyi (painter)   24
Jiu Ding (*see also* bronze vessels)   19
Jonsson, Hjorleifur   130

Kang, Youwei (intellectual)   35
Kangxi Emperor (1662–1722)   83
Kuomintang (Nationalist government)   20–1, 78, 125, 135

lacquer   12, 83, 108, 112, 135, 116, 135, 160
Land Reform   29
landscape (in paintings)   12
Lévi-Strauss, Claude   145, 148, 150
Li, Xuan   49
Li, Xueqin   49, 85
Liangzhu (neolithic culture)   90, 107
Livingstone, Ken   83
Long March   66

Longshan (neolithic culture)　90
Louis Vuitton Voyages exhibition (National
　Museum of China, 2011)　84
Lu, Jinmin　40
Lu, Xun (writer)　36, 44, 124
Lu, Xhangshen　41
Luo, Gongliu (painter)　24

Ma, Chengyuan　49, 109
Ma, Weidu　49
Ma, Zishu　30, 37
Ma Zu (divinity)　26
MacFarquhar, Roderick　97
Manchu　26, 78, 80
Mandate of Heaven (*see also* Chinese civilisation
　– origins of)　7, 91, 95
mannequins　137, 141, 142, 145–54
Mao, Zedong　22, 23, 24, 36, 60, 66, 73, 98,
　103, 117, 124, 125, 135
　Maoism　2, 11, 22, 23, 36, 98, 100, 104,
　　109, 112, 120
maps (as display techniques)　60, 62, 66, 115,
　145, 151, 153
'March Towards Science Campaign'　36
Marxism-Leninism (*see also* historical
　materialism)　7, 10, 11, 15, 22, 28, 35, 36,
　38, 41, 98, 104, 105, 107, 111, 112, 115, 117
May Fourth Movement (1919)　21, 36
Mawangdui archaeological site, Hunan　87
Memories of Mankind: Exhibition of Ancient
　Documents of the Yunnan Ethnic Groups
　exhibition (Yunnan Nationalities Museum,
　ongoing)　139
metonym　79, 80, 81, 141, 148, 153
Miao ethnic group　88, 137, 154, 155
miniature　77, 140, 141, 145–54
Morgan, Lewis Henry　105, 139
Mosuo ethnic group　142
museology (*see also* museum studies)
　Chinese museology　5, 6, 28, 30, 35–7, 41,
　　42, 50, 51, 67, 111
　Japanese museology　35, 51
　Soviet museology　35, 36, 104
　Western museology　35–6
museum
　museum actors　3, 6, 34, 43–57, 132, 158,
　　160, 161
　museum architecture　6, 41, 52, 67, 70–5,
　　160, 161, 162

museum audiences　6, 24, 33, 34, 40, 47,
　54–7, 61, 62, 81, 85, 88, 127, 143, 147,
　152, 153, 154, 160, 162
'museum diplomacy'　21
museum donors　6, 52–4, 66, 160
'museum effect'　59
industrial museums　44, 45, 47, 123–5, 160
museum professionals　6, 13, 24, 29, 30,
　50–2, 54, 160
private museums　48–50, 160
proto-museums　25–6, 35
public museums　10, 25, 28, 34, 43, 50, 53,
　79, 103, 161
university museums　44, 111, 133
museum world　43
museums
　Arthur Sackler Museum of Art and
　　Archaeology, Beijing　72, 94
　Auto Museum, Shanghai　45
　Bank Museum, Shanghai　45, 125
　British Museum, London　54, 83, 88, 96,
　　97
　Capital Museum, Beijing　39, 41, 64, 66,
　　72, 74, 83, 161
　Car Museum, Beijing　125
　China Dairy Museum, Shanghai　125
　China Fire Museum, Beijing　125
　China Millennium Monument, Beijing　68,
　　72, 73, 74
　China National Film Museum, Beijing　125
　China National Silk Museum, Hangzhou
　　45, 122
　China Science and Technology Museum,
　　Beijing　32, 126
　Donghua Porcelain Museum, Shanghai　48
　Ethnic Minorities Park, Beijing　133, 149
　Fuzhou Museum, Fujian　28
　Gong-mi-a Village Museum, Leishan,
　　Guizhou　155
　Guanfu Classical Art Museum, Beijing　2,
　　49
　Guggenheim Museum, Bilbao　71
　Ili Kazak Autonomous Prefecture Museum,
　　Xinjiang　131
　Institute of Clothing Technology, Beijing
　　45, 134
　Liu Dalin Sex Culture Museum, Shanghai
　　48
　Lu Xun Museum, Shanghai　36, 44

Mao Zedong Mausoleum, Beijing 73
Memorial Museum of the Chinese People's War of Resistance to Japan, Beijing 62, 100
Memorial Museum of the War Against Japan, Nanjing 100
Mengle Museum, Jinghong 137
Metropolitan Museum of Art, New York 17, 19, 42
Military Museum, Beijing 1, 10, 29, 32, 39, 44, 60, 66, 73, 74, 83, 106, 109
Ming Tomb Museum, north of Beijing 83
Musée du Quai Branly, Paris 88
Musée Guimet, Paris 88
Museum of Anthropology, University of Xiamen 132
Museum of Anthropology, Yunnan University, Kunming 111, 132, 136, 138, 143, 147
Museum of Chinese Revolution, Beijing 29, 105, 106, 112
Museum of the Cultural Revolution, Shantou 120
Museum of the Southwest University for Nationalities, Chengdu 133, 136, 139, 145, 147, 149, 150, 153
Museum of the University of Ethnic Minorities, Kunming 133, 135, 137
Museum of the University of Sichuan, Chengdu 66, 132
Nanjian Village Museum, Yunnan 155
Nanjing Museum 27, 72, 108
Nantong Museum, Jiangsu 27, 48
National Art Museum of China (NAMOC), Beijing 22, 23, 51, 66, 72, 106
National Gallery, Beijing 24
National Gallery of Greece, Athens 82
National Museum of China, Beijing 1, 14, 24, 39, 41, 42, 44, 63, 68, 69, 71, 75, 83, 84, 85, 90, 94, 106, 107, 110, 113–18, 122, 136, 160
National Museum of Chinese History, Beijing 27, 29, 39, 68
National Museum of Telecommunications, Beijing 44
National Portrait Gallery, London 83
National Palace Museum, Taipei 20
Natural History Museum, London 83

Natural History Museum, Shanghai 29, 50, 126
Nelson-Atkins Museum of Art, Kansas City 82
Oriental Musical Instruments Museum, Shanghai 123
Palace Museum, Beijing (see also Forbidden City) 20, 27, 28, 44, 52, 72, 83, 112, 161
Poly Art Museum, Beijing 49–50, 53, 66, 85, 86
Post Museum, Shanghai 45, 125
Revolutionary Museum, Beijing 39, 74
Sanxingdui Museum, Sichuan 63, 69, 73, 92, 93, 94, 95, 161
Science and Technology Museum, Shanghai 45
Shanghai Arts and Crafts Museum 73, 112
Shanghai Children's Museum 127
Shanghai History Museum 33, 45–6
Shanghai Museum 26, 39, 40, 41, 49, 53, 54, 55, 56, 63, 64, 65, 66, 67, 68, 69, 72, 73, 74, 83, 86, 108, 109, 112, 127, 132, 134, 135, 142, 143, 147, 160, 161, 162
    Kadoorie Gallery of Chinese Minority Nationalities 134
Shanghai Museum of Glass 125
Shanghai Public Security Museum 45, 124
Shanghai Urban Planning Exhibition Centre 73, 127
Shenyang Palace Museum 72
Site of the First Congress of the Communist Party, Shanghai 13, 15, 39, 55, 56, 60, 62, 74, 100, 106, 109
South Korea National Museum, Seoul 71
Summer Palace, Beijing 72, 86
Te Papa Tongarewa, Wellington 71
Tea Museum, Hangzhou 122, 123, 149, 150
Temple of Heaven, Beijing 72
Textile Museum, Shanghai 45
Tianjin Provincial Museum 27
Tibet Museum, Lhasa 131
Tobacco Museum, Shanghai 45, 60, 72, 73, 108, 123–4
Traditional Medicine Museum, Hangzhou 123
Victoria & Albert Museum, London 83
Virtual Museum of the Cultural Revolution 120

Yidu Museum, Anyang   26
Yunnan Nationalities Museum, Kunming
    133, 135, 137, 138, 139, 140, 147, 148,
    150, 152
Xiao-Huang Village Dong Chorus Museum,
    Congjiang, Guizhou   155
Xinjiang Uyghur Autonomous Region
    Museum, Urumqi   131
Xujiahui Museum, Shanghai   26
Zhejiang Provincial Museum   28, 106–7
museum studies (see also museology)   4, 5

Nanjie village, Henan   118
Nanjing   20–1, 27
National Conference of Museum Work (1956)
    36
National Research Institute of Cultural Heritage
    32
Naxi ethnic group   137, 138
New China   25, 29, 32, 36, 66, 78, 112, 126,
    131
New Cultural Movement (c. 1915)   27
New Democratic Revolution   106
Ni, Xingxiang   100
Ningxia Province   32
Nixon, Richard   82
nostalgia   104, 118–19, 149
Nuosu ethnic group   154

objectification   80
Old Democratic Revolution   105
Olympic Games, Beijing, 2008   41, 68, 82, 83,
    126, 129, 157
'Open Door' policies   30, 34, 44, 81
Opium War   86
oracle bones   20
Oriental Pearl Tower   47, 119
Orientalism   87, 130

Pan of Zi Zhong Jiang   54, 64
Pan, Shouyong   51
panopticon   149, 151, 153
patina (of age on objects)   16
peasants   22
Peking Man   74, 92, 107
People's Art (art review)   23
People's Liberation Army   49
People's Literature (literature review)   23
political legitimacy   95–101

porcelain (see also ceramics)   12, 48, 49, 62,
    64, 81, 83, 108
postcolonialism   4, 71, 132
Preziosi, Donald   68, 70
primitive art   87
private property   108
propaganda
    anti-Japanese propaganda   23
    Communist propaganda   22, 23, 24, 28,
        33, 39, 66, 79, 96, 97, 99, 125
proprioception   150

Qianlong (Emperor) (1736–95)   83
Qin Shihuangdi (Emperor)   96
Qing Dynasty   12
Qiu, Mingzhen   99
Qufu (Shandong Province)   25

Red Army (or Red Guards)   22, 29, 60, 66,
    116, 150
repatriation   6, 50, 53, 80, 85–7, 88
replicas (see also authenticity)   12–13
1911 Republican Revolution   4
resonance   60, 64, 67
restoration (of museum objects)   13
Review of Foreign Art (Guowai Meishu Ziliao);
    later Journal of Art Translation (Meishu
    Yicong)   24
Rising Sun in the East: Marxism in China
    and 90th Founding Anniversary of People's
    Publishing House exhibition (National
    Museum of China, 2011)   117
Rivière, Georges Henri   154
Royal Asiatic Society   26
Ru ware ceramics   63

Saunders, Barbara   100, 162
Sayers, Andrew   75
Schein, Louisa   138, 140
Schneider, Florian   121
scholar-officials   11
Selected African Sculptures in the Collection of
    the National Museum of China exhibition
    (National Museum of China, 2012)   85
shamanism   141
Shanghai World Expo 2010   1, 41, 83
Shan, Jixiang   44
Shaoshan village   118
Shelton, Anthony   62

shiguan 50
Shikumen Open House, Shanghai 118
singularisation 63, 64, 66, 67
Sino-Japanese War (1937–45) 23, 28
Social Forms, Reform and Development of Yunnan Ethnic Minorities exhibition (Yunnan Nationalities Museum, 2006) 135
'Socialist Realism' in painting 23
Song, Meiling 119
Song, Qingling 60, 72
source communities 4, 132
Soviet Union 2, 23, 36, 96, 104
Spiritual Civilisation Campaign (late 1980s) 24
Stalin, Joseph 129
Standing Committee of the National People's Congress 32
State Administration of Cultural Heritage (SACH) 1, 31, 32, 34, 37, 40, 43–4, 45, 49, 51, 81, 82, 112
State Bureau of Cultural Relics 30, 32, 37, 49
state-owned enterprises 6, 44, 45, 49, 123
Stewart, Susan 149, 152, 153
Su, Donghai 17, 25, 28, 35, 36, 38, 155
Sui ethnic group 139
Sun, Jianzheng 37
Sun, Yat-Sen 27, 60, 72
Suoga Miao village, Guizhou 154

Taiping Rebellion (1850–64) 26
Taiwan 16, 20–1, 23, 80, 100, 151
Tanahashigen, Tao (Japanese museologist) 35 n.10
Taotieh 19, 108
tea 123
Terracotta Army 83, 87, 88, 96, 97
The Art of the Enlightenment exhibition (National Museum of China, 2011) 84
The First Emperor: China's Terracotta Army exhibition (British Museum, 2007–08) 83, 96, 97
The treasures of a nation: China's cultural heritage 1949–99 exhibition (National Museum of Chinese History, 1999) 94, 112–13, 114
The Yellow River: Exhibition of Nakamura Sadao's Oil Paintings exhibition (National Museum of China, 2012) 84
'three natures and two tasks' theory 30, 36
Tian An Men Square 1, 2, 24, 73, 74, 100, 117

Tianjin 4, 30
Tibet 32, 78, 80, 100, 117, 130, 131, 138, 142, 149, 150, 151, 156
Tibetan ethnic group 131, 138, 142, 149, 150
Treasures from the Bronze Age of China exhibition, 1980 82
Tsui T T family 54

UNESCO *Convention on the Protection of World Cultural and Natural Heritage* ('The World Heritage Convention') (1972) 32
UNESCO *Convention on the Means of Prohibiting and Preventing the Illicit Import, Export and Transfer of Ownership of Cultural Property* (1970) 32, 50, 87
UNESCO Intangible Cultural Heritage list 157
UNESCO *Museum International* (journal) 40
UNIDROIT *Convention on Stolen or Illegally Exported Cultural Objects* (1995) 32
Universal Exhibition Paris (1867) 10
Uyghur ethnic group 131, 147, 157

de Varine, Hugues 154

Wang, Hongjun 16, 26, 38, 40, 50
Watson, Rubie 20, 103
wonder 64, 65, 66, 67, 117
World Art (*Shijie Meishu*) (art journal) 24
Wright, I S (missionary) 26
Wuyue State (Tang Dynasty, AD 618–906) 107

Yan'an Forum on Literature and Art (1942) 22
Yang, Mei-Hui 3
Yang, Xiaoneng 82
Yangtze River 94
Yanshao (neolithic culture) 90
Yao ethnic group 130
Yellow Emperor 78
Yellow River theory (*see also* Chinese civilisation – origins of) 92
Yi Marquis of Zeng, Hupei 87
Yip, Sunny 54
Yongzheng (Emperor) (1723–35) 83
Yu, King of the Xia Dynasty 19
Yuan, Kejian 35
Yves Saint Laurent art collection 86

Xia Dynasty   17, 19
Xi'an, Shaanxi   87
Xintiandi area, Shanghai   119
Xu, Beihong   21

Zhan Jianjun (painter)   24
Zhang, Qian   27, 48

Zhang, Taiyan   91
Zhang, Xiaoming   51
Zhang, Wenbin   31, 37, 40, 44
Zhou, Enlai   82, 106
Zhu, Xi   11
Zhuang ethnic group   139
zodiac fountain (Summer Palace, Beijing)   86

Heritage Matters

Volume 1: The Destruction of Cultural Heritage in Iraq
Edited by Peter G. Stone and Joanne Farchakh Bajjaly

Volume 2: Metal Detecting and Archaeology
Edited by Suzie Thomas and Peter G. Stone

Volume 3: Archaeology, Cultural Property, and the Military
Edited by Laurie Rush

Volume 4: Cultural Heritage, Ethics, and the Military
Edited by Peter G. Stone

Volume 5: Pinning Down the Past: Archaeology, Heritage, and Education Today
Mike Corbishley

Volume 6: Heritage, Ideology, and Identity in Central and Eastern Europe:
Contested Pasts, Contested Presents
Edited by Matthew Rampley

Volume 7: Making Sense of Place: Multidisciplinary Perspectives
Edited by Ian Convery, Gerard Corsane, and Peter Davis

Volume 8: Safeguarding Intangible Cultural Heritage
Edited by Michelle L. Stefano, Peter Davis, and Gerard Corsane

Volume 9: Museums and Biographies: Stories, Objects, Identities
Edited by Kate Hill

Volume 10: Sport, History, and Heritage: Studies in Public Representation
Edited by Jeffrey Hill, Kevin Moore, and Jason Wood

Volume 11: Curating Human Remains: Caring for the Dead in the United Kingdom
Edited by Myra Giesen

Volume 12: Presenting the Romans:
Interpreting the Frontiers of the Roman Empire World Heritage Site
Edited by Nigel Mills